THE COOK'S ENCYCLOPEDIA OF
VEGETABLES

THE COOK'S ENCYCLOPEDIA OF
VEGETABLES

CHRISTINE INGRAM

LORENZ BOOKS

This edition published by Lorenz Books
27 West 20th Street, New York, NY 10011

LORENZ BOOKS are available for bulk purchase for sales
promotion and for premium use. For details, write or call the
sales director, Lorenz Books, 27 West 20th Street, New York,
NY 10011; (800) 354-9657

Lorenz Books is an imprint of Anness Publishing Inc.

www.lorenzbooks.com

ISBN 0-7548-0369-4

Publisher: Joanna Lorenz
Senior Cookery Editor: Linda Fraser
Editor: Rosemary Wilkinson
Designer: Patrick McLeavey
Food for photography: Jane Stevenson
Photography and styling: Patrick McLeavey and Thomas Odulate

Previously published as *The Vegetable Ingredients Cookbook*

Printed and bound in China

© Anness Publishing Limited 1996, 1999,
Updated © 2000, 2001

10 9 8 7 6 5 4 3 2

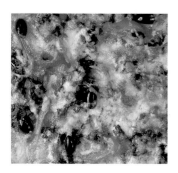

CONTENTS

INTRODUCTION

As A CHILD, THERE WERE TWO BASIC types of vegetables for me: the ones my mother cooked and the ones given to us at school. My mother only ever bought fresh vegetables and she knew how to cook them, so they were simple but good. Vegetables at school were overcooked and invariably tasteless. Travel then broadened my outlook.

From my first teenage sojourns around Europe, I recall, even now, the stalls in a Barcelona produce market, piled high with tomatoes, bell peppers and eggplants. The exotic-looking produce of The Orient, Asia and Caribbean countries cannot fail to spark off an inquisitive, creative enthusiasm in those who are unfamiliar with them and even basic ingredients - potatoes, onions and carrots - do not look like sorry, everyday necessities when they are displayed with pride.

HISTORY

Plants have formed an essential part of our diet since the early existence of mankind. Hunter-gatherers progressed towards a more settled life as they learned how to cultivate crops and rear animals. Archaeological evidence indicates that forms of wheat and barley, believed to be the first crops, were farmed in the Middle East as early as 8000 BC. Many edible plants are native to this area, so we can assume that vegetables were also eaten, not least to relieve a monotonous diet.

As plants became a regular part of the diet for satisfying appetites, and those that caused stomach upsets were discovered and avoided, people realized the necessity of growing edible crops. Beans and

Left: Italian Roast Peppers.
Above: Roast Asparagus Crêpes.

Left: Shallots.

were commonly grown.

By the Middle Ages, a wealth of vegetables was available and recipes for them were recorded in the first cookery books.

Early explorers displayed exotic ingredients, the spoils of their travels, in their native countries and created a huge appetite for new tastes among the wealthy classes of Europe. Marco Polo traveled to China and carried aromatic spices on his return to Europe. Christopher Colombus and subsequent explorers found potatoes, tomatoes, peppers, squashes and corn. Such produce was greeted with a somewhat lukewarm reception and potatoes and tomatoes were received with suspicion and grave misgivings!

It is only in recent generations that people all over the world have expressed interest in vegetables cultivated in different climates.

Nowadays, of course, we have the option of buying exactly what we want, when we want it. This is a luxury we have come to expect and we are ready to pay the price for international variety. Gluts of vegetables, once common seasonal occurrences when produce was cultivated and marketed on a local scale, are not a feature of modern food stores, but seasons still hold good for home-grown produce.

Unlike storecupboard ingredients, the great characteristic of many vegetables is that they still have natural seasons. So, in addition to taking advantage of the fantastic multi-national displays in cosmopolitan supermarkets, it pays also to buy from local growers who offer freshly harvested produce. It is important to enjoy summer vegetables during the season to which they traditionally belong and to savor

peas were among the first vegetables farmed in Thessaly and Macedonia. These legumes would have been enormously important to early societies as they grew easily to provide seeds which were a starchy food, high in protein and which dried well for long storage.

Many of our familiar vegetables were cultivated in historic times: the Egyptians grew onions, garlic, radishes, lettuce and fava beans;

the Greeks and Romans farmed produce which was native to their own countries and they also discovered a wider range of plants thanks to their contact with other cultures.

Not only did the Romans discover the fruits of other lands, but their armies also introduced ingredients to the countries they invaded. In Britain, for example, at the beginning of the first century AD, beans, peas, leeks, parsnips and turnips

Above: Spinach.

winter produce in dishes like whole-some stews and broths that are well suited to cooler weather.

NUTRITION

The total contribution of carbohy-drate (starchy) foods and vegetables in a well-balanced diet may not be entirely understood, but the benefits and protective role they play in ensuring good health is widely rec-ognized. Expert opinions agree on the fact that we should eat a high proportion of vegetables in our everyday diets.

Although the nutritional value of vegetables varies according to type, freshness, preparation and cooking method, they are a main source of many vitamins, especially vitamin C.

Some of the B-group vitamins are also found in vegetables, particularly in green vegetables and pulses. Carrots and dark green vegetables also include carotene which is used by the body to manufacture vitamin A. Vegetable oils are a useful source of vitamin E.

Vegetables also contain calcium, iron, potassium and magnesium, as well as some trace elements which are required in small quantities.

Starchy vegetables are an impor-tant source of energy-giving carbo-hydrate and they may include useful quantities of fiber.

In a vegetarian diet, vegetables, particularly peas, pulses and sprout-ing seeds, also make a valuable contribution to the overall protein intake.

Where specific vegetables are a rich source of nutrients, a note is

included under the relevant heading.

Vegetables have the highest nutri-tional content when they are freshly picked. The vitamin content dimin-ishes with staleness and exposure to sunlight. Use fresh vegetables as soon as possible after purchase and always avoid stale limp specimens. The peel and the layer directly beneath it contain a high concentra-tion of nutrients, so it is best to avoid peeling vegetables or to remove the thinnest layer for maximum nutrient retention.

Minerals and vitamins C and B are water soluble and they are lost by seepage into cooking water or the liquid over which vegetables are steamed. To minimize loss of nutri-ents, do not cut up vegetables finely as this creates a greater surface area for seepage. Vitamin C is also destroyed by long cooking and by exposure to alkalines.

Raw and lightly cooked vegetables provide the best nutritional value and source of fiber. Any cooking liquid should, whenever possible, be used in stocks, gravies or sauces.

ABOUT THIS BOOK

Vegetables can play a starring role in a recipe or they may be combined with other ingredients in a harmony of flavors. Some of the best vegetable soups are examples of well-tuned mixtures - minestrone, for instance, is a blend of onions, carrots, tomatoes and cabbage; or a good old-fashioned vegetable soup brings together simple ingredients such as carrots, turnips and leeks. These, and many others, are loved for the sum of their parts rather than for the taste of individual vegetables.

In general, however, in this book you will find recipes which make the most of each vegetable, so that their particular virtues can be appreciated to the full.

Above: Tomato and Basil Tart.
Left: Red, orange and green bell peppers.

This is not a vegetarian book; however, there are plenty of recipes which are vegetarian. In many instances, substituting vegetable stock for chicken stock will ensure that the recipe is acceptable.

The recipes are an eclectic mix of classic dishes from around the world and others devised over years of cooking. The great thing about cooking with vegetables is, however, that once you have got the hang of using them, a recipe becomes unnecessary. You will discover how you most enjoy carrots, asparagus or less-common vegetables and will learn to experiment in your own way. Good Luck!

ONIONS
AND
LEEKS

Onions

Shallots

Chives

Garlic

Leeks

ONIONS

There are bound to be vegetables you like better than others but a cook would be lost without onions. There are many classic recipes specifically for onion dishes so they can be appreciated in their own right. Onion tarts or French onion soup, for instance, have a sublime flavor, and only onions are appropriate. But also, there is hardly a recipe where onions, or their cousins – garlic, leeks or shallots – are not used. Gently fried until soft, or fried more fiercely until golden brown, they add a unique, savory flavor to dishes.

History

Onions, along with shallots, leeks, chives and garlic, belong to the *Allium* family which, including wild varieties, has some 325 members. All have the characteristic onion smell which is caused by volatile acids beneath the skin.

Archaeological and historical records show that onions have been eaten for thousands of years. They are believed to have originally come from the Middle East and their easy cultivation suggests that their use spread quickly. There are references to the onion in the Bible and it was widely eaten in Egypt. There was, we are told, an inscription on the Great Pyramid stating that the slaves who built the tomb ate their way through 1,600 talents worth of onions, radishes and garlic – presumably a lot, given that the Great Pyramid was made using more than two million 2^1/$_2$-ton blocks of stone.

By the Middle Ages, onions were a common vegetable throughout Europe and would have been used in soups, stews and sauces when strong flavoring was preferred.

Varieties

As they keep well in a cool place, most people keep a handy stock of onions, usually a general purpose type that can be sautéed or browned. However, onions come in a variety of different colors and strengths, and for certain recipes particular onions are needed.

Right: Spanish onions.
Far right top: Yellow onions.
Far right below: Red onions.

Spanish Onions: Onions raised in warm areas are milder in taste than onions from cooler regions, and Spanish onions are among the mildest cultivated onions. They are a beautiful pale copper color and are noticeably larger than yellow onions. They have a delicate, sweet flavor which makes them ideal for serving raw in salads, thinly sliced, while their size makes them suitable for stuffing and baking whole.

Yellow Onions: These are the widely available onions you find everywhere and, though called yellow onions, their skins are more golden brown. They are the most pungent of all the onions and are a good, all-purpose variety. The smallest ones, referred to as baby, button or pickling onions, are excellent for pickling but can also be added whole to a casserole or sautéed in butter to make a delicious vegetable accompaniment.

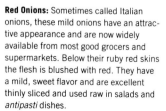

Red Onions: Sometimes called Italian onions, these mild onions have an attractive appearance and are now widely available from most good grocers and supermarkets. Below their ruby red skins the flesh is blushed with red. They have a mild, sweet flavor and are excellent thinly sliced and used raw in salads and *antipasti* dishes.

White Onions: These come in all sorts of interesting shapes and sizes – squat, round and oval, big and small. The very small white onions, with shimmery silver skins, are mild and best added whole to stews or served in a creamy sauce. Larger white onions can be mild or strong – there is no way of telling. Like yellow onions, white onions are extremely versatile whether used raw or cooked. The very small white onions, called Paris Silverskin, are the ones used for dry martinis and for commercial pickling.

Vidalia Onions: These popular American onions are a specialty of and named after a town in Georgia. They are a large, pale yellow onion and are deliciously sweet and juicy. Used in salads, or roasted with meat or with other vegetables, they are superb.

Bermuda Onions: These are similar in size to Spanish onions but are more squat. They have a mild flavor and are good thinly sliced, fried until golden and served with steaks or burgers.

remove the next layer of onion, as it is often dry or damaged. Unless slicing onions for stir-fries, for which it is customary to slice the onion into wedges, always slice the onion through the rings, widthwise. Make whole rings, or for half-rings, cut in half lengthwise through the root before slicing (*below*). For finely chopped onion, slice again lengthwise.

Cooking

The volatile acids in onions are driven off during cooking, which is why cooked onion is never as strong as raw onion. The method of cooking, even the way of frying an onion, affects its eventual taste. Boiled onion or chopped onion added neat to soups or casseroles has a stronger, more raw taste. Frying or sautéing briefly, or sweating (frying in a little fat with the lid on) until soft and translucent gives a mild flavor. When fried until golden brown, onions develop a distinct flavor, both sweet and savory, that is superb with grilled meats and is essential for French onion soup.

Scallions or Spring Onions: These are also true onions but harvested very young while their shoots are still green and fresh. They have a mild, delicate taste and both the small white bulb and the green tops can be used in salads, omelets and stir-fries, or indeed any dish which requires a mild onion flavor.

Nutrition

As well as tasting good, onions are good for you. They contain vitamins B and C together with calcium, iron and potassium. Like garlic, they also contain cycloallin, an anticoagulant which helps protect against heart disease.

Buying and Storing

It used to be a common sight in Europe to see an onion seller traveling around the streets on a bicycle with strings of onions hanging from every available support, including his own neck.

Strings of onions are hard to come by although, if you do find them in stores, they are a good way of buying and storing the vegetable.

Onions, more than almost any other vegetable, keep well provided they are stored in a cool, dry place, such as a larder or an outhouse. Do not store them in the fridge as they will go soft, and never keep cut onions in the fridge – or anywhere else – unless you want onion-flavored milk and an onion-scented home. Onions do not keep well once cut and it is worth buying onions in assorted sizes so that you do not end up having bits left over. Unused bits of onion can be added to stocks; otherwise throw them away.

Preparing

Onions contain a substance which is released when they are cut and causes the eyes to water, quite painfully sometimes. There are all sorts of ways which are supposed to prevent this, including cutting onions under running water, holding a piece of bread between your teeth or wearing goggles!

As well as the outer brown leaves,

Above far left: Vidalia onions.
Left: White onions.
Above left: Large and small scallions.

SHALLOTS

Shallots are not baby onions but a separate member of the onion family. They have a delicate flavor, less intense than most onions and they also dissolve easily into liquids, which is why they are favored for sauces. Shallots grow in small, tight clusters so that when you break one open there may be two or three bunched together at the root.

Their size makes them convenient for a recipe where only a little onion is required. Use shallots when only a small amount of onion is needed or when only a fine onion flavor is required. Shallots are a pleasant, if maybe extravagant, alternative to onions, but where recipes specify shallots (especially sauce recipes), they should be used if possible.

Although classic cooking frequently calls for particular ingredients, the art of improvisation should not be ignored. For instance, Coq au Vin is traditionally made with walnut-size white onions, but when substituted with shallots, the result is delightful.

History

Shallots are probably as ancient as onions. Roman commentators wrote eloquently about the excellence of shallots in sauces.

Varieties

Shallots are small slender onions with long necks and golden, copper-colored skins. There are a number of varieties, although there is unlikely to be a choice in the supermarkets. In any case, differences are more in size and color of skin than in flavor.

Buying and Storing

Like onions, shallots should be firm without any green shoots. They will keep well for several months in a cool dry place.

Preparing and Cooking

Skin shallots in the same way as onions, i.e. top and tail them and then peel off the outer skin. Pull apart the bulbs. Slice them carefully and thinly using a sharp knife – shallots are so small, it is easy to slip and cut yourself. When cooking them whole, fry over very low heat without browning too much.

CHIVES

Chives: In culinary terms, chives are really classed as a herb, but as members of the onion family they are worth mentioning here. As anyone who has grown them knows, chives are tufts of aromatic grass with pretty pale lilac flowers, which are also edible.

Preparing and Serving

Chives are often snipped with scissors and added to egg dishes, or used as a garnish for salads and soups, adding a pleasant but faint onion flavor. Along with parsley, tarragon and chervil, they are an essential ingredient of *fines herbes*.

Chives are also a delicious addition to soft cheeses – far nicer than commercially bought cheeses, where the flavor of chives virtually disappears. Stir also

into soft butter for an alternative to garlic butter. This can then be spread onto bread and baked like garlic bread.

If adding to cooked dishes, cook only very briefly, otherwise their flavor will be lost.

Garlic Chives: Garlic chives, sometimes called Chinese chives, have a delicate garlic flavor, and if you see them for sale in your local Chinese supermarket, they are worth buying as they add a delicate onion flavor to stir-fries and other oriental dishes.

Preparing and Serving

Use them as you would chives – both the green and white parts are edible. They are also delicious served on their own as a vegetable accompaniment.

Buying and Storing

For both types of chives, look for plump, uniformly green specimens with no brown spots or signs of wilting. They can be stored for up to a week in the fridge. Unopened flowers on garlic chives are an indication that the plant is young and therefore more tender than one with fully opened flowers.

Above left: Chives.
Above right: Garlic chives.

GARLIC

Garlic is an ingredient that almost any-one who does any cooking at all, and absolutely everyone who enjoys cooking, would not be without.

History

Garlic is known to have been first grown in around 3200 BC. Inscriptions and models of garlic found in the pyramids of ancient Egypt testify to the fact that gar-lic was not only an important foodstuff but that it had ceremonial significance as well. The Greeks and Romans likewise believed garlic to have magical qualities. Warriors would eat it for strength before going into battle, gods were appeased with gifts of garlic, and cloves of garlic were fastened round the necks of babies to ward off evil. Hence, vampire myth-ology has ancient precedents.

The Greeks and Romans also used garlic for its therapeutic qualities. Not only was it thought to be an aphrodisiac but also it was believed to be good for eczema, toothache and snake bites.

Although garlic found its way all over Europe – vats of butter, strongly flavored with garlic, have been found by archae-ologists working in Ireland which date back 200-300 years – fundamen-tally, its popularity today derives from our liking for Mediterranean, Indian and Asian food, in which garlic plays a very impor-tant part.

Nutrition

As is often the case, what was once dis-missed as an old wives' tale is, after thor-ough scientific inquiry, found to be true. Garlic is a case in point; most authorities accept that it has many therapeutic properties. The most significant of these is that it lowers blood cholesterol, thus helping prevent heart disease. Also, raw garlic contains a powerful antibiotic and there is evidence that it has a beneficial effect against cancer and strokes, and increases the absorption of vitamins. Many garlic enthusiasts take their garlic in tablet form, but true devotees prefer to take it as it comes.

Right: A string of pink-skinned garlic.

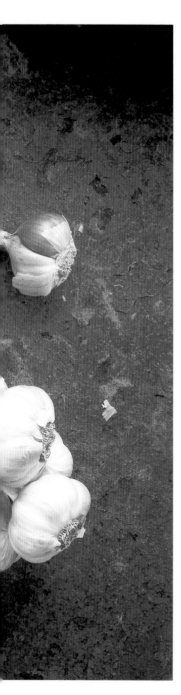

Varieties

There are numerous varieties of garlic, from the large "elephant" garlic, to small tight bulbs. Their papery skin can be white, pink or purple. Color makes no difference to taste but the particular attraction of the large purple bulbs is that they make a beautiful display in the kitchen.

As a general rule, the smaller the garlic bulb, the stronger it is likely to be. However, most garlic sold in stores is not classified in either shape or form (unless it is elephant garlic) and in practice you will simply pick up whatever you need, either loose, in bunches or on strings.

Garlic grown in a hot climate is likely to be the most pungent, and fresh new season's garlic has a subtle, mild flavor that is particularly good if it is to be used raw, for example, in salads and for dressings.

Above: Elephant garlic beside normal-size bulbs.

Buying and Storing

Garlic bulbs should be firm and round with clear, papery skins. Avoid any that are beginning to sprout. Garlic bulbs keep well stored in a cool, dry place; if the air is damp they will sprout and if it is too warm the cloves will eventually turn to gray powder.

Preparing and Cooking

First break the garlic bulb into cloves and then remove the papery skin. You can blanch this off with hot water but using a fingernail or knife is just as effective. When a garlic clove is split lengthwise a shoot is revealed in the center, which is occasionally green, and some people remove this whatever the color. Cloves are the little segments which make up the bulb and most recipes call for one or more cloves of garlic. (Don't use a bulb when you just need a clove!)

Crush cloves either with the blade of a knife or use a garlic crusher. Crushed garlic cooks more evenly and distributes its flavor in food better than when it is used sliced or finely chopped (stir-fries are the exception). Prepare garlic according to the strength of flavor required: thinly sliced garlic is milder than chopped, which in turn is milder than crushed garlic and, of course, cooking mutes the pungency.

Garlic Breath

The taste and smell of garlic tends to linger on the breath and can be a problem to get rid of. Chewing parsley is a well-known remedy but is only moderately successful. Chewing the seeds of cardamom pods is also said to work but is rather unpleasant. The best suggestion is to eat garlic with your friends so that nobody notices!

LEEKS

Leeks are very versatile, having their own distinct, subtle flavor. They are excellent in pies and casseroles with other ingredients, braised in cream and served by themselves, or simmered in butter as an accompanying vegetable.

Leeks are also wonderful in soups and broths and have rightly earned the title, "king of the soup onions." Cock-a-leekie from Scotland and *Crème Vichyssoise*, invented by the chef of New York's Ritz-Carlton, are two classic leek soups, but many other soups call for leeks.

History

Leeks, like onions and garlic, have a long history. They were grown widely in ancient Egypt and were also eaten and enjoyed throughout the Greek and Roman period. In England, there is evidence that leeks were enjoyed during the Dark Ages. There is little mention of them during the Middle Ages, and history suggests that between the sixteenth and eighteenth centuries eating leeks was not considered fashionable.

However, while they may not have enjoyed a good reputation among the notoriously fickle aristocracy, the rural communities probably continued to eat leeks. They grow in all sorts of climates and are substantial enough to make a reasonable meal for a poor family. It was probably during this time that they were dubbed "poor man's asparagus" – a name which says more about people's snobbishness about food than it does about leeks.

Many place names in England, such as Leckhampstead and Leighton Buzzard, are derived from the word leek and, of course, the leek has been a national emblem of Wales for hundreds of years.

Varieties

There are many different varieties of leeks but among them there is little difference in flavor. Commercially grown leeks tend to be about 10 inches long and about 3/4 inch in diameter. Leeks nurtured in home gardens can be left to grow to an enormous size, but these may develop a woody center.

RAMP

Among the many wild onions and leeks, the Canadian ramp is perhaps the best known. Also called the wild leek, it looks a little like a scallion, but has a stronger and more assertive garlic-onion flavor. Choose unblemished, clear white specimens with bright, fresh leaves and keep in a cool place, wrapped in a plastic bag to store.

Prepare and cook as you would scallions, by trimming the root end and then slicing thinly. Use in cooking or in salads but remember the onion flavor is stronger, so use sparingly.

Buying and Storing

Buy leeks which look fresh and healthy. The white part should be firm and unblemished and the leaves green and lively. As leeks do not keep particularly well, it is best to buy them as and when you need them. If you need to store them, trim away the top of the leaves and keep them in the salad drawer of the fridge or in a cool place. After several days they will begin to shrivel.

Preparing

It is important to wash leeks thoroughly before cooking as earth and grit lodges itself between the white sections at the base. To prepare leeks, cut away the flags (leaves) and trim the base. Unless the leek is extremely fresh or home-grown, you will probably have to remove the first layer of white; then cut a slit from one end to the other through to the center of the leek *(below)*. Wash under cold running water, pulling the sections apart so that the water rinses out any stubborn pieces of earth. If you slice the leeks – either slice thickly or thinly – place them in a colander and rinse thoroughly under cold water.

Cooking

Leeks can be steamed or boiled and then added to your recipe, or you can fry sliced leeks gently in butter for a minute or so and then cover with a lid to sweat so they cook without browning. Unlike onions, leeks shouldn't be allowed to brown; they become tough and unappetizing. They can be stir-fried, however, with a little garlic and ginger. If they begin to cook too fiercely, splash in a little stock and soy sauce and simmer until tender.

Left: Leeks.
Above: Ramp.

SHOOTS
AND
STEMS

ASPARAGUS

Asparagus is definitely a luxury vegetable. Its price, even in season, sets it apart from cabbages and cauliflowers, and it has a taste of luxury too. The spears, especially the thick, green spears, at their best in early summer, have an intense, rich flavor that is impossible to describe but easy to remember. If the gods eat, they will eat asparagus – served simply with a good hollandaise!

History

The ancient Greeks enjoyed wild asparagus, but it was not until the Roman period that we know it was cultivated. Even then asparagus was highly thought of: it is recorded that Julius Caesar liked to eat it with melted butter. There is little mention of asparagus being eaten in England until the seventeenth century. Mrs Beeton has 14 recipes for asparagus and from the prices quoted in her cookbook it is apparent that it was expensive even in Victorian times.

Nutrition

Asparagus provides vitamins A, B2 and C and is also a good source of potassium, iron and calcium. It is a well-known diuretic.

Varieties

There are many varieties of asparagus and many different ways of raising it too. Spanish and some Dutch asparagus is white with ivory tips; it is grown under mounds of soil and cut just as the tips begin to show. The purple variety is mostly grown in France, where the spears are cut once the tips are about $1^1/_2$ inches above the ground. Consequently, the stalks are white and the tops tinged with green or purple. In contrast, American and English asparagus grows above the ground and the spears are entirely green. Arguments continue over which has the better flavor, most growers expressing a preference for their own asparagus!

Thin, short asparagus are excellent when briefly steamed or stir-fried and added to salads. In Italy, they are served by themselves, scattered with grated Parmesan cheese.

Preparing

Unless the asparagus comes straight from the garden, cut off the bottom of the stalk as it is usually hard and woody. If the bottom parts of the stem also feel hard, pare this away with a potato peeler *(below)*. However, if the asparagus is very fresh, this is not necessary, and thin asparagus rarely needs trimming at all.

Buying and Storing

Asparagus has a relatively short growing season, from late spring to early summer. Nowadays, it is available in stores almost all year through, but outside the season it will have been imported. It is still good, but it is expensive and will not have the flavor of home-produced asparagus, since it starts to lose its flavor once it is cut.

When buying asparagus, the tips should be tightly furled and fresh looking, and the stalks fresh and straight. If the stalks are badly scarred or droopy, it indicates that they have been hanging around for too long and it is not worth buying. Asparagus will keep for several days if necessary. Untie the bundles and store in the salad drawer of the fridge.

Cooking

The problem with cooking asparagus is that the stalks take longer to cook than the tender tips, which need to be only briefly steamed. Ideally, use an asparagus steamer. Place the asparagus spears with the tips upward in the wire basket and then lower into a little boiling salted water in the steamer. Cover and cook until the stems are tender.

Alternately, if you don't have an asparagus steamer, place the bundle upright in a deep saucepan of boiling salted water. (The bundle can be wedged into place with potatoes.) Cover with a dome of foil and cook for 5-10 minutes or until the spears are tender. The cooking time depends largely on the thickness of the spears, but it is important not to overcook; the spears should still have a "bite" to them.

Asparagus can also be roasted in a little olive oil. This cooking method intensifies the flavor and is gratifyingly simple. Serve with just a sprinkling of sea salt – it's quite delicious! If steaming asparagus, serve simply with melted butter, which perfectly complements the luxury of the vegetable.

Left: Asparagus.
Above: White asparagus.

ARTICHOKES

Artichokes have an exquisite flavor and are a very sociable food to eat. They grow in abundance in Brittany, and during July and August farmers can frequently be seen selling them by the roadside. The globes are huge hearty specimens and are extremely fresh, so they make a good buy.

History

It is not known for certain whether artichokes were eaten in antiquity. Although they are mentioned by writers, they could have been referring to the cardoon, which is the uncultivated form of artichoke. Cardoons grew wild in many southern European countries, and, as far as we know, cultivated artichokes first became a popular food in Italy. However, Goethe did not share the Italians' liking for the vegetable and remarks in his book, *Travels Through Italy*, that "the peasants eat thistles," something he didn't care for at all.

Nowadays, artichokes are grown all over southern Europe and in California. People in Italy, France and Spain eat artichokes while the vegetable is still young, before the choke has formed and the entire artichoke is edible. Unfortunately, such young delicacies are not exported, but look out for them if you are in these countries.

Buying and Storing

It is only worth buying artichokes when they are in season, although they are available in supermarkets almost all year through. In winter, however, they are sad looking specimens, small and rather dry, and are really not worth the bother of cooking. At their best, artichokes should be lively looking with a good bloom on their leaves, the inner leaves wrapped tightly round the choke and heart inside. Artichokes will keep for 2-3 days in the salad drawer of the fridge but are best eaten as soon as possible.

Preparing and Cooking

First twist off the stalk which should also remove some of the fibers at the base and then cut the base flat and pull away any small base leaves. If the leaves are very spiky, trim them with a pair of scissors if liked *(above)*, then rinse under running water. Cook in boiling water, acidulated with the juice of half a lemon. Large artichokes need to be simmered for 30-40 minutes until tender. To test if they are done, pull off one of the outer leaves. It should come away easily and the base of the leaf should be tender.

heart. Eat the heart with a knife and fork, dipping it in the garlic butter or vinaigrette.

CARDOONS

This impressively large vegetable is closely related to the globe artichoke and has a superb flavor, a cross between arti-chokes and asparagus. Cultivated plants frequently grow to 6 feet in height, and once mature, cardoons, like celery, are blanched as they grow. This process involves wrapping the stalks with news-paper and black bags for several weeks, so that when harvested, in late fall, before the frosts, the stalks are a pale green.

The cardoon is a popular vegetable in southern Europe but less commonly available elsewhere. In Spain, for instance, it is much appreciated and often appears on the table, poached and served with chestnuts or walnuts. Only the inner ribs and heart are used.

Artichokes and Drink

Artichokes contain a chemical called cynarin, which in many people (although surprisingly not all) affects the taste buds by enhancing sweet flavors. Among other things, this will spoil the taste of wine. Consequently, don't waste good wine with artichokes but drink ice water instead, which should taste pleasantly sweet.

Eating Artichokes

Artichokes are fun to eat. They have to be eaten with fingers, which does away with any pomp and ceremony, always a handicap for a good dinner party. Serve one artichoke between two, so that people can share the fun of pulling off the leaves and dipping them into garlic butter or vinaigrette. If you want to serve one each, serve them in succession. The dipping sauces are an essential part of eating artichokes; people can either spoon a little onto their plates or have a little bowl each. After dipping, draw the leaf through your teeth, eating the fleshy part.

When most of the leaves have been eaten, a few thin pointed leaves remain in the center, which can be pulled off altogether. Then pull or cut away the fine prickly choke and discard, leaving the

Far left: Artichokes.
Top: Baby artichokes.
Above: Cardoons.

CELERY

Some people say that the very act of
eating celery has a slimming effect
because chewing it uses up more calories than the vegetable itself contains!
Although it may be insubstantial, celery
nevertheless has a distinct and individual flavor, sharp and savory, which
makes it an excellent flavoring for soups
and stuffings, as well as good on its own
or in salads. The astringent flavor and
crunchy texture of celery contrasts well
with the other ingredients in salads
such as Waldorf salad or Walnut and
avocado salad.

History

Celery is known to have been commonly
eaten in salads in Italy for hundreds of
years.

Nutrition

Celery is very low in calories but contains
potassium and calcium.

Varieties

Most grocers and supermarkets,
depending on the time of year, sell both
green and white celery. When celery is
allowed to grow naturally, the stalks are
green. However, by banking up earth
against the shoots celery is blanched:
the stalks are protected from sunlight
and remain pale and white.
Consequently, white celery is often
"dirty" – covered loosely in soil – while
green celery will always be clean.
White celery, which is frost hardy, is only
available in winter. It is more tender and
less bitter than green celery and is generally considered superior. Celery is
therefore thought of as a winter
vegetable and is traditionally used at
Christmas time, for stuffing and as a
sauce to go with turkey or ham.

Buying and Storing

White celery is in season during the
winter months. If possible, buy "dirty"
celery which hasn't been washed. It has
a better flavor than the pristine but
rather bland supermarket variety. Look
for celery with green fresh-looking leaves
and straight stems. If the leaves or any
outer stalks are missing, it is likely to be
old, so worth avoiding.

Celery will keep for several days in the salad drawer of the refrigerator. Limp celery can be revived by wrapping it in absorbent paper and standing it in a jar of water.

Preparing

Wash if necessary and pull the stalks apart, trimming the base with a sharp knife. Cut into thick or thin slices according to the recipe. When served raw and whole, the coarse outer "strings" should be removed from each stalk by pulling them up from the base.

Cooking and Serving

Serve celery raw and finely sliced in salads, mixed with cream cheese or sour cream. Braised celery is tasty, either whole or sliced. Celery has a distinctive, savory, astringent flavor so is excellent in soups or stuffings.

CELERY ROOT

Strictly speaking, celery root is classified as a root vegetable rather than a shoot or stem. It is knobbly with a patchy brown/white skin and has a similar but less pronounced flavor than celery. Grated and eaten raw, it has a crunchy texture, but when cooked it is more akin to potatoes. Thin slices of potato and celery root cooked *au gratin* with cream is a popular way of serving this vegetable.

Buying and Preparing

If possible, buy smallish bulbs of celery root. The flesh discolors when exposed to light, so as soon as you have peeled, sliced, diced or grated the celery root, plunge it into a bowl of acidulated water (water with lemon juice added).

Cooking

Celery root can be used in soups and broths, or can be diced and boiled and eaten in potato salads.

Left: Green celery.
Above: White celery.
Right: Celery root.

FIDDLEHEAD FERN

Sometimes called the ostrich fern, these shoots are a rich green color and are normally about 2 inches long. They have an unusual flavor, something like a cross between asparagus and okra, and have a slightly chewy texture, which makes them a popular choice for oriental dishes.

Preparing and Cooking

To prepare and cook, trim the ends and then steam or simmer in a little water or sauté in butter until tender. Use in salads or serve as a first course with a hollandaise sauce.

Right: Fiddlehead ferns.
Below left: Alfalfa sprouts.
Below right: Mung bean sprouts.

ORIENTAL SHOOTS

BAMBOO SHOOTS

In the Far East, edible bamboo shoots are sold fresh in the market. The young shoots are stripped of their brown outer skins and the insides are then eaten. Although fresh bamboo shoots can occasionally be found in oriental stores, the most readily available variety is sold in cans. The flavor is undoubtedly spoiled. Fresh bamboo shoots have a mild but distinct taste, faintly reminiscent of artichokes, while canned ones really taste of nothing at all. However, the texture, which, in Chinese cuisine particularly, is as important as the flavor, is not so impaired, and bamboo shoots have a pleasantly crunchy bite.

Preparing and Cooking

Peel away the outer skin and then cook in boiling water for about half an hour. They should feel firm, but not "rock" hard. Once cooked, slice thinly and serve by themselves as a side dish, with garlic butter or a sauce, or add to stir-fries, spring rolls or any oriental dish

where you need a contrast of textures. Since canned bamboo shoots have been preserved in brine, always rinse well before using.

BEAN SPROUTS

Bean sprouts are a neglected vegetable, used almost carelessly for oriental dishes but otherwise passed by as being insipid and not very interesting. It's a reputation they don't deserve: not only do they have a lovely fresh flavor, but they are also good for you.

All sorts of seeds can be sprouted, but the bean family are favorites among the sprouted vegetables. The bean sprouts most commonly available in the shops are sprouted mung beans, but aduki beans, alfalfa, lentils and soy beans can all be sprouted and taste delicious.

Nutrition

Beans sprouts contain a significant amount of protein, Vitamin C and many of the B vitamins. They have an excellent flavor too, best appreciated eaten raw in salads or sandwiches, and for slimmers they are an ideal food, low in calories, yet with sufficient substance to be filling, and with a flavor and texture that can be enjoyed without a dressing.

Buying and Storing

Bean sprouts should only be bought when absolutely fresh. They don't keep for long and they will taste sour if past their best. The sprouts should be firm, not limp, and and the tips should be green or yellow; avoid any that are beginning to turn brown.

Cooking

If stir-frying, add the bean sprouts at the last minute so they cook for the minimum period to keep plenty of crunch and retain their nutritional value. Most health food shops will have instructions on sprouting your own beans. Only buy seeds intended for sprouting.

PALM HEARTS

Fresh palm hearts are the buds of cabbage palm trees and are considered a delicacy in many parts of the world. They are available canned from oriental stores, but are most prized when fresh. These should be blanched before being cooked to eliminate any bitterness. They can be braised or sautéed and then served hot with a hollandaise sauce, or cold with a simple vinaigrette.

WATER CHESTNUTS

Water chestnut is the common name for a number of aquatic herbs and their nutlike fruit, the best known and most popular variety being the Chinese water chestnut, sometimes known as the Chinese sedge. In China they are grown in exactly the same way as rice, the plants needing the same conditions of

high temperatures, shallow water and good soil. In spring, the corms are planted in paddy fields which are then flooded to a depth of some 4 inches. These are drained in fall, and the corms are harvested and stored over the winter. Water chestnuts are much used in Chinese cooking and have a sweet crunchy flavor with nutty overtones.

They are edible cooked or raw and are excellent in all sorts of Chinese dishes.

Above: Sprouting mung beans.
Below: Clockwise from top left: Canned Water chestnuts, canned Bamboo shoots, fresh Water chestnuts, canned Palm hearts.

FENNEL

The vegetable fennel is closely related to the herb and spice of the same name. It is called variously bulb fennel, Florence fennel, sweet fennel, *finocchio dulce* or Italian fennel.

Like the herb, Florence fennel has the distinct flavor of anise, a taste that seems to go particularly well with fish, so the vegetable is often served with fish dishes while the herb or spice is commonly used in fish stocks, sauces or soups. The leaves are edible and can be used in soups and stocks as well as for garnishing.

History

Bulb fennel has only been popular for the last ten or so years, although it has a long history of cultivation, having been eaten by the ancient Egyptians, Greeks and Romans. In Italy, fennel has been eaten for several centuries: many of the best fennel recipes come from Italy and other parts of the Mediterranean.

Buying and Storing

If possible, buy small tender bulbs. The bulbs should be clean and white with no bruises or blemishes and the feathery leaves should be green and lively. Fennel will keep for a day or two in the salad drawer of the fridge.

Preparing

Unless the bulbs are very young and tender, remove the first layer of skin, as it is likely to be tough (this can be used for a stock). Fennel can then be sliced into slivers by cutting downward or into rings by cutting across the bulb. When used raw in salads, it must be cut into smaller pieces.

Cooking and Serving

Fennel can be served raw if it is thinly sliced and dressed with a light vinaigrette. In salads, its flavor contrasts well with apple, celery and other crunchy ingredients. Fennel is also excellent braised with onions, tomatoes and garlic.

Right: Bulb fennel.
Far right: Marsh samphire.

SAMPHIRE

There are two types of samphire. Marsh samphire grows in estuaries and salt marshes while rock samphire, sometimes called sea fennel, grows on rocky shores. The two are understandably confused since they are both connected with the sea, yet they are completely different plants.

The type likely to be sold by a fish dealer is marsh samphire. It is also known as glasswort and is sometimes called sea asparagus, as its shoots are similar to small asparagus shoots.

Although marsh samphire grows easily and is commonly found all over North America and Europe, it is not cultivated and is only available for a short time while it is in season, normally in late summer and early autumn.

Samphire has a distinctly salty, iodine flavor and a pleasant crisp texture. The flavor is reminiscent of the sea and goes particularly well with fish and seafood. However, samphire can be enjoyed simply steamed and dipped into melted butter.

Buying and Storing

When in season, good fish dealers get regular stocks of marsh samphire, and it should look bright and fresh. Buy it as you need it, as it will not keep for long.

Preparing and Cooking

If necessary, wash marsh samphire under cold running water. It is best steamed over a pan of boiling water for no more than 3 minutes. Alternately, blanch it in boiling water for 3-5 minutes and then drain. Samphire can be eaten raw but blanching it removes some of the saltiness.

To eat samphire, draw the shoots through the teeth to peel the succulent part from the thin central core.

ROOTS

POTATOES

History

The potato originates from South America. Most people learned at school that Sir Walter Raleigh brought the tubers to England from Virginia, but this never convinced historians as the potato was completely unknown in North America until the eighteenth century. They now believe that Sir Francis Drake was responsible. In 1586, after battling against the Spaniards in the Caribbean, Drake stopped to pick up provisions from Cartegena in northern Colombia – and these included tobacco and potato tubers. En route home, he stopped off at Roanoke Island, off the coast of Virginia. The first group of English colonists had been sponsored to settle there by Sir Walter Raleigh, but by this time they had had enough. Drake brought them back to England, along with some of Raleigh's men and, of course, the provisions – including the potato tubers.

Potatoes apparently fascinated Queen Elizabeth and intrigued horticulturists, but they were not an overnight success among the people. The wealthy frequently reviled them as being flavorless and the food of the poor. People distrusted the fact that they reached maturity underground, believing them to be the work of the devil. In Scotland, Presbyterian ministers darkly advised their congregations that there was no mention of potatoes in the Bible, and thus the eating of them was an ungodly act!

In spite of such a bad press, potatoes nevertheless were slowly recognized for their merit. By 1650 they were the staple food of Ireland, and elsewhere in Europe potatoes began to replace wheat as the most important crop, both for people and for livestock. In an early English cookbook, *Adam's Luxury and Eve's Cookery*, there are 20 different recipes for cooking and serving potatoes.

The first mention of potatoes in America is in 1719 in Londonderry, New Hampshire. They arrived not from the south, but via Irish settlers who brought their potatoes with them.

The current popularity of potatoes is probably thanks to a Frenchman called Antoine-Auguste Parmentier. A military pharmacist of the latter part of the eighteenth century, Parmentier recognized the virtues of the potato, both for its versatility and as an important food for the poor, and set out to improve its image. He persuaded Louis XVI to let him ostentatiously grow potatoes on royal land around the palace in Versailles to impress the fashion-conscious Parisians. He also produced a court dinner in which each course contained potatoes. Gradually, eating potatoes became chic, first among people in the French court and then in French Society. Today, if you see *Parmentier* in a recipe or on a menu, it means "with potato."

Nutrition

Potatoes are an important source of carbohydrate. Once thought to be fattening, we now know that, on the contrary, potatoes can be an excellent part of a calorie-controlled diet – provided, of course, they are not fried in oil or mashed with too much butter. Potatoes are also a very good source of vitamin C, and during the winter potatoes are often the main source of this vitamin. They also contain potassium, iron and vitamin B.

Varieties

There are more than 400 international varieties of potato, but unless you are a gardener, you will find only some 15 varieties generally available. Thanks to labeling laws, packaged potatoes carry their names, which makes it easier to learn to differentiate between the varieties and find out which potato is good for what.

New Potatoes

Carlingford: Available as a new potato or as main crop, Carlingford has a close white flesh.

Jersey Royal: Often the first new potato of the season, Jersey Royals have been shipped from Jersey for over a hundred years and have acquired an enviable reputation among everyone who enjoys good food. Boiled or steamed and then served with butter and a sprinkling of parsley, they cannot be beaten.

Jersey Royals are kidney-shaped, with yellow firm flesh and a distinctive flavor. Don't confuse Jersey Royals with Jersey Whites, which are actually Maris Pipers, grown in Jersey.

Maris Bard: A regularly shaped, slightly waxy potato with white flesh.

Maris Peer: This variety has dry firm flesh and a waxy texture and doesn't disintegrate when cooked – consequently, it is good in salads.

Main Crop Potatoes

Desiree: A potato with a pink skin and yellow soft-textured flesh. It is good for baking, frying, roasting and mashing.

Yukon Gold: A good masher with yellow flesh and pale skin.

Idaho: A russet-skinned potato that was the original favorite for making chips. It has an excellent, distinctive flavor, and should you find them for sale, buy them at once for baked potatoes. They are also good boiled or roasted.

Kerr's Pink: A good cooking potato with pink skin and creamy flesh.

King Edward: Probably the best known of potatoes, although not the best in flavor. King Edwards are creamy white in color with a slightly floury texture.

Red King Edwards are virtually identical except for their red skin. Both are good roasted or baked. However, the flesh disintegrates when boiled, so while good for mashing do not use King Edwards if you want whole boiled potatoes.

Maris Piper: This is a widely grown variety of potato, popular with growers and cooks because it is good for all kinds of cooking methods – baking, frying, roasting and mashing. It has a pale, smooth skin and creamy white flesh.

Left: Maris Bard potatoes.
Above: Kerr's pink (left) and Maris Piper (right) potatoes.
Right: Romano potatoes.

Pentland Dell: A long, oval-shaped potato with a floury texture that tends to disintegrate when boiled. For this reason, it is popular for roasting as the outside becomes soft when parboiled and then crisps up with the fat during roasting.

Romano: The Romano has a distinctive red skin with creamy flesh and is a good all-rounder, similar to Desiree.

Wilja: Introduced from Holland, this is a pale, yellow-fleshed potato with a good, sweet flavor and waxy texture.

Other Varieties

Although most of these varieties are also main crop, they are less widely available than those listed above but are increasingly sold in supermarkets. They are recommended for salads but many are also excellent sautéed or simply boiled.

Cara: A large main crop potato, which is excellent baked or boiled but is a good all-rounder.

Fingerlings: Thumb-sized, long baby potatoes are sometimes called finger potatoes. Among the many varieties are the German Lady's Finger. Since they are new crop potatoes, they need simply be boiled and then served either in salads or with a little butter and a sprinkling of parsley.

La Ratte: A French potato with a smooth skin and waxy yellow flesh. It has a chestnut flavor and is good in salads.

Linzer Delikatess: These small, kidney-shaped potatoes look a little like Jersey Royals but have a pale smooth skin. They do not have much taste and are best in salads where their flavor can be enhanced with other ingredients.

Pink Fir Apple: This is an old English variety, with pink skin and a smooth yellow flesh. It is becoming increasingly popular and has a distinctive flavor.

Above left: Cara (left) and Yukon Gold (right) potatoes.
Left: Linzer Delikatess potatoes.
Above: Desiree (left) and King Edward (right) potatoes.
Right: Fingerlings.

Blue: If you want to startle your friends, serve some of these striking purple-blue potatoes. There are several varieties of blue potato, ranging from a pale lavender to a wonderful deep purple. They have a dense texture, which makes them good for boiling. They are best served simply with a little butter and do retain their color when cooked.

Truffe de Chine: Another deep purple, almost black potato, of unknown origin but now grown in France. It has a nutty, slightly mealy flavor and is best served in a salad with a simple dressing. Like the Blue Potato, it retains its color after being cooked.

Recommended Varieties for Cooking

Baking: As for roasting, use potatoes with a floury texture, such as Idaho, Pentland Dell, King Edward and Maris Piper.

Boiling: Jersey Royal, Maris Bard and Maris Peer, or any of the Egyptian or Belgian new crop varieties. In addition, Pink Fir Apple, La Ratte and Linzer Delikatess are excellent.

Frying: King Edward, Idaho, Romano, Maris Piper and Desiree.

Mashing: Idaho, Maris Piper, King Edward, Wilja, Romano and Pentland Dell and Yukon Gold.

Roasting: Pentland Dell, Idaho, Maris Piper, King Edward, Desiree and Romano are among the best roasting potatoes. Ideally, use potatoes with a floury texture.

Salads: All the small, specialist potatoes, such as La Ratte, Pink Fir Apple and Linzer Delikatess as well as Fingerlings and small new potatoes.

Sautéing: Any waxy type of potato, such as Maris Bard, Maris Peer, any of the

specialist potatoes, and Romano and Maris Piper.

Buying and Storing

Potatoes should always be stored in a dark, cool, dry place. If they are stored exposed to the light, green patches will develop which can be poisonous, and they will go moldy if kept in the damp. When buying potatoes in bulk, it is best to buy them in paper sacks rather than plastic bags as humid conditions will cause them to go rotten. Similarly, if you buy potatoes in plastic bags, remove them when you get home and place them in a vegetable rack or in a paper bag, in a dark place.

Main crop potatoes will keep for several months in the right conditions but will gradually lose their nutritional value. New potatoes should be eaten within two or three days as they will go moldy if stored for too long.

Preparing

Most of the minerals and vitamins contained in potatoes are contained in or just below the skin. It is therefore better to eat potatoes in their skins. New potatoes need only be washed under running water; older potatoes need to be scrubbed.

If you peel potatoes, use a peeler that removes only the very top surface (*below left*) or, alternately, for salads and cold dishes, boil the potatoes in their skins and peel when cool.

Cooking

Baking: Cook baked potatoes in a low oven for well-browned and crunchy skins and fluffy flesh. Baked potatoes can be cooked more quickly in a microwave oven; for a crunchy texture to the skin place them in a hot oven for 10 minutes.

Boiling: It is impossible to generalize on how long to boil as it depends so much on the variety of potato. Try to cut potatoes to an even size (new potatoes should not need to be cut), salt the water if liked, cover and cook over a moderate heat. Don't boil potatoes too fiercely; old ones especially may disintegrate and leave you with a pan of starchy water.

French fries: Home-cooked French fries are a treat worth occasionally giving the family instead of the convenient but otherwise disappointing oven fries. However, they are fatty and therefore not good for you when eaten in great quantities or too often.

To make them, cut the potatoes into even-size pieces and place in a bowl of cold water for about 10 minutes before frying. Drain and then dry in a piece of muslin or an old dish towel before frying. Fry only as many pieces as will comfortably sit in the fat. Halfway through cooking, drain them and allow the oil to come back to temperature before plunging the fries back in. This browns the fries and they don't soak up excessive amounts of oil. Be warned; the cooking smells from making fries tend to linger!

Mashing: Boil the potatoes until tender, drain thoroughly and then tip them back into the pan; mash with a little milk and butter using a potato masher (*below right*), and season to taste with a little salt, if necessary, and pepper. Never use a food processor or blender: the potatoes will turn into an inedible thick gray paste. You may lightly whisk potatoes with a fork after mashing to fluff them up, but no more – for once modern machines have not improved on the basic utensil.

Roast Potatoes: The best roast potatoes are made using a floury textured potato such as Maris Piper or King Edward. Wash and cut them into even-size chunks and parboil them in lightly salted water until they begin to go tender and the outside looks soft. Drain them through a strainer or colander and then tip them back into the saucepan, put the lid on and shake the pan two or three times. This roughens up the surface of the potato. Place the potatoes in a dish of hot oil or fat, or around a joint of meat, and turn them over so that they are evenly coated. Roast them in the oven for 40-50 minutes until golden. Serve as soon as possible once cooked as the outsides become leathery if they are kept in a warm oven for too long.

Sautéing: There are various ways to sauté potatoes and no one way is better than another. For sautéed sliced potatoes, parboil whole potatoes for 5-10 minutes until they begin to soften. Drain them thoroughly and then slice into thick rounds. Using sunflower oil or a mixture of sunflower and olive oil (not butter as it will burn), fry them in a large frying pan. Turn the potatoes occasionally and cook until evenly browned. For sautéed, diced potatoes, cut the potatoes into small cubes, blanch for 2 minutes and then drain well. Either fry them on the stove or cook them in a little oil in the oven; turn them once or twice to brown evenly.

Steaming: New potatoes are excellent steamed. Place them on a bed of mint in a steamer or a colander over a pan of boiling water for 15-20 minutes.

Above left: Blue potatoes.
Below left: Truffe de Chine (left) and Pink Fir Apple (right) potatoes.

PARSNIPS

There's something very old-fashioned about parsnips. They conjure up images of cold winter evenings and warm comforting broths supped in front of a blazing wood fire. Nowadays parsnips are available all year through, but many people still feel they belong to winter, adding their characteristic flavor to soups and stews.

Parsnips are related to carrots, similarly sweet but with a distinct earthy flavor that blends well with other root vegetables and is also enhanced with spices and garlic.

History

Parsnips have a long history. The Romans grew and cooked them to make broths and stews. When they conquered Gaul and Britain, the Romans discovered that root vegetables grown in northerly areas had a better flavor than those grown in the south – they may have been the first to decree that parsnips should be eaten after the first frost!

Throughout the Dark Ages and early Middle Ages, parsnips were the main starchy vegetable for ordinary people (the potato had yet to be introduced). Parsnips were not only easy to grow but were a welcome food to eat during the lean winter months. They were also valued for their sugar content. Sweet parsnip dishes like jam and desserts became part of traditional English cookery, and they were also commonly used for making beer and wine. Parsnip wine is still one of the most popular of the country wines, with a beautiful golden color and a rich sherry-like flavor.

Nutrition

Parsnips contain moderate amounts of vitamins A and C, along with some of the B vitamins. They are also a source of calcium, iron and potassium.

Buying and Storing

Parsnips are really a winter crop, although nowadays they are available all year through. Tradition has it that parsnips are best after the first frost, but many people like the very young tender parsnips available in the early summer. When buying parsnips, choose small or

medium-size specimens as the large ones tend to be rather fibrous. They should feel firm and be a pale ivory color without any sprouting roots. Store parsnips in a cool place, ideally an airy larder or cool outhouse, where they will keep well for 8-10 days.

Preparing

Very small parsnips need little or no peeling; just trim the ends and cook according to your recipe. Medium-size and large parsnips must be peeled. Larger parsnips also must have the woody core removed; if it is cut out before cooking, the parsnips will cook more quickly and evenly.

Cooking

Roast parsnips are best parboiled for a few minutes before adding to the roasting dish. Very young parsnips can be roasted whole but larger ones are best halved or quartered lengthwise. Roast in butter or oil for about 40 minutes in an oven preheated to 400°F.

To boil parsnips, cut them into pieces about 2 inches long and boil for 15-20 minutes until tender. When boiled briefly like this, they keep their shape, but when added to a casserole or stew they eventually disintegrate. Don't worry if this happens; parsnips need plenty of cooking so that the flavor can blend with the other ingredients.

JERUSALEM ARTICHOKES

Jerusalem artichokes are related to the sunflower and have nothing to do with Jerusalem. One explanation for their name is that they were christened girasole, "Jerusalem," because their yellow flowers turned toward the sun. The Italian name for the Jerusalem artichoke is *girasole articocco.*

These small knobbly tubers have a lovely distinct flavor and are good in Palestine soup, a popular classic recipe. They are also delicious baked or braised.

History

Jerusalem artichokes are thought to have come from the central United States and Canada, where they were cultivated by the Native Americans as long ago as the fifteenth century. However, many writers have alluded to the fact that they cause "wind," which tempers their popularity.

Buying and Storing

Jerusalem artichokes are at their best during winter and early spring. They are invariably knobbly, but if possible buy neat ones with the minimum of knobs to save waste. The skins should be pale brown without any dark or soft patches. If they are stored in a cool dark place they will keep well for up to 10 days.

Preparing

The white flesh of artichokes turns purplish brown when exposed to light, so when peeling or slicing them raw, place them in a bowl of acidulated water (water to which the juice of about half a lemon has been added). Because artichokes are so knobbly, it is often easier to boil them in acidulated water in their skins and peel them afterward – the cooked skins should slip off easily.

Cooking

Jerusalem artichokes can be cooked in many of the ways in which you would cook potatoes or parsnips. They are excellent roasted, sautéed or dipped in batter and fried, but first parboil them for 10-15 minutes until nearly tender. For creamed artichokes, mix with potatoes in equal amounts; this slightly blunts their flavor, making a tasty side dish which is not too overpowering.

Left: Parsnips.
Below: Jerusalem artichokes.

TURNIPS AND RUTABAGAS

Turnips and rutabagas are both members of the cabbage family and are closely related to each other – so close that it is not surprising that their names are often confused. For instance, rutabagas are sometimes called Swedish turnips or swede-turnips and in Scotland, where they are thought of as turnips, they are called neeps.

Nowadays, the confusion is not so acute. Many grocers and supermarkets sell early or baby turnips or, better still, French turnips – *navets*.

Both are small and white, tinged either with green or in the case of *navets*, with pink or purple. Consequently, people are learning to tell their rutabagas from their turnips and also discovering what a delicious vegetable the turnip is.

History

Turnips have been cultivated for centuries, principally as an important livestock feed but also for humans. Although they were not considered the food of gourmets, they have been grown by poorer families as a useful addition to the winter table.

Rutabagas were known as turnip-rooted cabbages until the 1780s, when Sweden began exporting the vegetable to Britain and the shorter name resulted.

Until recently, turnips and rutabagas have not enjoyed a very high reputation among cooks in many parts of the world. This is partly because they are perceived as cattle food and partly because few people have taken the trouble to find acceptable ways of cooking them. Many cooks

tend to boil and then mash them to a watery pulp, and for many people this is the only way they have eaten either vegetable.

The French, in contrast, have had far more respect for the turnip, at least. For centuries they have devised recipes for their delicate *navets*, roasting them, caramelizing them in sugar and butter or simply steaming and serving with butter. Young, tender turnips have also been popular all over the Mediterranean region for many years, and there are many dishes using turnips with fish, poultry, or teamed with tomatoes, onions and spinach.

Nutrition

Both turnips and rutabagas are a good source of calcium and potassium.

Varieties

French *navets*, small round, squash-shaped turnips tinged with pink or purple, are increasingly available in grocers and supermarkets in the spring. Less common, but even more prized by the French, are the long carrot-shaped turnips, called *vertus*. English turnips are generally larger and are mainly green and white. Both have the characteristic peppery flavor, but this is less pronounced in *navets* which are generally sweeter.

Rutabagas generally have a more substantial, fuller-bodied flavor than turnips but at their best have a subtle, pleasant taste. The Marian is a yellow fleshed variety with a distinct "rutabaga" flavor. White-fleshed swedes, like Merrick, have a more watery, turnip-like flavor.

Buying and Storing

Turnips: If possible, buy French *navets* or failing that, the smallest and youngest turnips, available in stores from spring. They should be firm, smooth and unblemished, ideally with fresh green tops. Store in a cool dry place.

Rutabagas: Unlike turnips, rutabagas generally seem to come large. However, if possible, choose small rutabagas with smooth and unblemished skins as large ones are likely to be tough and fibrous. Store as for turnips.

Preparing and Cooking

Turnips: Young turnips should not require peeling; simply trim, then simmer or steam until tender. They are delicious raw, thinly sliced or grated into salads.

Peel older turnips (*below*) and then slice or dice before cooking. Remember, turnips are members of the cabbage family and older specimens particularly can show signs of that unpleasant cabbage rankness if overcooked. To avoid this, blanch turnips if they are to be served as a vegetable dish, or add sparingly to soups and casseroles, so that the rank flavor is dispersed.

Rutabagas: Peel to remove the skin and then cut into chunks (*below*). Rutabagas will disintegrate if overcooked, and they are unpleasantly raw tasting if not cooked sufficiently. The only answer is to check frequently while they are cooking. Rutabagas are particularly good when teamed with other root vegetables in soups and casseroles, adding a pleasant, slightly nutty flavor.

Far left: Navets and Turnips.
Below: Rutabagas.

CARROTS

After potatoes, carrots are without doubt our best-known and best-loved root vegetable. In the days when vegetables were served merely as an accessory to meat, carrots always made an appearance – often overcooked but still eaten up because, we were told, they helped you to see in the dark.

Carrots have many different flavors, depending on how they are cooked. Young, new season carrots braised in butter and a splash of water are intensely flavored and sweet; when steamed, they are tender and melting. Carrots grated into salads are fresh and clean tasting, while in casseroles they are savory with the characteristic carrot flavor. In soups they are fragrant and mild, and in cakes their flavor can hardly be detected, yet their sweetness adds richness.

History

Until the Middle Ages, carrots were purple. The orange carrots came from Holland, from where they were exported in the seventeenth and eighteenth centuries. Although purple and white carrots continued to be eaten in France, nowadays they are something of a rarity.

Nutrition

Carrots contain large amounts of carotene and vitamin A, along with useful amounts of vitamins B3, C and E. When eaten raw, they also provide good quantities of potassium, calcium, iron and zinc, but these are reduced when carrots are boiled.

The idea that carrots are good for your night sight originated in the Second World War. Early radar stations were established along the south and east coasts of England in 1939 to detect aggressors in the air or at sea. The Germans attributed this sudden remarkable night vision to the British habit of eating carrots. Indeed, the vitamin A in carrots forms retinal, a lack of which brings on night blindness.

Buying and Storing

Home-grown carrots are so much nicer than shop bought ones. Almost all vegetables have a better flavor if grown organically, but this is particularly true of carrots.

When buying carrots, look out for the very young, pencil-thin ones, which are beautifully tender either eaten raw or steamed for just a few minutes. Young carrots are commonly sold with their feathery tops intact, which should be fresh and green. Older carrots should be firm and unblemished. Avoid tired looking carrots as they will have little nutritional value.

Carrots should not be stored for too long. They will keep for several days if stored in a cool, airy place or in the salad drawer of the fridge.

Preparing

Preparation depends on the age of the carrots. The valuable nutrients lie either in or just beneath the skin, so if the carrots are young, simply wash them under cold running water. Medium-size carrots may need to be scraped and large carrots will need either scraping or peeling.

Cooking

Carrots are excellent cooked or raw. Children often like raw carrots as they have a very sweet flavor. They can be cut into julienne strips, with a dressing added, or grated into salads and coleslaw – their juices run and blend wonderfully with the dressing. Carrots can be cooked in almost any way you choose. As an accompaniment, cut them into julienne strips and braise in butter and cider, or cook in the minimum of stock and toss in butter and a sprinkling of caraway seeds.

Roasted carrots are delicious, with a melt-in-the-mouth sweetness. Parboil large ones first, but younger carrots can be quickly blanched or added directly to the pan with a joint of meat.

HORSERADISH

Horseradish is grown for its pungent root, which is normally grated and mixed with cream or oil and vinegar and served with roast beef. Fresh horseradish is available in many supermarkets in the spring, and you can make your own horseradish sauce by simply peeling the root and then mixing 3 tablespoons of grated horseradish with $^2/_3$ cup heavy or whipping cream and adding a little Dijon mustard, vinegar and sugar to taste. As well as being excellent with hot or cold beef, horseradish sauce is delicious with smoked trout or mackerel or spread thinly on sandwiches with a fine pâté.

Left: Carrots.
Right: Horseradish.

BEETS

Experience of vinegar-sodden beets has doubtlessly put many people off them. Those who love them know to buy their beets fresh, so that they can cook them themselves. They can be served in a number of different ways: baked and served with sour cream, braised in a creamy sauce, grated in a salad or used for the classic soup *borscht*.

History

Beets are closely related to sugar beets and mangelwurzels. As the demand for sugar increased over the centuries, when sugar could successfully be extracted from beets, sugar production became a big industry in Britain and Europe.

Mangelwurzels were eaten in parts of Europe and in England in times of famine, although they were primarily grown as cattle fodder.

Beets, however, have probably been eaten since Roman times. By the mid-nineteenth century they were clearly a popular vegetable, and Mrs Beeton in her famous cookbook has 11 recipes for them, including a beet and carrot jam and beet fritters.

Nutrition

Beets are an excellent provider of potassium. The leaves, which have the flavor of spinach, are high in vitamin A, iron and calcium.

Buying and Storing

If possible, buy small beets which have their whiskers intact and have at least 2 inches of stalk at the top; if they are too closely cropped they will bleed during cooking. Beets will keep for several weeks if stored in a cool place.

Preparing

To cook beets whole, first rinse under cold running water. Cut the stalks to about 1 inch above the root and don't cut away the root or peel it – or the glorious deep red color will bleed away. When serving cold in salads, or where the recipe calls for chopped or grated beets, peel away the skin with a potato peeler or sharp knife.

Cooking

To bake in the oven, place the cleaned beet in a dish with a tight-fitting lid, and add 4-5 tablespoons of water. Lay a double layer of foil over the dish before covering with the lid, then bake in a low oven for 2-3 hours or until the beets are tender. Check occasionally to ensure the pan doesn't dry out and to see whether the beets are cooked. They are ready when the skin begins to wrinkle and can be easily rubbed away with your fingers. Alternately, simply wrap the beets in a double layer of foil and cook as above. To boil beets, prepare as above and simmer for about 1 1/2 hours.

BEET GREENS

The tops of several root vegetables are not only edible, but are also extremely nutritious. Beet greens are particularly good, being very high in vitamins A and C, and indeed have more iron and calcium than spinach itself. They are delicious, but not easily available unless you grow your own. If you are lucky enough to get some, boil the greens for a few minutes, then drain well and serve with butter or olive oil.

Left: Beets.
Above right: Scorzonera.
Below right: Salsify.

SALSIFY AND SCORZONERA

These two root vegetables are closely related to each other as well as to members of the same family as dandelion and lettuce. All have long tapering roots.

Salsify has a white or pale brownish skin and scorzonera, sometimes called black salsify, has a black skin. They both have a pale creamy flesh and a fairly similar flavor reminiscent of artichokes and asparagus. Salsify is said to have the superior flavor and has been likened to oysters (it is sometimes referred to as the oyster plant), although many people fail to detect this.

Both salsify and scorzonera make an unusual and pleasant accompaniment, either creamed or fried in butter. They can also be also used in soups.

History

Salsify is native to the Mediterranean but now grows in most areas of North America and Europe. Scorzonera is a southern European plant.

Both roots are classified as herbs and, like many wild plants and herbs, their history is bound up with their use in medicines. The roots, together with their leaves and flowers, were used for the treatment of heartburn, loss of appetite and various liver diseases.

Buying and Storing

Choose specimens that are firm and smooth and, if possible, still with their tops on, which should look fresh and lively. Salsify will keep for several days stored in a cool dark place.

Preparing

Salsify and scorzonera are difficult to clean and peel. Either scrub the root under cold running water and then peel after cooking, or peel with a sharp stainless steel knife (*below*). As the flesh discolors quickly, place the trimmed pieces into acidulated water (water to which lemon juice has been added).

Cooking

Cut into short lengths and simmer for 20–30 minutes until tender. Drain well and sauté in butter, or serve with lemon juice, melted butter or chopped parsley.

Alternately, they can be puréed for soups or mashed. Cooked and cooled salsify and scorzonera can be served in a mustard or garlic vinaigrette with a simple salad.

EXOTIC ROOTS

Throughout the tropical regions of the world all sorts of tubers are grown and used for a fabulous variety of dishes. Yams, sweet potatoes, cassava and taro, to name but a few, are for many people a staple food, not only cooked whole as a vegetable accompaniment, but ground or pounded for bread and cakes. There is an enormous variety of these tropical and subtropical tubers, and while they cannot be cultivated in a moderate climate, the more common tubers are now widely available in specialist shops and in most supermarkets.

SWEET POTATOES

Sweet potatoes are another one of those vegetables that once tasted, are never forgotten. They are, as the name suggests, sweet, but they also have a slightly spicy taste. It's this distinct sweet and savory flavor which makes them such an excellent foil to many savory dishes and

they are fittingly paired with meat dishes that need a touch of sweetness, like turkey or pork.

History

Sweet potatoes are native to tropical America, but today they are grown all over the tropical world. They have been grown in South America from before the Inca civilizations and were introduced into Spain before the ordinary potato. They also have a long history of cultivation in Asia spreading from Polynesia to New Zealand in the fourteenth century.

They are an important staple food in the Caribbean and southern United States, and many famous recipes feature these vegetables. Candied sweet potatoes, for instance, are traditionally served with ham or turkey at Thanksgiving all over the United States, while Jamaica and the West Indies abound with sweet potato dishes, from the simple baked

potato to Caribbean pudding, a typically sweet and spicy dish with sweet potatoes, coconut, limes and cinnamon.

Sweet potatoes appear to have been introduced to England even earlier than regular potatoes. Henry VIII was said to have been very partial to them baked in a pie, believing they would improve his love life! If Henry VIII was eating sweet potatoes in the early/mid-sixteenth century, then it's likely he received them via the Spanish, who, thanks to Christopher Columbus, were busy conquering the New World, thus experiencing a whole range of tropical vegetables and fruit.

Varieties

The skin color ranges from white to pink to reddish brown. The red-skinned variety, which has a whitish flesh, is the one most commonly used in African and Caribbean cooking.

Buying and Storing

Choose small or medium-size ones if possible as larger specimens tend to be rather fibrous. They should be firm and evenly shaped; avoid those that seem withered, have damp patches or are sprouting. They will keep for several days in a cool place.

Preparing and Cooking

If baking, scrub the potatoes well and cook exactly as you would for ordinary potatoes. To boil, either cook in their skins and remove these after cooking, or peel and place in acidulated water (water to which lemon juice has been added). This prevents them turning brown and it's worth boiling them in lightly acidulated water for the same reason. Sweet potatoes can be cooked in any of the ways you would cook ordinary potatoes - roast, boiled, mashed or baked. However, avoid using them in creamy or gratin-type dishes. They are both too sweet and too spicy for that.

It is preferable to roast or sauté them with onions and other savory ingredients to bring out their flavor, or mash them and serve them over chunks of chicken for a crusted chicken pie.

Preparing

Peel away the skin thickly to remove the outer skin and the layer underneath that contains the poison dioscorine. This in fact is destroyed during cooking, but discard the peel carefully. Place the peeled yam in salted water as it discolors easily.

Cooking

Yams, like potatoes, are used as the main starchy element in a meal, boiled and mashed, fried, sautéed or roasted. They tend to have an affinity with spicy sauces and are delicious cut into discs, fried and sprinkled with a little salt and cayenne pepper. African cooks frequently pound boiled yam to make a dough which is then served with spicy stews and soups.

TARO/EDDO

Like yams, taro is another hugely important tuber in tropical areas, and for thousands of years it has been a staple food for many people. It goes under many different names; in South-east Asia, South and Central America, all over Africa and in the Caribbean it is called variously eddo and dasheen.

There are two basic varieties of taro – a large barrel-shaped tuber and a smaller variety, which is often called eddo or dasheen. They are all a dark mahogany brown with a rather shaggy skin, looking like a cross between a beet and a rutabaga.

Although they look very similar, taro belongs to a completely different family from yam and in flavor and texture is noticeably different. Boiled, it has a completely unique flavor, something like a floury water chestnut.

Buying and Storing

Try to buy small specimens; the really small smooth bulbs are tiny attachments to the larger taro and are either called eddoes, or rather sweetly, "sons of taro." Stored in a cool, dark place, they should keep for several weeks.

YAMS

Yams have been a staple food for many cultures for thousands of years. There are today almost countless varieties, of different shapes, sizes and colors and called different names by different people. Most varieties are thought to have been native to China, although they found their way to Africa during a very early period and became a basic food, being easy to grow in tropical and subtropical conditions, and containing the essential carbohydrate of all staple foods.

Although cush-cush or Indian yam was indigenous to America, most yams were introduced to the New World as a result of the slave trade in the sixteenth century. Today with such a huge variety of this popular vegetable available, there are innumerable recipes for yam, many probably not printed and published, but handed down by word of mouth from mother to daughter and making their appearance at mealtimes all over the hot regions of the world.

Varieties

The greater yam, as the name suggests, can grow to a huge size. A weight of 137 pounds has been recorded. The varieties you are likely to find in stores will be about the size of a small marrow, although smaller yams are also available such as the sweet yam, which looks like a large potato and is normally covered with whiskery roots. All sizes have a coarse brown skin and can be white or red-fleshed.

In Chinese stores, you may find the Chinese yam, which is a more elongated, club-like shape and is covered with fine whiskers.

Buying

Look out for firm specimens with unbroken skins. The flesh inside should be creamy and moist and if you buy from a grocery, the storekeeper may well cut open a yam so you can check that it is fresh. They can be stored for several weeks in a cool, dark place.

Left: Sweet potatoes.
Above: Yams.

Preparing

Taros, like yams, contain a poison just under the skin which produces an allergic reaction. Consequently, either peel taros thickly, wearing rubber gloves, or cook in their skins. The toxins are completely eliminated by boiling, and the skins peel off easily.

Cooking

Taros soak up large quantities of liquid during cooking, and this can be turned to advantage by cooking in well-flavored stock or with tomatoes and other vegetables. For this reason, they are excellent in soups and casseroles, adding bulk and flavor in a similar way to potatoes. They can also be steamed or boiled, deep-fried or puréed for fritters, but must be served hot as they become sticky if allowed to cool.

CALLALOO

Callaloo are the leaves of the taro plant, poisonous if eaten raw, but used widely in Asian and Caribbean recipes. They are cooked thoroughly, then used for wrapping meat and vegetables. Callaloo can also be shredded and cooked together with pork, bacon, crab, shrimp, okra, chili, onions and garlic, together with lime and coconut milk to make one of the Caribbean's most famous dishes, named after the leaves themselves, Callaloo.

JICAMA

Also known as the Mexican potato, this large root vegetable is a native of central America. It has a thin brown skin and white, crunchy flesh which has a sweet, nutty taste. It can be eaten cooked in the same way as potatoes or sliced and added raw to salads.

Buy specimens that are firm to the touch. Jicama in good condition will keep for about two weeks if stored in a plastic bag in the refrigerator.

Top: Taros (Eddoes).
Above: Jicama.
Left: Callaloo.

CASSAVA

This is another very popular West Indian root, used in numerous Caribbean dishes. It is native to Brazil, and found its way to the West Indies surprisingly via Africa, where it also became a popular vegetable. Known as cassava in the West Indies, it is called manioc or mandioc in Brazil, and juca or yucca is used in other parts of South America.

Cassava is used to make tapioca, and in South America a sauce and an intoxicating beverage are prepared from the juice. However, in Africa and the West Indies it is eaten as a vegetable either boiled, baked or fried, or cooked and pounded to a dough to make *fufu,* a traditional savory African pudding.

Right: Cassava.
Below left: Ginger.
Below right: Galangal.

GINGER <u>AND</u> GALANGAL

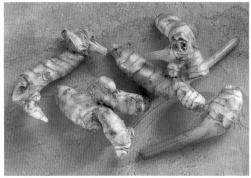

GINGER

This is probably the world's most important and popular spice and is associated with a number of different cuisines - Chinese, Indian and Caribbean, to name but a few. It was known in Europe during the Roman period, but was still fairly rare until the spice routes opened up trade in the sixteenth and seventeenth centuries. Like many spices, ginger has the quality of enhancing and complementing both sweet and savory food, adding a fragrant spiciness to all sorts of dishes. However, while ground ginger is best in recipes which will be baked, and preserved ginger, where the ginger is preserved in syrup, tastes wonderful in desserts, for savory dishes, always use fresh ginger.

Nowadays, the pale, knobbly roots of fresh ginger are widely available in supermarkets and whenever possible, buy just a small quantity, as you will not need a great deal and fresh ginger will not keep indefinitely.

To prepare, simply peel away the skin with a sharp knife and grate or thinly slice according to the recipe.

GREATER GALANGAL

Galangal looks similar to ginger except that the rhizome is thinner and the young shoots are bright pink. The roots should be prepared in the same way as ginger and can be used in curries and satay sauces.

— FOUR —

GREENS

Spinach

Brussels Sprouts

Cauliflower

Sprouting Broccoli
and Calabrese

Turnip Tops

Cabbage

Kale and Curly Kale

Garden and Wild Leaves

Chinese Greens

Kohlrabi

Chard

SPINACH

For many people, spinach is inextricably linked with Popeye, the cartoon character who used to eat huge amounts of spinach. It is a wonderfully versatile vegetable, popular worldwide, with nearly every cuisine featuring spinach somewhere in its repertoire. The Italians are particularly partial to spinach and have hundreds of dishes using the vegetable. The words *à la florentine* mean the dish contains spinach.

As well as being delicious on its own, chopped or puréed spinach can be mixed with a range of other ingredients with superb results. It has a particular affinity with dairy products and in the Middle East, feta or helim cheese is used to make boreks or other spinach pies. The Italians mix spinach with ricotta or Parmesan cheese for a huge range of recipes, and the English use eggs and sometimes Cheddar for a spinach soufflé.

History

Spinach was first cultivated in Persia several thousands of years ago. It came to Europe via the Arab world; the Moors introduced it to Spain, and Arabs in the Middle East took it to Greece. It first appeared in England in the fourteenth century, probably via Spain. It is mentioned in the first known English cookbook, where it is referred to as *spynoches*, which echoes the Spanish word for spinach, *espinacas*. It quickly became a popular vegetable, probably because it is quick and easy to grow and similarly easy and quick to cook.

Nutrition

Spinach is an excellent source of vitamin C if eaten raw, as well as vitamins A and B, calcium, potassium and iron. Spinach was originally thought to provide far more iron than it actually does, but the iron is "bound" up by oxalic acid in cooked spinach, which prevents the body absorbing anything but the smallest amounts. Even so, it is still an extremely healthy vegetable whether eaten cooked or raw.

Buying and Storing

Spinach grows all year through, so you should have no difficulty in buying it fresh. Frozen spinach is a poor

substitute, mainly because it has so little flavor, so it is worth the effort to use the fresh product.

Spinach leaves should be green and lively; if they look tired and the stalks are floppy, shop round until you find something in better condition. Spinach reduces significantly when cooked: about 1 pound will serve two people. Store it in the salad drawer of the fridge, where it will keep for 1-2 days.

Preparing

Wash well in a bowl of cold water and remove any tough or large stalks.

Cooking

Throw the leaves into a large pan with just the water that clings to the leaves and place over a low heat with a sprinkling of salt. Cover the pan so the spinach steams in its own liquid and shake the pan occasionally to prevent the spinach sticking to the bottom. It cooks in 4-6 minutes, wilting down to about an eighth of its former volume. Drain and press out the remaining liquid with the back of a spoon.

Spinach can be used in a variety of ways. It can be chopped and served with lots of butter, or similarly served with other spring vegetables such as

BRUSSELS SPROUTS

baby carrots or young fava beans. For frittatas, chop the spinach finely, stir in a little Parmesan cheese, a good sprinkling of salt and pepper and a dash of cream, if liked, and stir into the omelet before cooking. Alternately, purée it for sauces or blend it for soups. Spinach is also delicious raw, served with chopped bacon or croûtons. A fresh spinach salad is delicious as the leaves have just the right balance of flavor – sharp but not overpowering.

Below: Spinach.
Below right: Brussels sprouts.

Brussels sprouts have a pronounced and sweet nutty flavor, quite unlike cabbage, although the two are closely related. They are traditionally served at Christmas with chestnuts and indeed have a definite affinity for certain nuts – particularly the sweet flavored nuts, e.g. almonds, pair well rather than hazelnuts or walnuts.

History

Brussels sprouts were cultivated in Flanders (now Belgium) during the Middle Ages. They are basically miniature cabbages which grow in a knobbly row on a long tough stalk. The Germans call sprouts *rosenkohl* – rose cabbage – a pretty and descriptive name as they look like small rosebuds.

Buying and Storing

Buy Brussels sprouts as fresh as possible as older ones are more likely to have that strong unpleasant "cabbage" flavor. They should be small and hard with tightly wrapped leaves. Avoid any that

are turning yellow or brown or have loose leaves.

Brussels sprouts will keep for several days in a cool place such as a larder or salad drawer of a fridge, but it is far better to buy them as you need them.

Preparing

Cut away the bottom of the stalk and remove the outer leaves. Some people cut a cross through the bottom of the stalk although this is not really necessary. If you haven't been able to avoid buying big Brussels sprouts, cut them in half or into quarters, or slice them thinly for stir-frying.

Cooking

As with cabbage, either cook Brussels sprouts very briefly or braise slowly in the oven. Cook in small amounts of fast boiling water for about 3 minutes until just tender. To stir-fry Brussels sprouts, slice into three or four pieces and then fry in a little oil and butter – they taste great with onions and ginger.

CAULIFLOWER

Cauliflower is a member of the cabbage family, *Brassica oleracea*. Like all cabbages, cauliflower suffers terribly from overcooking. A properly cooked cauliflower has a pleasant fresh flavor but when overcooked it turns grey and becomes unpalatably soft, taking on a nasty rank flavor with an unpleasant aftertaste. Children often like raw cauliflower even though they may not connect it with the same vegetable served up as boiled.

History

Cauliflower is thought to have come originally from China and thence to the Middle East. The Moors introduced it to Spain in the twelfth century and from there it found its way to England via established trading routes. The early cauliflower was the size of a tennis ball but is has gradually been cultivated to the enormous sizes we see today. Ironically, baby cauliflowers are now fashionable.

Varieties

Green and occasionally purple cauliflowers are available in the stores. The purple variety was originally grown in Sardinia and Italy but is increasingly grown by other market gardeners. They look pretty and unusual but are otherwise similar to white cauliflower. Dwarf varieties of cauliflower are now commonly available in stores.

Broccoli Romanescoes: As well as baby white cauliflowers, broccoli romanescoes are also avaliable. These pretty green or white vegetables look like a cross between broccoli and cauliflower, but are more closely related to cauliflower. They taste very much like cauliflower, but since they are quite small, they are less likely to be overcooked and consequently retain their excellent flavor.

Broccoflower: A cross between broccoli and cauliflower, this looks like a pale green cauliflower. It has a mild flavor and should be cooked in the same way as you would cauliflower.

Right: Baby cauliflowers.
Far right top: Broccoli romanescoes.
Far right bottom: Green cauliflowers.

Nutrition

Cauliflower contains potassium, iron and zinc, although cooking reduces the amounts. It is also a good source of vitamins A and C.

Buying and Storing

In top condition, a cauliflower is a creamy white color with the outer leaves curled round the flower. The head should be unblemished with no black or discolored areas and the outer leaves should look fresh and crisp. Keep cauliflower in a cool place for no longer than 1-2 days; after that it will deteriorate and valuable nutrients will be lost.

Preparing

To cook a cauliflower whole, first trim away the coarse bottom leaves (leave the inner ones on, if liked). Very large cauliflowers are best halved or broken into florets, as the outside will overcook before the inside is tender. Some people trim away the stalk, but others like this part and only trim off the very thick stalk at the bottom of the plant.

Cooking

Cauliflowers are excellent steamed, either whole or in florets. Place in a steamer or colander over a pan of boiling water, cover and steam until just tender and immediately remove from the heat. The florets can then be fried in olive oil or butter for a few minutes to give a lightly browned finish.

When cooking a cauliflower whole, start testing it after 10 minutes; it should feel tender but still have plenty of "bite" left in it. Cauliflower is a popular vegetable accompaniment, either served with just a little butter, or with a tomato or cheese sauce. It is also good stir-fried with onions and garlic together with a few tomatoes and capers.

Cauliflower is excellent in salads or used for crudités. Either use it raw or blanch it in boiling water for 1-2 minutes, then refresh under cold running water.

Small cauliflowers and broccoli romanescoes are intended to be cooked whole, and can be steamed or boiled, covered with a lid, in the minimum of water for 4-5 minutes until just tender.

SPROUTING BROCCOLI AND CALABRESE

Varieties

Calabrese Broccoli: This is the vegetable we today commonly call broccoli, with large beautiful, blue-green heads on succulent stalks. It is named after the Italian province of Calabria where this variety was first developed.

Purple Sprouting Broccoli: The original variety – it has long thin stalks with small flowerheads that are normally purple but can be white or green. Heads, stalks and tender leaves are all edible. The purple heads turn green when cooked but the others keep their color. Purple sprouting broccoli is more seasonal than the easily available calabrese; it is usually available from late winter onward.

Buying and Storing

If possible, buy loose broccoli rather than the pre-wrapped bundles, because it is easier to check that it is fresh and also because wrapped vegetables tend to deteriorate more quickly.

Purple sprouting broccoli can also be sold loose or prepacked. Check that the stalk, flower head and leaves all look fresh and that the florets are tightly closed and bright green. Neither type will keep for long.

Broccoli or calabrese is a relatively modern vegetable and is one of the most popular. It is quick and easy to prepare with little or no waste and similarly easy to cook. It is attractive, whether served raw or cooked, and you can buy it in the quantity you require, unlike cauliflower or cabbage.

History

Before calabrese came into our stores, people bought and ate purple sprouting broccoli. This is basically an "untidy" version of calabrese, with long shoots and clusters of flowerheads at the end – the broccoli we know today has neat tidy heads. The stalks of purple sprouting broccoli have a faint asparagus flavor.

The Romans cooked purple sprouting broccoli in wine or served it with sauces and it is still a popular vegetable today in Italy, cooked in the oven with anchovies and onions or served with pasta in a garlic and tomato sauce.

Preparing and Cooking

Trim the ends and remove any discolored leaves.

Calabrese Broccoli: Break into even-size pieces, dividing the stem and floret lengthwise if they are thick. Cook in a little boiling water for 4-5 minutes until just tender and then drain. Do not steam this variety of broccoli as its vibrant green color tends to turn gray.

Purple Sprouting Broccoli: Either steam in long, even-size lengths in a steamer or, if you have an asparagus steamer, cook as you would asparagus. Alternately, tie the stems loosely together and stand in a little water – if necessary, wedge it in with a potato or rolled up piece of foil. Cover with a dome of foil and steam for 4-5 minutes until tender.

Serving

Serve both varieties simply with butter and lemon juice or with a hollandaise or béarnaise sauce as an accompaniment. They are also excellent stir-fried.

Above far left: Purple cauliflower.
Below far left: Purple sprouting broccoli.
Above: Calabrese broccoli.
Below: Turnip tops.

TURNIP TOPS

Turnip tops, like beet greens, are both delicious and nutritious. They are not widely available but if you are able to buy some or if you grow your own, slice them *(below)* and boil or steam for a few minutes, then drain and serve with butter.

CABBAGE

Cabbage, sliced and cooked, can be one of two things: deliciously crisp, with a mild pleasant flavor – or overcooked and horrible! Cabbage and other brassicas contain the chemical hydrogen sulphide, which is activated during cooking at about the point the vegetable starts to soften. It eventually disappears, but during the in-between time, cabbage acquires its characteristic rank smell and flavor. So, either cook cabbage briefly, or cook it long and slow, preferably with other ingredients so that flavors can mingle.

History

Cabbage has a long and varied history. However, because there are many varieties of cabbage under the general heading of "brassica", it is difficult to be sure whether the variety the Greeks and Romans enjoyed is the same as today's round cabbage, or something more akin to kale or even Chinese cabbage.

The round cabbages we know today were an important food during the Dark Ages, and by the Middle Ages they were in abundance, as you will see if you study the paintings of that period. These commonly show kitchen tables or baskets at market positively groaning with fruit and vegetables, and cabbages in all their shapes and sizes were often featured.

Medieval recipes suggest cooking cabbages with leeks, onions and herbs. In the days when all except the very wealthy cooked everything in one pot, it is fair to assume that cabbages were cooked long and slow.

Varieties

Savoy Cabbage: This is a variety of green cabbage with crimped or curly leaves. It has a mild flavor and is particularly tender, thus needing less cooking than other varieties.
Spring Greens: These have fresh loose heads with a pale yellow-green heart. They are available in spring and are delicious simply sliced, steamed and served with butter.

Right: Savoy cabbage.
Above far right: Green cabbage.
Below far right: Spring greens.

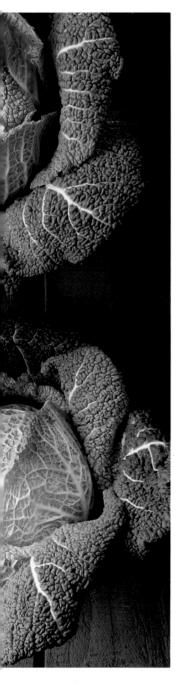

Green Cabbage: The early green, or spring, cabbages are dark green, loose-leafed and have a slightly pointed head. They have little or no heart as they are picked before this has had time to develop. Nevertheless, they are a very good cabbage and all but the very outside leaves should be tender. As the season progresses, larger, firmer and more pale green cabbages are available. These are a little tougher than the spring cabbages and need longer cooking.

Red Cabbage: A beautifully colored cabbage with smooth firm leaves. The color fades during cooking unless a little vinegar is added to the water. Red cabbage can be pickled or stewed with spices and flavorings.

White Cabbage: Sometimes called Dutch cabbages, white cabbages have smooth firm pale green leaves. They are available throughout the winter. They are good cooked or raw. To cook, slice them thinly, then boil or steam and serve with butter. To serve raw, slice thinly and use in a coleslaw.

Buying and Storing

Cabbages should be fresh looking and unblemished. When buying, avoid any with wilted leaves or those that look or feel puffy. Savoys and collard greens will keep in a cool place for several days; firmer cabbages will keep happily for much longer.

Preparing

Remove the outer leaves, if necessary, and then cut into quarters. Remove the stalk and then slice or shred according to your recipe or to taste.

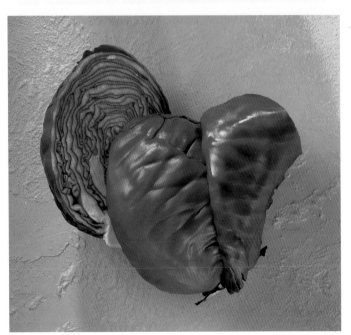

Cooking

For green or white cabbages, place the shredded leaves in a pan with a pat of butter and a couple of tablespoons of water to prevent burning. Cover and cook over a medium heat until the leaves are tender, occasionally shaking the pan or stirring.

Red cabbage is cooked quite differently and is commonly sautéed in oil or butter and then braised in a low oven for up to 1 1/2 hours with apples, currants, onions, vinegar, wine, sugar and spices.

KALE AND CURLY KALE

Kale is the name used for a variety of green-leafed vegetables of the brassica family. Most kales have thick stems and robust leaves that do not form a head. Many kales have curly leaves, which are the variety most commonly eaten. Large coarse-leafed kales are grown for cattle and sheep feeds.

History

Kale is thought to be one of the first cultivated brassicas. Colewort, the wild ancestor, still grows along the coasts of western Europe.

Varieties

Collards: Collards, or collard greens, are a popular green vegetable in the southern United States. They are grown in summer and autumn for harvesting in the spring and are a good source of vitamin A.
Curly Kale: With its crimped, curly leaves, this is the most commonly available kale, although even this can be quite hard to come by. If you are a big fan and don't grow your own, try farm stores in early spring.
Purple or Silver Kale: This is an ornamental variety, and is grown almost exclusively for display.

Preparing and Cooking

Kale is probably the strongest tasting of the brassicas and is best cooked simply, paired with a bland-flavored vegetable, such as potatoes. To prepare, break the leaves from the stalk and then cut out any thick stalk from the leaf. This can then be rolled and sliced or cooked whole. Boil the leaves in a little salted water for 3-5 minutes until tender. Owing to its robust nature, kale is frequently teamed with fairly hot spices and is consequently popular in many Indian dishes.

Above far left: White cabbage.
Below far left: Red cabbage.
Left: Collards.
Above: Curly kale.

GARDEN AND WILD LEAVES

VINE LEAVES

All leaves from vines that produce grapes can be eaten when young. They make an ideal wrapping for various meats and vegetables as they are surprisingly strong and of course edible. Most countries that produce wine will have dishes where vine leaves appear. *Dolmades*, commonly eaten in Greece and the Middle East is perhaps the best known dish, but in France, Spain and Italy, there are recipes using vine leaves to wrap small birds, like quail or snipe.

Vine leaves have a faintly lemon/cabbage flavor which can be detected at its best in a good *dolmades*. The leaves must be cooked briefly before using, so that they are pliable and don't crack or break as you wrap the food. Bring to the boil and simmer for about 1 minute. The leaves should then be drained and separated until you are ready to use them.

DANDELION

Any child who has picked dandelions for his or her rabbits or guinea pigs and has watched them gobble them up greedily will know that this weed, though hated by the gardener in the family, has something going for it. Some gardeners, of course, are partial to dandelion and raise the plant carefully so that the leaves are fresh and tender for the salad, and in France dandelions can often be seen for sale at market.

Look in any book of herbal remedies, and dandelions will feature prominently.

They are a well-known diuretic, their French name – *pissenlits* (piss-a-bed) – attesting to this in no uncertain terms.

Although it's gratifying to pick your own vegetables for free, it is generally recommended, if you like dandelions, that you buy the domestic seeds and grow your own. These are likely to be the juiciest and least bitter plants. If you do pick

your own, do so well away from the roadside and wash the leaves carefully.

Dandelion leaves can be added to salads or used in *pissenlits au lard*, where whole young dandelion plants are dressed in vinaigrette and then covered in finely chopped pieces of salt pork or bacon and bacon fat.

SORREL

Sorrel is not always available commercially, although it is in France and is greatly prized. However, it grows wild in cool soils, or can be grown in your own garden. Young leaves are delicious in salads, or, later in the year, can be used in soups or sauces to accompany fish. It has a sharp, distinct, lemon flavor and is commonly teamed with eggs and cream.

ORACHE

Although not related to spinach, this beautiful red or golden-leafed plant is called mountain spinach and its large leaves can be treated like spinach.

GOOD KING HENRY AND FAT HEN

These are both members of the goose-foot family and were popular vegetables in Europe in the sixteenth century. Today, Good King Henry has all but disappeared, and Fat Hen only grows wild as a weed. Both were superseded by spinach, which they are said to resemble in taste, although Fat Hen is milder.

NETTLES

Wild food enthusiasts get very excited about nettles as food, perhaps because they are plentiful and free and maybe because they take pleasure in eating something that everyone else avoids. Of course, once cooked, the sting completely disappears. They should be picked when they are very young and are good used in soups.

Above far left: Fresh vine leaves.
Above left: Dandelion.
Below left: Sorrel.
Right: Good King Henry.
Below: Nettles.

CHINESE GREENS

CHINESE CABBAGE/LEAVES (PE-TSAI)

Chinese cabbage, also called Napa cabbage, has pale green, crinkly leaves with long, wide, white ribs. Its shape is a little like a very fat head of celery, which gives rise to another of its alternative names, celery cabbage. It is pleasantly crunchy with a faint cabbage flavor, and, since it is available all year through, it makes a useful winter salad component. Chinese cabbage is also very good stir-fried with a tasty sauce. It is an essential ingredient of many oriental recipes.

Buying and Storing

For some reason, Chinese leaves almost always look fresh and perky when on sale in the supermarket, which probably indicates that they travel well and are transported quickly. Avoid any with discoloured or damaged stems. The leaves should be pale green and straight without blemishes or bruises. They will keep for up to six days in the salad drawer of the fridge.

Preparing

Remove the outside leaves and slice as much as you need.

Many Chinese greens are members of the brassica family. If you go into a popular and reasonably large Chinese supermarket, you'll be astonished at the varieties of green vegetables for sale. Discovering the names of these vegetables, on the other hand, can be a bit of a hit-and-miss undertaking, as the storekeepers, although always well intentioned, rarely know the English name, if indeed there is one.

CHINESE MUSTARD GREENS

Mustard greens are worth buying if you can, as they are very good to eat. The plant is a member of the cabbage family, but is grown in Europe solely for its mustard seed. In India and Asia it has long been grown for its oil seed, but the Chinese developed the plant for its leaves as well. These are deep green and slightly puckered-looking and have a definite mustard flavor, which can be quite fiery.

If you grow your own, then you'll be able to enjoy the young leaves which can be added to lettuce to spice up salads. Older leaves are best stir-fried and then dressed with a light Chinese sauce. They are also good cooked with onion and garlic and served as a side dish to accompany pork or bacon.

Preparing and Cooking

Break apart the stalks, rinse, then cut both stalks and leaves into thick or thin slices. These can then be stir-fried with garlic and onions, or cooked and served as you would chard. It has a pleasant flavor, milder than mustard greens, yet with more bite than the bland Chinese cabbage.

CHINESE BROCCOLI

This is another leafy vegetable, but with slender heads of flowers that look a little like our own broccoli, except that the flowers are usually white or yellow. Once the thicker stalks are trimmed, the greens can be sliced and cooked and served in the same way as Chinese mustard greens.

Far left: Chinese mustard greens.
Left: Chinese leaves.
Above: Chinese broccoli.
Below: Pak-choi.

Cooking and Serving

If adding to salads, combine Chinese cabbage with something fairly forceful, like Belgian endive or arugula, and add a well-flavored dressing. If adding to a stir-fry, cook with garlic, ginger and other fairly strong flavors. While the faint cabbage flavor will be lost, you will still get the pleasant crunchy "bite" of the stalk, and the leaves will carry the sauce.

PAK-CHOI

If you frequent your local Chinese super-market, you will almost certainly have come across *Pak-Choi*. In English it should correctly be called Chinese celery cabbage and its thick stalks, joined at the end in a small root, are vaguely celery-like. Its leaves, on the other hand, are generally large and spoon shaped. There are many different species of this vegetable, and smaller specimens look more like the tops of radishes and have small slim stalks. Consequently the vegetable can be known by all sorts of picturesque names, like "horse's ear" and "horse's tail." There's no rule for discovering exactly what you are buying, but the important thing is to choose a fresh plant whatever its size: look for fresh green leaves and crisp stalks.

KOHLRABI

Kohlrabi looks like a cross between a cabbage and a turnip and is often classified as a root vegetable, even though it grows above ground. It is a member of the brassica family, but, unlike cabbages, it is the bulbous stalk that is edible rather than the flowering heads.

There are two varieties of kohlrabi: one is purple and the other pale green. They both have the same mild and fresh tasting flavor, not dissimilar to water chestnuts. Kohlrabi is neither as peppery as turnip nor as distinctive as cabbage, but it is easy to see why people think it a little like both. It can be served as an alternative to carrots or turnips.

History

Although kohlrabi is not a very popular vegetable in North America, it is commonly eaten in Europe, as well as in China, India and Asia. In Kashmir, where it is grown, there are many recipes – the bulbs are often finely sliced and eaten in salads and the greens are cooked in mustard oil with garlic and chilies.

Buying and Storing

Kohlrabi is best when small and young, since larger specimens tend to be coarse and fibrous. It keeps well for 7-10 days if stored in a cool place.

Preparing

Peel the skin with a knife and then cook whole or slice.

Cooking

Very small kohlrabies are tender and can be cooked whole. However, if they are any bigger than 2 inches in diameter, they can be stuffed. To do this, hollow out a little before cooking and then stuff with fried onions and tomatoes, for instance. For sliced kohlrabi, cook until just tender and serve with butter or a creamy sauce. They can also be cooked long and slow in gratin dishes, with, for instance, potatoes as a variation of *gratin Dauphinois*. Alternately, parboil them and bake in the oven covered with a cheese sauce.

CHARD

Chard is one of those vegetables that needs plenty of water when growing, which explains why it is a popular garden vegetable in many places which have a high rainfall. Gardeners are very fond of chard, not only because it is delicious to eat but also because it is so very striking.

Chard is often likened to spinach. The leaves have similarities, although they are not related and chard is on an altogether larger scale. Chard leaves are large and fleshy with distinctive white ribs, and the flavor is stronger and more robust than spinach. It is popular in France where it is baked with rice, eggs and milk in *tians*, and cooked in a celebrated pastry from Nice – *tourte de blettes* – which is a sweet tart filled with raisins, pine nuts, apples and chard bound together with eggs. It is also often combined with eggs in frittatas and tortillas.

Chard is a member of the beet family and is called by several names on this theme, including sea kale beet and spinach beet.

Ruby or rhubarb chard has striking red ribs and leaf beet is often cultivated as a decorative plant, but they both have the same flavor, and unlike sugar beet and beets, they are cultivated only for their leaves.

Buying and Storing

Heads of chard should be fresh and bright green; avoid those with withered leaves or flabby stems. It keeps better than spinach but should be eaten within a couple of days.

Preparing

Some people buy or grow chard for the white stems alone and discard the leaves (or give them to pet guinea pigs), but this is a waste of a delicious vegetable. The leaf needs to be separated from the ribs, and this can be done roughly with a sharp knife (*right*) or more precisely using scissors. The ribs can then be sliced. Either shred the leaves, or blanch them and use them to wrap little parcels of fragrant rice or other food. If the chard is young and small, the ribs do not need to be removed.

Cooking

For pies, frittatas and gratins, the leaves and ribs can be cooked together. Gently sauté the ribs in butter and oil and then add the leaves a minute or so later. Alternately, the ribs can be simmered in a little water until tender and the leaves added a few minutes later or steamed over the top.

Above far left: Kohlrabi.
Left: Purple kohlrabi.
Above: Chard.

BEANS, PEAS AND SEEDS

FAVA BEANS

One of the delights of having a garden is discovering how truly delicious some vegetables are when garden fresh. This seems particularly true of fava beans, which have a superb sweet flavor that sadly can never be reproduced in the frozen product. If you're lucky enough to grow or be given fresh fava beans, don't worry about recipes; just cook them until tender and serve with butter. It will be a revelation! However, if you're not one of those lucky few, don't dismiss fava beans, as they are still a wonderfully versatile vegetable. They can be used in soups or casseroles, and, since they have a mealy texture, they also purée well.

History

People have been eating fava beans almost since time began. A variety of wild fava bean grew all over southern Europe, North Africa and Asia, and it would have been a useful food for early man. There is archaeological evidence that by Neolithic times fava beans were being farmed, making them one of the first foods to be cultivated.

Fava beans will grow in most climates and most soils. They were a staple food for people throughout the Dark Ages and the Middle Ages, grown for feeding people and livestock until being replaced by the potato in the seventeenth and eighteenth centuries. Fava beans were an important source of protein for the poor, and because they dry well, they would have provided nourishing meals for families until the next growing season.

Nutrition

Beans are high in protein and carbohydrates and are also a good source of vitamins A, B1 and B2. They also provide potassium and iron as well as several other minerals.

Buying and Storing

Buy beans as fresh as possible. The pods should preferably be small and tender. Use as soon as possible.

Preparing

Very young beans in tender pods, no more than 3 inches in length, can be eaten pod and all; top and tail, and then

slice roughly. Usually, however, you will need to shell the beans. Elderly beans are often better skinned after they are cooked to rid them of the strong, bitter flavor that puts many people off this vegetable.

Cooking

Plunge shelled beans (or in their pods if very young) into rapidly boiling water and cook until just tender. They can also be parboiled and then finished off braised in butter. For a simple broad bean purée, blend the cooked beans with garlic cooked in butter, cream and a pinch of fresh herbs, such as savory or thyme.

LIMA BEANS

These are popular in the US, named after the capital of Peru, and are sold mainly shelled. They are an essential ingredient in the Native American dish *succotash*. Lima beans should be cooked in a little boiling water until tender. Elderly beans need skinning after they are cooked. The dried bean, also known as the butter bean, can be large or small. These large beans tend to become mushy when cooked so are best used in soups or purées.

Above: Fava beans.
Below: Lima beans.
Right: Wax beans.

WAX BEANS

The wax bean is native to South America, where it has been cultivated for more than 2000 years, and there is archaeological evidence of its existence much earlier than that.

It is a popular vegetable to grow. Most home vegetable gardeners have a patch of wax beans – they are easy to grow and, like all legumes, their roots contain bacteria that help renew nitrogen supplies in the soil.

They have a more robust flavor and texture than French beans and are distinct from green beans in several ways: they are generally much larger with long, flattened pods; their skin is rough textured, although in young beans this softens during cooking; and they contain purple beans within the pods, unlike green beans whose beans are mostly white or pale green. Nevertheless, runner beans belong to the same family as all the green beans.

Buying and Storing

Always buy young beans as the pods of larger beans are likely to be tough. The pods should feel firm and fresh; if you can see the outline of the bean inside the pod it is likely to be fibrous – although you could leave the beans to dry out and use the dried beans later in the season. Ideally, the beans inside should be no larger than your small fingernail.

Use as soon as possible after buying; they do not store well.

Preparing

Wax beans need to be topped and tailed and may also need stringing. Carefully put your knife through the top of the bean without cutting right through, and then pull downward; if a thick thread comes away, the beans need stringing, so do the same on the other side. The beans can then be sliced either using a sharp knife or a slicer.

Slice through lengthwise, not diagonally, so that you will be able to serve the beans with just a little skin and lots of succulent flesh.

Cooking

Plunge the beans into boiling salted water and cook until *al dente*.

PEAS

Fresh peas are wonderful – try tasting them raw, straight from the pod. Unfortunately, the season for garden peas is short, and frozen peas, which are the next best thing, never quite come up to the mark. If you grow your own peas, for three or four weeks in early summer, you can eat like a king; otherwise you can buy them from a good grocer, who may be able to keep you supplied all through the early summer.

History

Peas have an even longer history than fava beans, with archaeological evidence showing they were cultivated as long ago as 5700 BC. High in protein and carbohydrates, they would have been another important staple food and were eaten fresh or dried for soups or potage.

"Pease" porridge is mentioned in a Greek play written in 5 BC. "Pease pudding," probably something similar, made with split peas with onion and herbs, is an old-fashioned but still very popular dish, especially in the north of England, traditionally eaten with ham and pork.

One of the first recipes for peas, however, comes from *Le Cuisinier Français*, which was translated into English in the middle of the seventeenth century and gives a recipe for *petits pois à la française* (peas cooked with small-hearted lettuces) – still a popular recipe today.

Varieties

Snow peas: These are eaten whole and have a delicate flavor, providing they are not overcooked. Unfortunately, they are easy to overcook and the texture then becomes rather slippery. Alternately, blanch or stir-fry them. They are also good served raw in salads.

Petits Pois: These are not, as you might expect, immature peas but are a dwarf variety. Gardeners grow their own, but they are not available fresh in the stores as they are mainly grown commercially for canning or freezing.

Sugar Peas, Sugar Snaps: These have the distinct fresh flavor of raw peas and are more plump and have more snap than snow peas.

Buying and Storing

Only buy fresh peas; if they are old they are bound to be disappointing and you would be better off buying them frozen. In top condition, the pods are bright green and lively looking; the more withered the pod, the longer they have been hanging around. It is possible to surreptitiously sample peas on occasion, to check if they are fresh (grocers don't seem to mind if you buy some). Use fresh peas as soon as possible.

Preparing

Shelling peas can be very relaxing. Press open the pods and use your thumb to push out the peas *(below)*. Snow peas and sugar snaps just need to be topped and tailed *(below right)*.

Cooking

Cook peas with a sprig of mint in a pan of rapidly boiling water or in a covered steamer until tender. Alternately, melt butter in a flameproof casserole, add the peas and then cover and sweat over low heat for 4–5 minutes. Cook snow peas and sugar snaps in any of these ways but for a shorter time.

Left: Peas.
Above right: Sugar snap peas.

GREEN BEANS

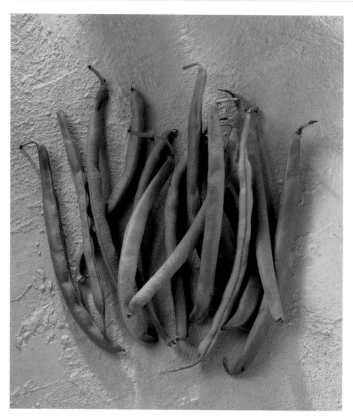

slim in shape. They should be eaten when very young, no more than 2¹/₂-3 inches in length.

Thai Beans: These long beans are similar to French beans and can be prepared and cooked in the same way.

Yellow Wax Beans: This is also a French bean and has a mild, slightly buttery taste.

Buying and Storing

Whatever variety, beans should be bright and crisp. Avoid wilted ones, or those with overly mature pods which feel spongy when lightly squeezed. They do not keep well, so use as soon as possible after buying or picking.

Preparing

To remove the ends of the beans: gather them together in one hand and then slice away the top ¹/4 inch *(below)*, then do the same at the other end. If necessary, pull off any stringy bits.

Whether you call beans French beans, haricots or green beans, they all belong to a large and varied family.

History

The bean is a New World vegetable that had been cultivated for thousands of years by native peoples in both the north and south of the continent, which accounts for its wide diversity.

Varieties

One variety or another is available all year through and so they are one of the most convenient fresh green vegetables.

French Beans: This name encompasses a range of green beans, including the snap bean and bobby bean. They are mostly fat and fleshy, and when fresh, should be firm so that they break in half with a satisfying snapping sound.

Haricots Verts: These are considered the best French beans and are delicate and

Cooking

Plunge beans into rapidly boiling salted water and cook until *al dente*. When overcooked, beans have a flabby texture and also lose much of their flavor. Drain and toss them in butter or serve in a sauce with shallots and bacon. For salads, cook until just tender and then refresh under cold water. They are excellent with a garlicky vinaigrette. Serve with carrots or other root vegetables and savor the contrast in flavors.

Above left: Bobby beans.
Below left: Yellow wax beans.
Right: Haricots verts.
Below: Thai beans.

CORN

Fresh corn, eaten on the cob with salt and a little butter, is deliciously sweet. Some gardeners who grow it have a pan ready on the boil, so that when they cut the corn it goes into the pan in only the time it takes to race up from the garden to the kitchen. Buying it from the supermarket is inevitably a bit hit-or-miss, although if purchased in season, corn can be very good indeed.

History

In 1492, as Christopher Columbus disembarked on the island now called Cuba, he was met by Native Americans offering two gifts of hospitality – one was tobacco and the other something the Native Americans called *maïs*. The English word for staple food was then corn, so that when Columbus and his crew saw that maize was the staple food for the Native Americans, it was dubbed "Indian corn."

Corn originated in South America and had enormous significance to the Native Americans of the whole continent, who were said to have lived and died by corn. They referred to it as their "first mother and father, the source of life." By far their most important food, corn was used in many other ways as well. They used the plant for their shelters and for fences, and they wore it and decorated their bodies with it.

The Aztecs had corn planting ceremonies that included human sacrifices, and other tribes had similar customs to appease the god "corn." Countless myths and legends have been woven around corn, each tribe telling a slightly different story, but each on the same theme of planting and harvesting corn. For anthropologists and historians, they make compelling study.

Nutrition

Corn is a good carbohydrate food and is rich in vitamins A, B and C. It contains protein, but less so than most other cereals. It is also a good source of potassium, magnesium, phosphorus and iron.

Varieties

There are five main varieties of corn – popcorn, sweet corn, dent corn, flint corn and flour corn. Dent corn is the

most commonly grown worldwide, for animal feeds and oil, and the corn we eat on the cobs is sweet corn. Baby corn cobs are picked when immature and are cooked and eaten whole.

Buying and Storing

As soon as corn is picked, its sugar begins to turn to starch and therefore the sooner it goes into the pot, the better. Wherever possible, buy locally grown corn.

Look for husks that are clean and green and tassels which are golden, with no sign of matting. The corn itself should look plump and yellow. Avoid cobs with pale or white kernels or those with older shriveled kernels which will undoubtedly be disappointing.

Preparing

Strip away the husks. To use the kernels for recipes, cut downward using a sharp knife from top to bottom *(left)*.

Cooking

Cook corn on the cob in plenty of boiling salted water until tender. Timing depends on the size of the cobs but 10-15 minutes will normally be enough. Serve them with sea salt and butter, but if the cobs are really sweet, leave out the butter. Stir-fry baby corn cobs briefly and serve in oriental dishes.

Far left: Corn cobs.
Below: Baby corn cobs.

OKRA

History

Okra originated in Africa. In the sixteenth century, when African people were enslaved by the Spanish and shipped to the New World, they took with them the few things they could, including the plants and seeds from home – dried peas, yams, ackee – and okra. This lantern-shaped pod containing rows of seeds oozes a sticky mucilaginous liquid when cooked, and it was popular not only for its subtle flavor but also for thickening soups and stews.

The plant thrived in the tropical climate and by the early nineteenth century, when the slave trade was finally abolished, okra was an important part of the cuisine of the Caribbean and the southern United States. In and around New Orleans, the Creoles, the American-born descendants of European-born settlers, adopted a popular Native American dish called *gumbo*. An essential quality of this famous dish was its thick gluey consistency. The Native Americans used filé powder (the dry pounded leaves of the sassafras tree), but okra was welcomed as a more satisfactory alternative.

Gumbos are now the hallmark of Creole cooking, and in some parts of America, the word "gumbo" is an alternative word for okra itself.

Buying and Storing

Choose young, small pods as older ones are likely to be fibrous. They should be bright green, firm and slightly springy when squeezed. Avoid any that are shriveled or bruised. They will keep for a few days in the salad drawer of the fridge.

Preparing

When cooking whole, trim the top but don't expose the seeds inside or the viscous liquid will ooze into the rest of the dish. If, however, this is what you want, slice thickly or thinly according to the recipe *(right)*. If you want to eliminate some of this liquid, first soak the whole pods in acidulated water (water to which lemon juice has been added) for about an hour.

Cooking

The pods can be steamed, boiled or lightly fried, and then added to or used

with other ingredients. If cooked whole, okra is not mucilaginous but is pleasantly tender. Whether cooked whole or sliced, use garlic, ginger or chili to perk up the flavor, or cook Native American-style, with onions, tomatoes and spices.

Above: Okra.

DRIED BEANS AND PEAS

Dried beans feature in traditional cuisines all over the world, from Mexican refried beans to Italy's *pasta e fagioli*. They are nutritious, providing a good source of protein when combined with rice, and are a marvelous store cupboard standby.

Black-eyed Peas: Sometimes called black-eyed beans, these small cream-colored beans have a black spot or eye. When cooked, they have a tender, creamy texture and a mildly smoky flavor. Black-eyed beans are widely used in Indian cooking.

Chana Dhal: Chana dhal is very similar to yellow split peas but smaller in size and with a slightly sweeter taste. It is used in a variety of vegetable dishes.

Chick-peas: These round beige-colored pulses have a strong, nutty flavor when cooked. As well as being used for curries, chick-peas are also ground into a flour which is widely used in many Indian dishes such as *pakoras* and *bhajees*.

Flageolet Beans: Small oval beans which are either white or pale green in color. They have a very mild, refreshing flavor and feature in classic French dishes.

Green Lentils: Also known as continental lentils, these have quite a strong flavor and retain their shape during cooking. They are very versatile and are used in a number of dishes.

Haricot Beans: Small, white oval beans which come in different varieties. Haricot beans are ideal for Indian cooking because not only do they retain their shape but they also absorb the flavors of the spices.

Kidney Beans: Kidney beans are one of the most popular pulses. They are dark red/brown, kidney-shaped beans with a strong flavor.

Mung Beans: These are small, round green beans with a slightly sweet flavor and creamy texture. When sprouted they produce the familiar bean sprouts.

Red Split Lentils: A readily available lentil that can be used for making dhal. Use instead of toovar dhal.

Toovar Dhal: A dull orange-colored split pea with a very distinctive earthy flavor. Toovar dhal is available plain and in an oily variety.

Soaking and Cooking Tips

Most dried pulses, except lentils, need to be soaked overnight before cooking. Wash the beans thoroughly and remove any small stones and damaged beans. Put into a large bowl and cover with plenty of cold water. When cooking, allow double the volume of water to beans and boil for 10 minutes. This initial boiling period is essential to remove any harmful toxins. Drain, rinse and cook in fresh water. The cooking time for all pulses varies depending on the type and their freshness. Pulses can be cooked in a pressure cooker to save time. Lentils, on the whole, do not need soaking. They should be washed in several changes of cold water before being cooked.

Left: Clockwise from bottom right: Mung beans, Flageolet beans, Chick-peas, Haricot beans, Black-eyed peas, Kidney beans.
Above: Clockwise from top: Red split lentils, Green lentils, Toovar dhal, Chana dhal.

SIX

SQUASHES

Zucchini

Marrows and Summer Squashes

Pumpkins and Winter Squashes

Exotic Gourds

Cucumbers

ZUCCHINI

Zucchini are the best loved of all the squashes as they are so versatile. They are quick and easy to cook and are succulent and tender with a delicate, un-assuming flavor. Unlike other squashes, they are available all year through.

Vegetables taste best when eaten immediately after they have been picked, and this particularly applies to zucchini. They have a long season and are good to grow since the more you cut, the more the plants produce. Left unchecked, they turn into marrows.

Varieties

The zucchini is classified as a summer squash, *cucurbita pepo*, along with marrows and pattypan squashes.

Zucchini: Sometimes called courgettes, zucchini are basically immature marrows. The word is a diminutive of the Italian *zucca*, meaning gourd, and similarly courgette means miniature *courge*, French for marrow. Zucchini have a deep green skin, with firm pale flesh. The seeds and pith found in marrows have yet to form but are visible in more mature zucchini. Conversely, the prized baby zucchini have no suggestion of seeds or pith and the flesh is completely firm.

Yellow Zucchini: These are bright yellow and somewhat straighter than green zucchini. They have a slightly firmer flesh than green zucchini but are otherwise similar.

Pattypan Squashes: These little squashes look like tiny custard squashes. They can be pale green, yellow or white and have a slightly firmer texture than zucchini, but a similar flavor. They can be sliced and broiled in the same way as zucchini but, to make the most of their size and shape, steam them whole until tender.

Summer Crooknecks: Pale yellow with curves at the neck and a bumpy skin, crooknecks are prepared and cooked in the same way as zucchini.

Italian Zucchini: These very long, thin zucchini are grown in Italy. They are treated liked ordinary zucchini but are strictly a bottle gourd.

Buying and Storing

Zucchini should be firm with a glossy, healthy looking skin. Avoid any that feel soft or generally look limp, as they will be dry and not worth using. Choose small zucchini whenever possible and buy in small quantities as needed.

Preparing

The tiny young zucchini need no preparation at all, and if they still have their flowers, so much the better. Other zucchini should be topped and tailed and then prepared according to the recipe, either sliced or slit for stuffing.

Cooking

Baby zucchini need little or no cooking. Steam them whole or just blanch them. Sliced larger zucchini can be steamed or boiled but take care that they do not overcook as they go soggy very quickly. Alternately, grill, roast or fry them. Try dipping slices in a light batter and then shallow frying in a blend of olive and sunflower oil. To roast, place them in a ovenproof dish, scatter with crushed garlic and a few torn basil leaves and sprinkle with olive oil; then bake in a very hot oven until tender, turning the slices occasionally.

Top left: Pattypan squashes.
Far left: Baby zucchini.
Left: Yellow zucchini.
Right: Italian zucchini beside white and green zucchini.

MARROWS AND SUMMER SQUASHES

Vegetable marrow is classified as a summer squash yet it is rather the poor relation of squashes. Most of the edible flesh is water and at best it is a rather bland vegetable, with a slightly sweet flavor. At worst, it is insipid and if cooked to a mush (which isn't unheard of), it is completely tasteless.

Marrows can be stuffed, although it involves a lot of energy expended for very little reward; but marrow cooked over low heat in butter with no added water (so that it steams in its own juice) brings out the best in it.

History

Marrows, like all the summer and winter squashes, are native to America. Squashes were eaten by Native Americans, traditionally with corn and beans, and in an Iroquois myth the three

vegetables are represented as three inseparable sisters. Although the early explorers would almost certainly have come into contact with them, they were not brought back home, and vegetable marrow was not known in England until the nineteenth century. Once introduced, however, it quickly became very popular. Mrs Beeton gives eight recipes for vegetable marrow and observes that "it is now extensively used." No mention at all is made of zucchini, which of course are simply immature marrows, as any gardener will know.

Varieties

The word "marrow" as a general term tends to refer to the summer squashes. At the end of summer and in the early fall a good variety of the large summer squashes is available.

Vegetable Marrows: This is the proper name for the large prize marrows, beloved of harvest festivals and country fairs. Buy small specimens whenever possible.

Spaghetti Squashes/Marrows: Long and pale yellow, like all marrows these squashes can grow to enormous sizes, but buy small specimens for convenience as well as flavor. They earned their name from the resemblance of the cooked flesh to spaghetti.

To boil a spaghetti squash, first pierce the end, so that the heat can reach the middle, then cook for about 25 minutes or until the skin feels tender. Cut the squash in half lengthwise, remove the seeds, and then fork the strands of flesh out onto a plate. It has a fragrant, almost honey and lemon flavor and tastes good with garlic butter or pesto.

Custard Marrows: These are pretty, pale green squashes with scalloped edges and a similar flavor to zucchini. If possible, buy small specimens, about 4 inches across. Boil these whole until tender, then cut a slice off the tops, scoop out the seeds and serve with a pat of butter.

Buying and Storing

Buy vegetables that have clear, unblemished flesh and avoid any with soft or brown patches. Vegetable marrows and spaghetti squashes will keep for several months provided they are kept in a cool, dark place. Custard marrows will keep up to a week.

Preparing

Wash the skin. For sautéing or steaming, or if the skin is tough, peel it away. For braised marrow, cut into chunks and discard the seeds and pith (*right*). For

stuffing, cut into thick slices or cut lengthwise and discard the seeds and pith.

Cooking

Place chunks of marrow in a heavy-based pan with a little butter, cover and cook until tender. It can then be livened up with garlic, herbs or tomatoes. For stuffed marrow, blanch first, stuff, then cover or wrap it in foil to cook.

Above: Vegetable marrows.
Far left: Spaghetti squashes.
Left: Custard marrows.

PUMPKINS <u>AND</u> WINTER SQUASHES

Pumpkins are the most famous of the winter squashes; aesthetically they are one of nature's most pleasing vegetables for their huge size, their color and the smoothness of their skin. They originated in America and, from a culinary point of view, they have their home here.

The name squash comes from America and as well as pumpkins, the family includes acorn, butternut and turban squashes to name but a few. There are simply hundreds of different squashes, including Sweet Dumpling, Queensland Blue (from Australia), Calabaza, Cushaw and Golden Nugget.

History

The tradition of eating pumpkin at Thanksgiving came from when the Pilgrim Fathers, who had settled in New England and proclaimed a day of thanksgiving and prayer for the harvest. The early tradition was to serve the pumpkin with its head and seeds removed, the cavity filled with milk, honey and spices, and baked until tender. The custom of eating pumpkin at Thanksgiving has remained, but it is now served in a different way: puréed pumpkin, either fresh or canned, is used to make golden tarts.

Varieties

There are a huge number of varieties of winter squashes and, confusingly, many are known by several different names. However, from a cooking point of view, most are interchangeable, although it is best to taste dishes as you cook them, as seasoning may differ from one to the other. In general, they all have a floury and slightly fibrous flesh and a mild, almost bland flavor tinged with sweetness. Because of this blandness, they harmonize well with other ingredients.

Acorn Squashes: These are small and heart-shaped with a beautiful deep green or orange skin, or a mixture of the two. Peel, then use as for pumpkins or bake whole, then split and serve with butter.

Butternut Squashes: Perfectly pear-shaped, these are a buttery color. Use in soups or in any pumpkin recipe.

Delicata Squashes: This pretty pale yellow squash has a succulent yellow

flesh, tasting like a cross between sweet potato and butternut squash.

English Pumpkins: These have a softer flesh than the American variety and are good for soups or, if puréed, combined with potatoes or other root vegetables.

Hubbard Squashes: These large winter squashes have a thick, bumpy, hard shell which can range in color from bright orange to dark green. If they are exceptionally large, they are sometimes sold in halves or large wedges. They have a grainy texture and are best mashed with butter and seasoning.

Kabocha Squashes: Attractive bright green squashes with a pale orange flesh.

They are similar in flavor and texture to acorn squashes and can be prepared and cooked in the same way.

Onion Squashes: Round, yellow or pale orange, onion squashes have a mild flavor, less sweet than pumpkin but still with a slightly fruity or honey taste. They are good in risottos or in most pumpkin recipes, but taste for flavor – you may need to add extra seasoning or sugar.

Above: Clockwise from right: A pumpkin hybrid, Kabocha squash, Acorn squash. Right: Clockwise from top right: Hybrid squash, two Golden Acorn squashes, two small and one large pumpkin.

Pumpkins: Large, bright yellow or orange squashes, with a deep orange flesh. They have a sweet, slightly honeyed, flavor and are very much a taste North Americans and Australians grow up with. However, they are not to everyone's liking and some people find them rather cloying. Pumpkin soup, pumpkin bread and pumpkin pie are part of the American tradition, as are faces carved from the shell at Halloween.

Buying and Storing

All winter squashes may be stored for long periods. Buy firm, unblemished vegetables with clear smooth skins.

Preparing

For larger squashes, or for those being used for soups or purées, peel and cut into pieces, removing the seeds (*left*).

Cooking

Boil in a little water for about 20 minutes until tender, then mash and serve with butter and plenty of salt and pepper. Smaller squashes can be baked whole in their skins, then halved, seeded and served with butter and maple syrup. Pumpkin and other squashes can also be lightly sautéed in butter before adding stock, cream or chopped tomatoes.

EXOTIC GOURDS

While the squashes are native to America, most gourds originated in the Old World – from Africa, India and the Far East. However, over the millennia, seeds crossed water and, over the centuries, people crossed continents so that squashes and gourds are now common all over the world. Both belong to the family *Cucurbitacea,* and both are characterised by their rapid-growing vines.

Bottle Gourds: Bottle gourds are still a familiar sight in Africa, where they are principally grown not for their fruit, but for their dried shells. The gourds can grow to enormous sizes and the shells are used for water bottles, cups and musical instruments. The young fruit can be eaten, but it is extremely bitter and is normally only added to highly flavored stews, like curries.

Chayotes: The chayote (pronounced chow-chow) is a popular gourd in all sorts of regions of the world and can be found in just about any ethnic supermarket, be it Chinese, African, Indian or Caribbean. In each it is known by a different name, christophine being the Caribbean term, but choko, shu-shu and chinchayote among its many other names used elsewhere. Unlike most gourds, it originated in Mexico but was widely grown throughout the tropics after the invasions of the Spanish.

It is a pear-shaped fruit with a large central pit and has a cream-colored or green skin. It has a bland flavor, similar to marrow, and a slightly firmer texture something like pumpkin. It is commonly used in Caribbean cooking, primarily as a side dish or in soufflés. Alternately it can be used raw in salads.

Chinese Bitter Melons: These are a common vegetable in all parts of Asia and go by a myriad of names – bitter gourd and bitter cucumber to name but two. They are popular throughout Asia, eaten when very young, but are extremely bitter and rarely eaten in the West. They are easily recognized as they have warty, spiny skins, looking like a toy dinosaur. The skins are white when young but will probably have ripened to a dark green by the time they appear in the shops.

Most recipes from China suggest halving the gourd, removing the pulp and then slicing before boiling for several minutes to remove their bitterness. They can then be added to stir-fries or other oriental dishes.

Far left: Sweet dumpling.
Left: Pumpkin.
Top right: Chinese bitter melon.
Middle right: Loofah.
Below: Chayote.

Smooth and Angled Loofahs: The smooth loofah must be one of the strangest plants. When young it can be eaten, although it is not much valued. However, the plant is grown almost exclusively for sponges, used everywhere as a back rub in the bath. The ripe loofahs are picked and, once the skin has been stripped off and the seeds shaken out, allowed to dry. The plant then gradually dries to a fibrous skeleton and thence to bathrooms everywhere - so now you know!

Angled or ribbed loofahs are more commonly eaten but again are only edible when young as they become unpleasantly bitter when mature. They taste something like zucchini and are best cooked in a similar way, either fried in butter or cooked with tomatoes, garlic and oil.

CUCUMBERS

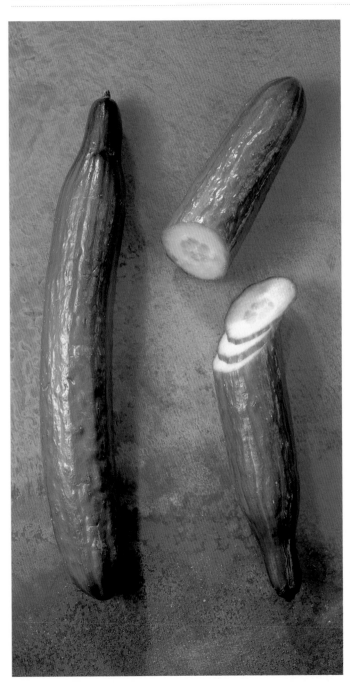

The Chinese say food should be enjoyed for its texture as well as flavor; cucumbers have a unique texture and refreshing cool taste. An afternoon tea with cucumber sandwiches, thinly sliced cucumber between wafer thin brown buttered bread, provides a delight of contrasts – the soft bread, the smooth butter and the cool crisp cucumber.

Varieties

English Cucumbers: These are the cucumbers the English are most familiar with. They have fewer seeds and thinner skin than the ridged cucumber.
Gherkins: These are tiny cucumbers with bumpy, almost warty skins and are mostly pickled in vinegar and eaten with cold meats or chopped into mayonnaise.
Kirbys: Small cucumbers, available in the United States and used for pickling.
Ridged Cucumbers: These are smaller than most cucumbers with more seeds and a thick, bumpy skin. The waxed ones need to be peeled before eating but most ridged cucumbers on the European Continent are unwaxed and good without peeling.

Buying and Storing

Cucumbers should be firm from top to bottom. They are often sold prewrapped in plastic and can be stored in the salad drawer of the fridge for up to a week. Remove the plastic packaging once you've "started" a cucumber. Discard once it begins to go soggy.

Preparing

Whether you peel a cucumber or not is a matter of personal preference, but wash it if you don't intend to peel it. Some producers use wax coatings to give a glossy finish and these cucumbers must be peeled. If you are in doubt, buy organic cucumbers. Special citrus peelers can remove strips of peel to give an attractive striped effect when sliced.

Left: Cucumbers.
Above right: Ridged cucumbers.
Above far right: Baby cucumbers.
Below right: Kirbys.

Serving

Thinly sliced cucumber is most frequently served with a light dressing or sour cream. In Greece cucumber is an essential part of a Greek country salad, *horiatiki salata*, cut into thick chunks and served with tomatoes, peppers and feta and dressed simply with olive oil and a little wine vinegar.

Iced cucumber soup is delicious, and cucumber can also be puréed with yogurt, garlic and herbs and served with sour cream stirred in.

Cooking

Cucumbers are normally served raw, but are surprisingly good cooked. Cut the cucumber into wedges, remove the seeds and then simmer for a few minutes until tender. Once drained, return the cucumber to the pan and stir in a little cream and seasoning.

FRUIT

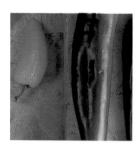

Tomatoes

Eggplant

Peppers

Chilies

Plantains and Green Bananas

Ackee

Avocados

Breadfruit

TOMATOES

Next to onions, tomatoes are one of the most important fresh ingredients in the kitchen. In Mediterranean cooking, they are fundamental. Along with garlic and olive oil, they form the basis of so many Italian, Spanish and Provençal recipes that it is hard to find many dishes in which they are not included.

History

Tomatoes are related to potatoes, eggplant and sweet and chili peppers, and all are members of the nightshade family. Some very poisonous members of this family may well have deterred our ancestors from taking to tomatoes. Indeed, the leaves of tomatoes are toxic and can result in a very bad stomach ache.

Tomatoes are native to western South America. By the time of the Spanish invasions in the sixteenth century, they were widely cultivated throughout the whole of South America and Mexico. Hernán Cortés, conqueror of the Aztecs, sent the first tomato plants, a yellow variety, to Spain (no doubt along with the plundered Aztec gold).

However, people did not instinctively take to this "golden apple." English horticulturists mostly grew them as ornamental plants to adorn their gardens and had little positive to say about them as food. Spain is recorded as the first country to use tomatoes in cooking, stewing them with oil and seasoning. Italy followed suit, but elsewhere they were treated with suspicion.

The first red tomatoes arrived in Europe in the eighteenth century, brought to Italy by two Jesuit priests. They were gradually accepted in northern Europe where, by the mid-nineteenth century, they were grown extensively, eaten raw, cooked or used for pickles.

Above right: Red and yellow cherry tomatoes.
Below right: Yellow pear tomatoes.
Opposite above: Round or salad tomatoes on the vine.
Opposite below: Beefsteak tomatoes.

Varieties

There are countless varieties of tomatoes, ranging from the huge beef tomatoes that measure 4 inches across, to tiny cherry tomatoes, not much bigger than a thumb nail. They come in all shapes, too – elongated, plum-shaped or slightly squarish and even pear-shaped.

Beefsteak Tomatoes: Large, ridged and deep red or orange in color, these have a good flavor so are good in salads.

Canned Tomatoes: Keep a store of canned tomatoes, especially in the winter when fresh ones tend to taste insipid. Tomatoes are one of the few vegetables that take well to canning, but steer clear of any that are flavored with garlic or herbs. It is far better to add flavoring yourself.

Cherry Tomatoes: These small, dainty tomatoes were once the prized treasures of gardeners but are now widely available. Although more expensive than round tomatoes, they have a delightful

sweet flavor and are worth paying the extra money for serving in salads or for cooking whole.

Plum Tomatoes: Richly flavored with fewer seeds than regular tomatoes, these Italian-grown tomatoes are usually recommended for cooking, although they can be used in salads.

Round or Salad Tomatoes: These are the common tomatoes found in grocers and supermarkets. They vary in size according to the exact type and season. Sun-ripened tomatoes have the best flavor, however; for through-the-year availability the fruit is often picked and ripened off the plant. These tomatoes are versatile in everyday cooking. Adding a pinch of sugar and taking care to season the dish well helps to overcome any weakness in flavor.

Sun-dried Tomatoes: This is one of the fashionable foods of the late Eighties and early Nineties. They add an evocative flavor to many Mediterranean dishes, but don't use them too indiscriminately.

Tomato Paste: This is good for adding an intense tomato flavor, but use carefully or the flavor will be overpowering. Tubes have screw tops and are better than cans

as, once opened, they can be kept for up to 4–6 weeks in the fridge.

Yellow Tomatoes: These are exactly like red tomatoes - they may be round, plum or cherry-sized - except they are yellow.

Buying and Storing

Ideally, tomatoes should be allowed to ripen slowly on the plant so that their flavor can develop. Consequently, home-grown tomatoes are best, followed by those grown and sold locally. When buying from a supermarket or grocer, look at the leafy green tops; the fresher they look the better. Buy locally grown beefsteak or cherry tomatoes for salads and plum tomatoes for rich sauces. Paler tomatoes or those tinged with green will redden if kept in a brown paper bag or the salad drawer of the fridge, but if you intend to use tomatoes right away, buy bright red specimens. Overripe tomatoes, where the skin has split and they seem to be bursting with juice, are excellent in soups. However, check for any sign of mold or decay, as this will spoil all your good efforts.

Preparing

Slice tomatoes across rather than downward for salads and pizza toppings. For wedges, cut downward; halve or quarter and cut into two or three depending on the size of the tomato.

Cooking

Among the many classic tomato dishes is tomato soup, cooked to a delicate orange color with stock or milk, or simmered with vegetables, garlic and basil. Recipes *à la provençale* indicate that tomatoes are in the dish; in Provençal cooking and Italian dishes, tomatoes are used with fish, meat and vegetables, in sauces and stuffings, with pasta and in superb salads. The Italian *tri colore salata* is a combination of large tomatoes, mozzarella and basil (the three colors of the Italian flag). The natural astringency of tomatoes means that, in salads, they need only be sprinkled with a fruity olive oil.

Chopped Tomatoes

Chopped tomatoes add a depth of flavor to all sorts of meat and vegetarian dishes. Ideally, even in fairly rustic meals, the tomatoes should be peeled, since the skin can be irritating to eat once cooked. Some sauces also recommend seeding tomatoes, in which case cut the tomato into halves and scoop out the seeds before chopping (*above*).

Skinning Tomatoes

Cut a cross in the tops of the tomatoes, then place in a bowl and pour over boiling water. Leave for a minute (*above*), then use a sharp knife to peel away the skin, which should come away easily. Do a few at a time (five at most) otherwise they will begin to cook while soaking; boil water for the next batch when you have finished peeling. The water must be boiling.

EGGPLANT

Many varieties of eggplants are cultivated and cooked all over the world. In Europe, Asia or America, they feature in a multitude of different dishes.

History

Although eggplant is a member of the nightshade family and thus related to potatoes, tomatoes and peppers, it was not discovered in the New World. The first mention of its cultivation is in China in 5 BC, and it is thought to have been eaten in India long before that. The Moors introduced the eggplant to Spain some 1200 years ago and it was grown in Andalucia. It is likely that they also introduced it to Italy, and possibly from there to other southern and eastern parts of Europe.

In spite of their popularity in Europe, eggplants did not become popular in the United States or Britain until very recently; although previous generations of food writers knew about them, they gave only the occasional recipe for cooking with them.

Above left: Plum tomatoes.
Top: Eggplants.
Above: Baby eggplants.
Left: Japanese eggplants.

Meanwhile, in the southern and eastern parts of Europe, eggplant had become extremely well liked, and today it is one of the most popular vegetables in the Mediterranean. Indeed, Italy, Greece and Turkey claim to have 100 ways of cooking it. In the Middle East, eggplant is also a central part of their cuisine.

Varieties

There are many different varieties of eggplants, differing in color, size and shape according to their country of origin. Small ivory-white and plump eggplants look like large eggs (hence their name in the States; they are called aubergines in the UK). Pretty striped eggplants may be either purple or pink and flecked with white irregular stripes. The Japanese or Asian eggplant is straight and very narrow, ranging in color from a pretty variegated purple and white to a solid purple. It has a tender, slightly sweet flesh. Most eggplants, however, are either glossy purple or almost black and can be long and slim or fat like zeppelins. All eggplants have a similar

flavor and texture; they taste bland yet slightly smoky when cooked, and the flesh is spongy to touch when raw, but soft after cooking.

Buying and Storing

Eggplants should feel heavy and firm to the touch, with glossy, unblemished skins. They will keep well in the salad drawer of the fridge for up to two weeks.

Preparing

When frying eggplants for any dish where they need slicing (e.g. ratatouille), it is a good idea to salt the slices first in order to draw out some of their moisture, otherwise, they absorb enormous quantities of oil during cooking (they absorb copious amounts anyway, but

salting reduces this slightly). Salting also used to be advised to reduce their bitterness but today's varieties are rarely bitter.

To salt eggplants, cut into slices, about $^{1}/_{2}$ inch thick for fried slices, *(top right)* or segments *(above right)* and sprinkle generously with salt. Leave them to drain in a colander for about one hour, then rinse well and gently squeeze out the moisture from each slice or carefully pat dry with a piece of cheesecloth.

Cooking

Eggplant slices can be fried in olive oil, as they are or first coated in batter – both popular Italian and Greek starters.

For moussaka, *parmigiana* and other dishes where eggplant is layered with

other ingredients, fry the slices briefly in olive oil. This gives them a tasty crust, while the inside stays soft.

To make a purée, such as for Poor Man's Caviar, first prick the eggplant all over with a fork and then roast in a moderately hot oven for about 30 minutes until tender. Scoop out the flesh and mix with scallions, lemon juice and olive oil. One of the most famous eggplant dishes is *Imam Bayaldi* – "the Iman fainted" – fried eggplant stuffed with onions, garlic, tomato, spices and lots of olive oil.

Above left: White eggplants.
Below left: Striped eggplants.
Above: Thai eggplants, including white, yellow and Pea eggplants.

PEPPERS

In spite of their name, peppers have nothing to do with the spice pepper used as a seasoning, although early explorers may have been mistaken in thinking the fruit of the shrubby plant looked like the spice they were seeking. It is thanks to this 400-year-old mistake that the name "pepper" has stuck.

History

The journeys Christopher Columbus and the conquistadors made were partly to find the spices Marco Polo had found a hundred years earlier in the Far East. Instead of the Orient, however, Columbus discovered the Americas, and instead of spices, he found maize, potatoes and tomatoes. He would have noted, though, that the Native Americans flavored their food with ground peppers, and since it was hot, like pepper, perhaps wishful thinking colored his objectivity. In any case, he returned with the new vegetables, describing them as peppers and advertising them as more pungent than those from Caucasus.

Varieties

Peppers and chilies are both members of the capsicum family. To distinguish between them, peppers are called sweet peppers, bell peppers and even bullnose peppers and come in a variety of colors – red, green, yellow, white, orange and a dark purple-black.

The color of the pepper tells you something about its flavor. Green peppers are the least mature and have a fresh "raw" flavor. Red peppers are ripened green peppers and are distinctly sweeter. Yellow/orange peppers taste more or less like red peppers, although perhaps slightly less sweet and if you have a fine palate you may be able to detect a difference. Black peppers have a similar flavor to green peppers but when cooked are a bit disappointing as they turn green; so if you buy them for their dramatic color, they are best used in salads.

In Greece and other parts of southern Europe, longer, slimmer peppers are often available which have a more pronounced sweet and pungent flavor than the bell-shaped peppers in the US – although this may be because they are locally picked and therefore absolutely fresh. Whichever is the case, they are quite delicious.

Buying and Storing

Peppers should look glossy and sprightly and feel hard and crisp; avoid any that look wrinkled or have damp soft patches. They will keep for a few days at the bottom of the fridge.

Preparing

To prepare stuffed peppers, cut off the top and then cut away the inner core and pith, and shake out the seeds. The seeds and core are easily removed when halving, quartering or slicing.

Cooking

There are countless ways of cooking peppers. Sliced, they can be fried with onions and garlic in olive oil and then braised with tomatoes and herbs. This is the basic ratatouille; other vegetables, such as zucchini and eggplant, can of course be added.

Peppers can be roasted, either with ratatouille ingredients or with only onions and garlic. Cut into large pieces, place in a roasting pan and sprinkle with olive oil, torn basil and seasoning. Roast in a very hot oven (425°F) for about 30 minutes, turning occasionally. Broiled peppers are another superb dish. Once broiled they can be skinned to reveal a soft, luxurious texture and added to salads.

Above far left: Red, green and orange bell peppers.
Below far left: Yellow bell peppers.
Above left: White bell peppers.
Above right: Purple bell peppers.

Skinning Peppers

Cut the pepper into quarters lengthwise and broil, skin side up (*above*), until the skin is charred and evenly blistered. Place the pieces immediately into a plastic bag (you will need tongs or a fork as they will be hot) and close the top of the bag with a tie or a loose knot. Leave for a few minutes and then remove from the bag and the skin will peel off easily.

CHILIES

Some people apparently become so addicted to the taste of hot food that they carry little jars of chopped dried chilies around with them and scatter them over every meal. Although this is a bit extreme, it is chilies more than any other ingredient that spice up our mealtimes.

Varieties

Chilies are the most important seasoning in the world after salt. Unlike peppers, to which they are closely related, the different varieties of chili can have widely different heat values – from the "just about bearable" to the "knock your head off" variety.

Anaheim Chili: A long, thin chili with a blunt end, named after the Californian city. It can be red or green and has a mild, sweet taste.

Ancho Chili/Pepper: These look like tiny peppers. They are mild enough to taste their underlying sweetness.

Birdseye or Bird Chili: These small red chilies are fiery hot. Also known as pequin chilies.

Cayenne Pepper: This is made from the dried, ground seeds and pods of chilies. The name comes from the capital of French Guiana, north of Brazil, although the cayenne chili does not grow there any longer and the pepper is made from chilies grown all over the world.

Early Jalapeño: A popular American chili, which starts dark green and gradually turns to red.

Habañero: Often called Scotch Bonnet, this is the hottest of all chilies and is small and can be green, red or yellow. Color is no real guide to its heat properties, so don't be fooled into thinking that green ones are mild. They are all *very* hot. The habañero comes from Mexico and is frequently used in Mexican and Caribbean dishes.

Hot Gold Spike: A large, pale, yellow-green fruit grown in the southwestern United States: it is very hot.

Above: Birdseye chilies.
Left: Habañero chilies (in and below bowl) and Yellow wax peppers.

Preparing

The capsaicin in chilies is most concentrated in the pith inside the pod and this, together with the seeds, should be cut away (*below*) unless you want maximum heat. Capsaicin irritates the skin and especially the eyes, so take care when preparing chilies. Either wear gloves or wash your hands thoroughly after handling chilies. If you rub your eyes, even if you have washed your hands carefully, it will be painful.

Poblano: A small, dark green chili, served whole in Spain either roasted or broiled. They are mostly mild but you can get the rogue fiery one, so beware if eating them whole.

Red Chili: These are long, rather wrinkled chilies which are green at first and then gradually ripen to red. They are of variable hotness and, because they are so long and thin, are rather difficult to prepare.

Serrano Chili: A long, red and extremely hot chili.

Tabasco: A sauce made with chilies, salt and vinegar and first made in New Orleans. It is a fiery sauce, popular in Creole, Caribbean and Mexican cookery – or indeed in any dish requiring last minute heat.

Yellow Wax Pepper: Pale yellow to green, these can vary from mild to hot.

Buying and Storing

Some fresh chilies look wrinkled even in their prime and therefore this is not a good guide to their freshness. They should, however, be unblemished, and avoid any which are soft or bruised.

The substance which makes the chili hot is a volatile oil called capsaicin. This differs not only from one type to another but also from plant to plant, depending on growing conditions; the more the plant has to struggle to survive in terms of light, water, soil, etc, the more capsaicin will be produced. It is therefore impossible to tell how hot a chili will be before tasting, although some types are naturally hotter than others. The belief that green chilies are milder than red ones does not necessarily follow; generally red chilies will have ripened for longer in the sun with the result that they will only be sweeter for all that sunshine. Chilies can be stored in a plastic bag in the fridge for a few days.

Cooking

In Mexican cooking chilies play a vital, and almost central role. It is difficult to think of any savory Mexican dish that does not contain either fresh chilies or some form of processed chili, whether canned, dried or ground. Other cuisines, however, are equally enthusiastic about chilies. They are essential in curries and similar dishes from India and the Far East, and in Caribbean and Creole food they are also used extensively.

If you have developed a tolerance for really hot food, then there is no reason why you shouldn't add as many as you wish. In general, however, use chilies discreetly, if for no better reason than you can't take the heat away if you make a mistake.

Above: Ancho chilies (left) and Anaheim chilies (on board).

PLANTAINS <u>AND</u> GREEN BANANAS

While bananas are well and truly fruit, eaten almost exclusively as a dessert or by themselves as fruit, plantains can reasonably be considered among the vegetable fraternity as they have a definite savory flavor, are normally eaten as a first or main course and can only be eaten once cooked.

Varieties

Plantains: Also known as cooking bananas, these have a coarser flesh and more savory flavor than sweet bananas. While superficially they look exactly like our own bananas, they are, on closer inspection, altogether larger and heavier looking. They can vary in color from the unripe fruit, which is green, through yellow to a mottled black color, which is when the fruit is completely ripe.

Green Bananas: Only certain types of green bananas are used in African and Caribbean cooking, and the "greenish" bananas you find in most western supermarkets are normally eating bananas, just waiting to ripen. If you need green bananas for a recipe, look out for them in West Indian or African stores.

Preparing

Plantains: These are inedible raw and must be cooked before eating. Unless very ripe, the skin can be tricky to remove. With yellow and green plantains, cut the fruit into short lengths, then slit the skin along the natural ridge of each piece of plantain. Gently ease the skin away from the flesh and pull the skin until it peels off completely (*below*).

Once peeled, plantains can be sliced horizontally or into lengths and then roasted or fried. Like bananas, plantains will discolor if exposed to the air so, if not using immediately, sprinkle with lemon juice or place in a bowl of salted water.

Green Bananas: These should be prepared in a similar way. As with plantains, green bananas should not be eaten raw and are usually boiled, either in their skins or not, according to the recipe.

If making green banana crisps, use a potato peeler to produce the thinnest slices (*left*).

If cooking plantains or green bananas in their skins, slit the skin lengthwise along the sides and place in a saucepan of salted water. Bring to the boil, simmer gently for about 20 minutes until tender and then cool. The peel can then easily be removed before slicing.

Cooking and Serving

Plantains and green bananas both have an excellent flavor. In many African and Caribbean recipes they are roasted or fried and then served simply with salt. However, if boiled, they can be sliced

and served in a simple salad with a few sliced onions, or added to something far more elaborate like a gado gado salad, with mango, avocado, lettuce and shrimp.

Plantains also make a delicious soup, where they are often teamed with corn. After frying an onion and a little garlic, add two sliced and peeled plantains, together with tomatoes, if liked. Fry gently for a few minutes and then add vegetable stock to cover and one or two sliced chilies, together with about 6 ounces of corn. Simmer gently together until the plantain is tender.

Above left: Plantains.
Below left: Green bananas.
Below: Canned ackee.

ACKEE

Ackee is a tropical fruit which is used in a variety of savory dishes, mainly of Caribbean origin, where the fruit is very popular. The fruit itself is bright red and, when ripe, bursts open to reveal three large black seeds and a soft, creamy flesh resembling scrambled eggs. It has a slightly lemony flavor and is traditionally served with saltfish to make one of Jamaica's national dishes. Only buy ripe fruit as, when under-ripe, certain parts of the fruit are toxic.

However, unless you are visiting the Caribbean you are probably only likely to find ackee in cans, and indeed most recipes call for canned ackee which is a good substitute for the fresh fruit.

Jamaican cooks also use ackee to add a subtle flavor to a variety of vegetable and bean dishes. The canned ackee needs very little cooking, and should be added to dishes in the last few minutes of cooking. Take care when stirring into a dish as it breaks up very easily.

AVOCADOS

The avocado has been known by many names – butter pear and alligator pear to name but two. It earned the title butter pear clearly because of its consistency, but alligator pear was the original Spanish name. Although you would be forgiven for thinking this was due to its knobbly skin (among some varieties anyway), the name in fact derives from the Spanish which was based on the Aztec word, the basically unpronounceable *ahuacatl*. From this to the easily-said alligator and thence to avocado was but a short step.

History

The avocado is a New World fruit, native to Mexico, but while it would have been "discovered" by the Old World explorers, it didn't become a popular food in Europe until the middle of this century, when modern transport meant that growers in California, who started farming avocados in the middle of the nineteenth century, could market this fruit worldwide. Avocados are now also exported by South Africa and Australia.

Nutrition

The avocado is high in protein and carbohydrate. It is one of the few fruits that contains fat, and it is also rich in potassium, Vitamin C, some B vitamins and Vitamin E. Its rich oils, particularly its Vitamin E content, mean that it is not only useful as food, but for skin and hair care too, something the Aztecs and Incas were aware of a thousand years ago. The cosmetic industry may have been in its infancy, but it still knew a good thing when it saw it.

Because of their valuable protein and vitamin content, avocados are a popular food for babies. They are easily blended, and small children generally enjoy their creamy texture and pleasant flavor.

Varieties

There are four varieties: Hass, the purple-black small knobbly avocado, the Ettinger and Fuerte, which are pear-shaped and have smooth green skin, and the Nabal, which is rounder in shape. The black-colored Hass has golden-yellow flesh, while green avocados have pale green to yellow flesh.

Buying and Storing

The big problem in buying avocados is that they're never ripe when you want them to be. How often do you see shoppers standing by the avocado shelves, feeling around for that rare creature, the perfectly ripe avocado? Most times they all feel as hard as rocks; that or else they're hopelessly soft and squashy and clearly past their best. The proper and sensible thing to do is to buy fruit a few days before you need it. An unripe avocado will ripen in between 4 -7 days at room temperature. Once it is ripe, it will keep well in the fridge for a few days, but you still need to plan well in advance if you want to be sure of the perfect avocado.

The alternative is to hope for the best and keep feeling around until you find a ripe fruit. A perfect avocado should have a clean, unblemished skin without any brown or black patches. If ripe, it should "give" slightly if squeezed gently in the hand, but not so much that it actually feels soft. Over-ripe avocados are really not worth bothering with, however persuasive and generous the offer from the man on the market. The flesh will be unattractively brown and stringy and the bits of good flesh you do manage to salvage will be soft and pulpy. Good for a dip, but nothing much else.

Preparing

Although they are simple fruits, avocados can be the devil to prepare. Once peeled, you are left with a slippery object which is then almost impossible to remove from the stone.

If you intend to eat the avocados in halves, it's fairly simple to just prise out the pit once halved. If you want to slice the fruit, use this tip. The only thing you need is a very sharp knife. Cut the avocado in half, remove the stone and then, with the skin still on, cut through the flesh and the skin to make slices. It is then relatively simple to strip off the peel. Remember to sprinkle the slices with lemon juice as the flesh discolors once exposed to the air.

Cooking

Most popular raw, avocados can also be baked, broiled or used in sautéed and sauced dishes.

Serving Ideas

As well as shrimp or vinaigrette, a half avocado can hold a mixture of chopped tomatoes and cucumber, a mild garlic cheese dip or a sour cream potato salad. Slices of avocado are delicious served with sliced tomatoes and mozzarella, sprinkled simply with olive oil, lemon juice and plenty of black pepper. Avocado can be chopped and added to a salad, or puréed for a rich dressing.

In Mexico, where avocados grow in abundance, there are countless avocado recipes. Guacamole is perhaps the best known, but they are also eaten in soups and stews and commonly used to garnish tacos and enchiladas.

BREADFRUIT

Breadfruit is the name for a tropical tree that grows on the islands of the South Pacific ocean. The fruit of the tree is about the size of a small melon with a rough rind and a pale, mealy flesh.

Preparing

The fruit should be peeled and the core removed.

Cooking

Breadfruit can be treated like potatoes: the flesh may be boiled, baked or fried. It is a staple food for the people of the Pacific islands who bake the flesh, or dry and grind it for biscuits, bread and puddings. It has a sweet flavor and soft texture when ripe.

Left: Clockwise from the right: Fuerte, Hass and Nabal avocados.
Right: Breadfruit.

SALAD
VEGETABLES

Lettuce

Arugula

Chicory and Radicchio

Radishes

Watercress

Mustard and Cress

LETTUCE

One aspect of lettuce that sets it apart from any other vegetable is that you can only buy it in one form – fresh.

History

Lettuce has been cultivated for thousands of years. In Egyptian times it was sacred to the god Min, and tubs of lettuce were ceremoniously carried before this fertility god. It was then considered a powerful aphrodisiac, yet for the Greeks and the Romans lettuce was thought to have quite the opposite effect, making one sleepy and generally soporific. Chemists today confirm that lettuce contains a hypnotic similar to opium, and in herbal remedies lettuce is recommended for insomniacs.

Varieties

There are hundreds of different varieties of lettuce. Today, an increasing variety is available in stores so that the salad bowl can contain a wealth of color and texture.

Round Lettuces

Sometimes called head or cabbage lettuces, round lettuces have cabbage-like heads and include:
Butterheads: These are the classic lettuces seen in kitchen gardens. They have a pale heart and floppy, loosely packed leaves. They have a pleasant flavor as long as they are fresh.
Crispheads: Crisp lettuces, such as Iceberg, have an excellent crunchy texture and will keep their vitality long after butterheads have faded and died.
Looseheads: These are non-hearting lettuce with loose leaves and include *lollo rosso* and *lollo biondo*, oakleaf lettuce and Red Salad Bowl. Although they are not particularly remarkable for their flavor, they look superb.

Cos Lettuces

The romaine is the only lettuce that would have been known in antiquity. It is known

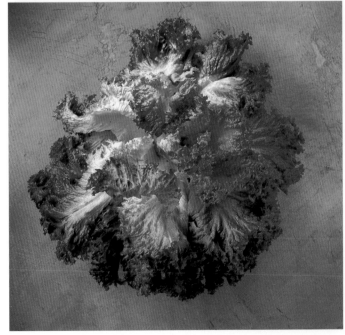

Above: Butterhead lettuce.
Right: Lollo rosso lettuce.
Above far right: Romaine lettuce.
Below far right: Lamb's lettuce.
Below extreme right: Bibb lettuce.

by two names: cos, derived from the Greek island where it was found by the Romans; and romaine, the name used by the French after it was introduced to France from Rome. There are two romaine lettuces, both with long, erect heads.

Romaine: Considered the most delicious lettuce, this has a firm texture and a faintly nutty taste. It is the correct lettuce for Caesar Salad, one of the classic salads.

Bibb: In appearance Bibbs look like something between a baby romaine and a tightly furled butterhead. They have firm hearts and are enjoyed for their distinct flavor. Like other lettuce hearts, they cope well with being cooked.

LAMB'S LETTUCE OR CORN SALAD

This popular winter leaf does not actually belong to the lettuce family (it is related to Fuller's teasel), but as it makes a lovely addition to salads, this seems a good place to include it. Called *mâche* in France, it has spoon-shaped leaves and an excellent nutty flavor.

Nutrition

As well as containing vitamins A, C and E, lettuce provides potassium, iron and calcium and traces of other minerals.

Buying and Storing

The best lettuce is that fresh from the garden. The next best thing is to buy lettuce from a farm store or pick-your-own (although if fertilizers and pesticides are used, their flavor will be disappointing compared to the organic product).

Nowadays, lettuce is frequently sold ready shredded and packed with herbs etc, an acceptable and convenient form of buying lettuce. Whether you buy lettuce prepacked or from the shelf, it must be fresh. Soil and bugs can be washed off but those with limp or yellow leaves are of no use. Eat lettuce as soon as possible after purchasing; in the meantime keep it in a cool dark place, such as the salad drawer of the fridge.

Making Salads

Salads can be made using only one lettuce or a mixture of many. There are no rules but, when mixing salads, choose leaves to give contrast in texture and color as well as flavor. Fresh herbs, such as parsley, cilantro and basil also add an interesting dimension.

Tear rather than cut the leaves of loose-leafed lettuce; icebergs and other large lettuces are commonly sliced or shredded. Eat as soon as possible after preparing.

Dressings should be well-flavored with a hint of sharpness, but never too astringent. Make them in a blender, a screw-top jar or in a large bowl so that the ingredients can be thoroughly blended. Always use the best possible oils and vinegars, in roughly the proportion of five oil to one vinegar or lemon juice. Use half good olive oil and half sunflower oil, or for a more fragrant dressing, a combination of walnut oil and sunflower oil. A pinch of salt and pepper is essential, French mustard is optional and the addition of a little sugar will blunt the flavor.

Add the dressing to the salad when you're ready to serve – never before.

ARUGULA

Arugula, also called rocket, has a wonderful peppery flavor and is excellent in a mixed green salad. It has small, bright green dandelion-shaped leaves. The Greeks and Romans commonly ate *arugula* in mixed salads, apparently to help counterbalance the dampening effect lettuce had on the libido – arugula's aphrodisiac properties in antiquity are well cataloged. It used to be sown around the statues of Priapus, the mythological Greek god of fertility and protector of gardens and herbs and son of Aphrodite and Dionysus.

Buying and Storing

Arugula is to be found either among the salads or fresh herbs in supermarkets. Buy fresh green leaves and use soon after purchasing. If necessary, the leaves can be kept immersed in cold water.

Preparing and Serving

Discard any discolored leaves. Add arugula to plain green salads, or grind with garlic, pine nuts and olive oil for a dressing for pasta.

Since it has such a striking flavor, a little arugula goes a long way, making it an excellent leaf for garnishing. It tastes superb contrasted with grilled goat cheese, or one or two leaves can be added to sandwiches, or loosely packed into pitta bread pockets along with tomatoes, avocado, peanuts and bean sprouts.

Above left: Oak Leaf lettuce.
Below left: Frisée.
Below: Arugula.

CHICORY AND RADICCHIO

Chicory, radicchio, endive and escarole are all related to each other and when they are tasted together you can easily detect their family resemblance. Their names are occasionally interchanged: chicory is often referred to as Belgian or French endive, and French and Belgian *chicorée* as the English curly endive and the American frisée.

CHICORY

During the late eighteenth century, chicory was grown in Europe for its root, which was added to coffee. A Belgian, M. Brezier, discovered that the white leaves could be eaten, a fact he kept secret during his lifetime; but after his death chicory became a popular vegetable, first in Belgium and later elsewhere in Europe. Its Flemish name is *witloof*, meaning "white leaf," and its characteristic pale leaf is due to its being grown in darkness; the paler it is, the less bitter its flavor.

Chicory can be eaten raw but is commonly cooked, either baked, stir-fried or poached. To eat raw, separate the leaves and serve with fruit, such as oranges or grapefruit, which counteract chicory's slight bitterness.

RADICCHIO

This is one of many varieties developed from wild chicory. It looks like a small lettuce with deep wine-red leaves and striking cream ribs and owes its splendid foliage to careful shading. If it is grown completely in the dark the leaves are marbled pink, and those that have been exposed to some light can be patched with a green or copper color. Its flavor tends to be bitter but contrasts well with green salads. Radicchio can be stir-fried or poached, although the leaves turn dark green when cooked.

FRISÉE AND ESCAROLE

These are robust salad ingredients in both flavor and texture. The curly-leaved frisée looks like a green frizzy mop and the escarole is broad-leaved, but both have a distinct bitter flavor. Serve mixed with each other and a well-flavored dressing. This dampens down the bitter flavor but gives the salad a pleasant "bite."

Preparing

To prepare chicory, take out the core at the base with a sharp knife (*left*) and discard any wilted or damaged leaves. Rinse thoroughly, then dry the leaves.

Above: Chicory.
Above right: Radicchio.
Below right: Escarole.

Preparing Salad Leaves

Pull the leaves away from the stalk, discarding any wilted or damaged leaves.

Wash the leaves in plenty of cold water, swirling gently to make sure all dirt and any insects are washed away.

Place the washed leaves in a soft dish towel and then gently pat dry.

Place in a dry dish towel in a large plastic bag. Chill in the fridge for about 1 hour.

RADISHES

Radishes have a peppery flavor that can almost be felt in the nostrils as you bite into one. Their pungency depends not only on the varieties but also on the soil in which they are grown. Freshly harvested radishes have the most pronounced flavor and crisp texture.

Varieties

Radishes were loved throughout antiquity and consequently there are many varieties worldwide. Both the small red types and the large white radishes are internationally popular.

Red Radishes: These small red orbs have many pretty names, but are mostly sold simply as radishes. They are available all year round, have a deep pink skin, sometimes paler or white at the roots and a firm white flesh. Their peppery flavor is milder in the spring and they are almost always eaten raw. Finely sliced and sandwiched in bread and butter, they make an interesting *hors d'oeuvre*.

French Breakfast Radishes: These are red and white and slightly more elongated than the red radish. They tend to be milder than the red radishes and are popular in France either eaten on their own or served with other raw vegetables as *crudités*.

Daikon or Mooli Radishes: Sometimes known as the oriental radish, the daikon is a smooth-skinned, long, white radish. Those bought in stores have a mild flavor, less peppery than the red radish – perhaps because they lose their flavor after long storage (daikons straight from the garden are hot and peppery). They can be eaten raw or pickled, or added to stir-fries.

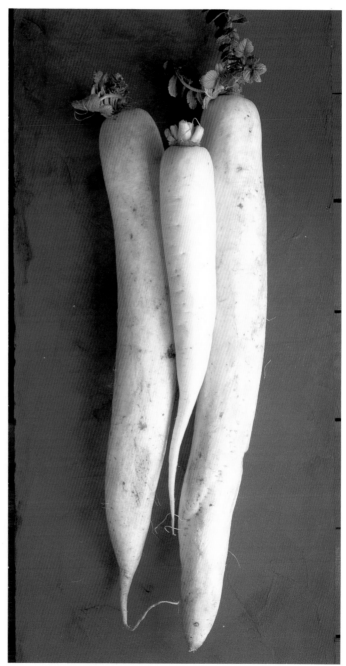

Buying and Storing

Buy red radishes that are firm with crisp leaves. If at all possible, buy daikons or moolis which still have their leaves; this is a good indication of their freshness as they wilt quickly. The leaves should be green and lively and the skins clear with no bruises or blemishes. They can be stored in the fridge for a few days.

Preparing and Serving

Red radishes need only to be washed. They can then be sliced or eaten whole by themselves or in salads. You can make a feature of them by slicing into a salad of, say, oranges and walnuts, perhaps with a scattering of arugula and dressed with a walnut oil vinaigrette. To use daikon in a stir-fry, cut into slices and add to the dish for the last few minutes of cooking. It adds not only flavor but also a wonderfully juicy and crunchy texture.

Left: Red radishes.
Above: French breakfast radishes.
Right: Daikon, or Mooli, radishes.

WATERCRESS

Watercress is perhaps the most robustly flavored of all the salad ingredients and a handful of watercress is all you need to perk up a rather dull green salad. It has a distinctive "raw" flavor, both peppery and slightly pungent and this, together with its bright green leaves, make it a popular garnish.

Watercress, as the name suggests, grows in water. It needs fast flowing clean water to thrive and is really only successful around freshwater springs on chalk hills. The first watercress beds were cultivated in Europe, but watercress is now grown worldwide.

WINTER CRESS

Winter cress or land cress is often grown as an alternative to watercress, when flowing water is not available. It looks like a robust form of watercress and indeed has a similar if even more assertive flavor, with a distinct peppery taste. Use as you would use watercress, either in salads or in soups.

Nutrition

Watercress is extremely rich in vitamins A, B2, C, D and E. It is also rich in calcium, potassium and iron and provides significant quantities of sulphur and chloride.

Buying and Storing

Only buy fresh-looking watercress – the darker and larger the leaves the better. Avoid any with wilted or yellow leaves. It will keep for several days in the fridge or better still, submerged in a bowl, or arranged in a jar of cold water, and kept in a cool place.

Preparing and Cooking

Discard any yellow leaves and remove thick stalks which will be too coarse for salads or soups. Small sprigs can be added to salads.

For soups and purées, either blend watercress raw or cook briefly in stock, milk or water. Cooking inevitably destroys some of the nutrients but cooked water-cress has a less harsh flavor, while still retaining its characteristic peppery taste.

MUSTARD <u>AND</u> CRESS

Mustard and cress are often grown together, to provide spicy greenery as a garnish or for salads. They are available all year through.

Mustard seedlings germinate 3-4 days sooner than the cress, so if you buy mustard and cress from the supermarket, or grow your own on the windowsill, initially the punnets will only show mustard seedlings.

History

Cress has been grown for thousands of years, known first to the Persians. There is a story that the Persians would always eat cress before they baked bread, and there are other references in antiquity to people eating cress with bread.

Serving

Today mustard and cress are often enjoyed in sandwiches, either served simply on buttered bread, or with avocado or cucumber added. Cress probably wouldn't be substantial enough as a salad in itself, but, with its faint spicy flavor, it can perk up a plain green salad, and it is also excellent in a tomato salad, dressed simply with olive oil and tarragon vinegar.

Above left: Watercress.
Below left: Winter cress.
Above right: Mustard seedlings.
Right: Cress seedlings.

NINE

MUSHROOMS

White Mushrooms

Field Mushrooms

Woodland Mushrooms

Wild Mushrooms
and Other Fungi

WHITE MUSHROOMS

wrapped cartons, transfer loose to the bottom of the fridge as soon as possible. They will keep only for a day or two.

Preparing

Mushrooms should not be washed but wiped with a damp cloth or a piece of paper towel (*below*). This is partly because you don't want to increase their water content, and also because they should be fried as dry as possible.

Unless the skins are very discolored, it should not be necessary to peel them, although you probably will need to trim the very base of the stem.

Mushrooms are generally cooked, although some white mushrooms are served raw in salads. Eat them quickly; after frying they can go soft and flabby.

History

In the past, mushrooms have had a firm association with the supernatural and even today their connection with the mysterious side of life hasn't completely disappeared. Fairy rings – circles of mushrooms – inexplicably appear overnight in woods and fields and thunder is still thought to bring forth fresh crops of mushrooms.

Many types of mushrooms and fungi are either poisonous or hallucinogenic, and in the past their poisons have been distilled for various murderous reasons.

The use of the term mushroom to mean edible species, and toadstool to mean those considered poisonous, has no scientific basis, and there is no simple rule for distinguishing between the two. Picking wild mushrooms is not safe unless you are confident about identifying edible types. In France during the autumn, people take the wild mushrooms they have gathered to the local pharmacy, where safe mushrooms are identified.

Varieties

White/Button Mushrooms: Cultivated mushrooms are widely available in stores and are sold when very young and tiny. The slightly larger ones are known as closed cap, while larger ones still are open capped, or open cup, mushrooms. They have ivory or white caps with pinky/beige gills that darken as they mature. All have a pleasant flavor.

Cremini Mushrooms: These have a thicker stem and a darker, pale brown cap. They have a more pronounced "mushroomy" flavor and a meatier texture than white mushrooms.

Buying and Storing

It is easy to see whether or not white mushrooms are fresh – their caps will be clean and white, without bruises or blemishes. The longer they stay on the shelves, the darker and more discolored the caps become, while the gills underneath turn from pink to brown.

If possible, use the paper bags provided in many supermarkets nowadays when buying mushrooms. Mushrooms in plastic bags sweat in their own heat, eventually turning slippery and unappetizing. If you have no choice or you buy mushrooms in cellophane-

Cooking

Mushrooms are largely composed of water and shrink noticeably during cooking. They also take up a lot of fat as they cook so it is best to use butter or a good olive oil for frying. Fry mushrooms briskly over a moderately high heat so that as they shrink the water evaporates and they don't stew in their own juice. For the same reason do not fry too many mushrooms at once in the same pan.

Most of the recipes in this book use fried mushrooms as their base and they are completely interchangeable – so if you can't get wild mushrooms or cremini mushrooms for instance, white mushrooms can be used instead.

Above: White mushrooms.
Top right: Flat mushrooms.
Far right: Field mushrooms.
Right: Cremini mushrooms (top) and open capped or cup mushrooms.

FIELD MUSHROOMS

Field mushrooms are the wild relatives of the cultivated mushroom and when cooked have a wonderful aroma. Flat mushrooms, although indistinguishable from field mushrooms in appearance, have probably been cultivated and are also excellent. Connoisseurs say that only wild mushrooms have any flavor but many would argue against this. However, if you know where to find field mushrooms, keep the secret to yourself (most mushroom devotees seem to know this) and count yourself lucky!

Buying and Storing

Field mushrooms are sometimes available during the autumn in farm stores. Since they are likely to have been picked recently, they should be fresh unless obviously wilting. Unless you intend to stuff them, don't worry if they are broken in places as you will be slicing them anyway. Use as soon as possible after purchase.

Preparing

Trim the stalk bottoms if necessary and wipe the caps with a damp cloth. Slice according to the recipe.

Cooking

For true field mushrooms, you need do nothing more complicated than simply fry them in butter or olive oil with a suggestion of garlic if liked. However, like flat mushrooms, field mushrooms can be used for stuffing, in soups or indeed any mushroom recipe. They are darker than white mushrooms and will color soups and sauces brown, but the flavor will be extremely good.

When stuffing mushrooms, gently fry the caps on both sides for a few minutes. The stalks can be chopped and added to the stuffing or can be used for soups or stocks.

WOODLAND MUSHROOMS

Varieties

Ceps: Popular in France, where they are known as *cèpes* and in Italy where they are called *porcini*, these meaty, bun-shaped mushrooms have a fine almost suede-like texture and a good flavor. Instead of gills they have a spongy texture beneath the cap and unless they are very young it is best to scrape this away as it goes soggy when cooked. Ceps are excellent fried in oil or butter over a brisk heat to evaporate the liquid and then added to omelets.

Alternately, an Italian way of cooking is to remove the stalk and the spongy tubes, and brush the tops with olive oil. Broil for about 10 minutes under a moderate broiler and then turn them over and pour olive oil and a sprinkling of garlic into the center. Broil for a further 5 minutes and then serve sprinkled with seasoning and parsley.

Chanterelles: Frilly, trumpet-shaped chanterelles are delicate mushrooms which range in color from cream to a vivid yellow. Later, winter chanterelles have grayish-lilac gills on the underside of their dark caps. Chanterelles have a delicate, slightly fruity flavor and a firm, almost rubbery texture. They are difficult to clean as their tiny gills tend to trap grit and earth. Rinse them gently under cold running water and then shake dry. Fry in butter over a gentle heat to start with so they exude their liquid and then increase the heat to boil it off. They are delicious

with scrambled eggs, or served by themselves with finely cut toast.

Horn of Plenty/Black Trumpets: Taking its name from its shape, this mushroom ranges in color from mid-brown to black. As it is hollow, it will need to be brushed well to clean or, if a large specimen, sliced in half. It is very versatile, but goes particularly well with fish.

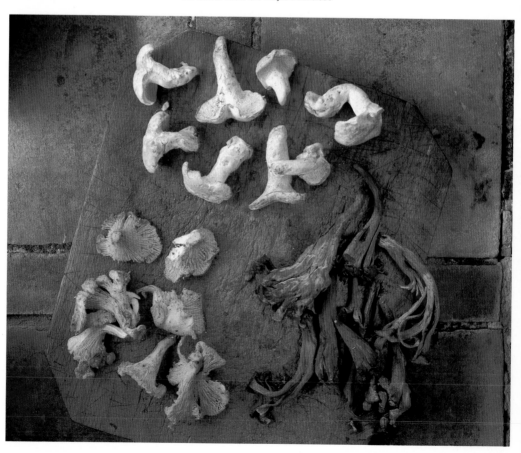

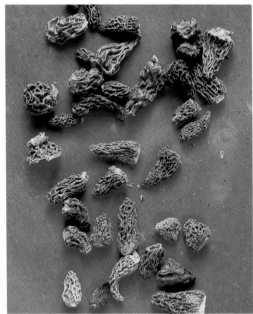

Morels: These are the first mushroom of the year, appearing not in autumn but in spring. In Scandinavia they are called the "truffles of the north" and are considered among the great edible fungi. They are cone-shaped with a crinkled spongy cap but are hollow inside. You will need to wash them well under running water as insects tend to creep into their dark crevices. Morels need longer cooking than most mushrooms: sauté them in butter, add a squeeze of lemon and then cover and simmer for up to an hour until tender. The juices can then be thickened with cream or egg yolks.

Dried Mushrooms: Most wild mushrooms are available dried. To reconstitute, soak in warm water for about 20-30 minutes; in the case of morels when they are added to stews, soak for about 10 minutes. Dried wild mushrooms, particularly ceps, have an intense flavor.

Left: Clockwise from the top: Ceps, Horn of Plenty, Chanterelles.
Above right: Dried mushrooms.
Above left: Morels.
Right: Winter chanterelles.

WILD MUSHROOMS <u>AND</u> OTHER FUNGI

Mushroom gathering, a seasonal event throughout Eastern Europe, Italy and France, is increasingly popular. The French are particularly enthusiastic: in autumn whole families drive to secret locations to comb the ground for prizes like shaggy ink caps or ceps. Wild mushrooms are sold in supermarkets.

OYSTER MUSHROOMS

These ear-shaped fungi grow on rotting wood. Cap, gills and stem are all the same color, which can be grayish brown, pink or yellow. They are now widely cultivated, although they are generally thought of as wild mushrooms. Delicious both in flavor and texture, they are softer than the white mushroom when cooked but seem more substantial, having more "bite" to them.

Buying and Storing

Fresh specimens are erect and lively looking with clear gills and smooth caps. They are often sold packed in plastic boxes under cellophane wrappings and

will wilt and go soggy if left on the shelf for too long. Once purchased, remove them from the plastic packaging and use as soon as possible.

Preparing

Oyster mushrooms rarely need trimming at all but if they are large, tear rather than cut them into pieces. In very large specimens the stems can be tough and should be discarded.

Cooking

Fry in butter until tender – they take less time to cook than white mushrooms. Do not overcook oyster mushrooms as the flavor will be lost and the soft texture will become more rubbery.

Left: Pink and yellow oyster mushrooms.
Above: Gray oyster mushrooms.

ENOKITAKI MUSHROOMS

This is another Japanese mushroom. The wild variety is orangy-brown with shiny caps but outside Japan, you will probably only be able to find the cultivated variety, which are similarly fine, with pin-size heads, but are pale colored with snowy white caps. They have a fine, sweet and almost fruity flavor. In Japanese cookery they are added to salads or used as a garnish for soups or hot dishes. Since they become tough if overcooked, add enokitaki mushrooms at the very last minute of cooking.

SHIITAKE MUSHROOMS

These Japanese fungi are now commonly available in supermarkets. They are among a variety of tree mushrooms (called *take* in Japan, the *shii* being the hardwood tree from which they are harvested). They have a meaty, slightly acid flavor and a distinct slippery texture. Shiitake mushrooms, though once only available in oriental stores, are now widely available in most supermarkets. Unlike white mushrooms that can be flash-fried, shiitake need to be cooked through, although even this only takes 3–5 minutes. Add them to stir-fries for a delicious flavor and texture. Alterna-tively, fry them in oil until tender. Sprinkle with sesame oil and then serve with a little soy sauce.

Above: Enokitaki mushrooms.
Right: Shiitake mushrooms.

COOKING
WITH
VEGETABLES

ONION AND LEEK RECIPES

BAKED ONIONS STUFFED WITH FETA

SERVES FOUR

INGREDIENTS
  4 large red onions
  1 tablespoon olive oil
  1 ounce pine nuts
  4 ounces feta cheese, crumbled
  1 ounce fresh white bread crumbs
  1 tablespoon chopped fresh cilantro
  salt and freshly ground black pepper

1 Preheat the oven to 350°F and lightly grease a shallow ovenproof dish. Peel the onions and cut a thin slice from the top and base of each. Place in a large saucepan of boiling water and cook for 10–12 minutes until just tender. Remove with a slotted spoon. Drain on paper towels and leave to cool slightly.

2 Using a small knife or your fingers, remove the inner sections of the onions, leaving about two or three outer rings. Finely chop the inner sections and place the shells in an ovenproof dish.

3 Heat the oil in a medium-size frying pan and fry the chopped onions for 4–5 minutes until golden, then add the pine nuts and stir-fry for a few minutes.

4 Place the feta cheese in a small bowl and stir in the onions and pine nuts, the bread crumbs and cilantro. Season well with salt and pepper and then spoon the mixture into the onion shells. Cover loosely with foil and bake in the oven for about 30 minutes and remove the foil for the last 10 minutes.

5 Serve as a starter or as a light lunch with warm olive bread.

ONION TARTS WITH GOAT CHEESE

A VARIATION OF A CLASSIC FRENCH DISH, TARTE A L'OIGNON, THIS DISH USES YOUNG GOAT CHEESE INSTEAD OF CREAM, AS IT IS MILD AND CREAMY AND COMPLEMENTS THE FLAVOR OF THE ONIONS. THIS RECIPE MAKES EITHER EIGHT INDIVIDUAL TARTS OR ONE LARGE 9-INCH TART.

SERVES EIGHT

INGREDIENTS
For the pastry
  6 ounces all-purpose flour
  2½ ounces butter
  1 ounce Cheddar cheese, grated
For the filling
  1–1½ tablespoons olive or
    sunflower oil
  3 onions, finely sliced
  6 ounces young goat cheese
  2 eggs, beaten
  1 tablespoon light cream
  2 ounces Cheddar cheese, grated
  1 tablespoon chopped fresh tarragon
  salt and freshly ground black pepper

1 To make the pastry, sift the flour into a bowl and rub in the butter until the mixture resembles fine bread crumbs. Stir in the grated cheese and add enough cold water to make a dough. Knead lightly, put in a plastic bag and chill. Preheat the oven to 375°F.

2 Roll out the dough on a lightly floured surface, and then cut into eight rounds using a 4½-inch pastry cutter and line eight 4-inch muffin pans. Prick the bases with a fork and bake in the oven for 10–15 minutes until firm but not browned. Reduce the oven temperature to 350°F.

3 Heat the olive or sunflower oil in a large frying pan and fry the onions over low heat for 20–25 minutes until they are a deep golden brown. Stir occasionally to prevent them burning.

4 Beat the goat cheese with the eggs, cream, Cheddar cheese and tarragon. Season with salt and pepper and then stir in the fried onions.

5 Pour the mixture into the part-baked pastry shells and bake in the oven for 20–25 minutes until golden. Serve warm or cold with a green salad.

CLASSIC FRENCH ONION SOUP

WHEN FRENCH ONION SOUP IS MADE SLOWLY AND CAREFULLY, THE ONIONS ALMOST CARAMELIZE TO A DEEP MAHOGANY COLOR. IT HAS A SUPERB FLAVOR AND IS A PERFECT WINTER SUPPER DISH.

SERVES FOUR

INGREDIENTS
4 large onions
2 tablespoons sunflower or olive oil, or
   1 tablespoon of each
1 ounce butter
3¾ cups beef stock
4 slices Italian bread
1½–2 ounces Gruyère or Cheddar
   cheese, grated
salt and freshly ground black pepper

1 Peel and quarter the onions and slice or chop them into ¼-inch pieces. Heat the oil and butter together in a deep heavy-based saucepan, preferably with a medium-size bottom so that the onions form a thick layer.

3 When the onions are a rich mahogany brown, add the beef stock and a little seasoning. Simmer, partially covered, for 30 minutes, then taste and adjust the seasoning according to taste.

4 Preheat the broiler and toast the bread. Spoon the soup into four oven-proof serving dishes and place a piece of bread in each. Sprinkle with the cheese and broil for a few minutes until golden.

2 Fry the onions briskly for a few minutes, stirring constantly, and then reduce the heat and cook gently for 45–60 minutes. At first, the onions need to be stirred only occasionally but as they begin to color, stir frequently. The color of the onions gradually turns golden and then more rapidly to brown, so take care to stir constantly at this stage so they do not burn on the bottom.

THAI NOODLES ᵂᴵᵀᴴ GARLIC CHIVES

THIS RECIPE REQUIRES A LITTLE TIME FOR PREPARATION, BUT THE COOKING TIME IS VERY FAST. EVERYTHING IS COOKED SPEEDILY IN A HOT WOK AND SHOULD BE EATEN AT ONCE.

SERVES FOUR

INGREDIENTS

    12 ounces dried rice noodles
    ½-inch piece fresh ginger, grated
    2 tablespoons light soy sauce
    3 tablespoons vegetable oil
    2 garlic cloves, crushed
    1 large onion, cut into thin wedges
    4 ounces fried bean curd,
      thinly sliced
    1 green chili, seeded
      and finely sliced
    6 ounces bean sprouts
    4 ounces garlic chives, cut into
      2-inch lengths
    2 ounces roasted peanuts, ground
    2 tablespoons dark soy sauce
    2 tablespoons chopped fresh
      cilantro
    1 lemon, cut into wedges

1 Place the noodles in a large bowl, cover with warm water and soak for 20–30 minutes, then drain. Blend together the ginger, light soy sauce and 1 tablespoon of the oil in a bowl. Set aside for 10 minutes. Drain, reserving the marinade.

2 Heat 1 tablespoon of the oil in a wok or large frying pan. Fry the garlic for a few seconds, then remove from pan and discard.

5 When hot, spoon onto serving plates and garnish with the remaining ground peanuts, cilantro and lemon wedges.

COOK'S TIP
This a vegetarian meal, however, thinly sliced pork or chicken could be used instead. Stir-fry it initially for 4–5 minutes.

3 Heat the remaining oil in the wok or frying pan and stir-fry the onion for 3–4 minutes until softened and tinged with brown. Add the bean curd and chili, stir-fry briefly and then add the noodles. Stir-fry for 4–5 minutes.

4 Stir in the bean sprouts, garlic chives and most of the ground peanuts, reserving a little for the garnish. Stir well, then add the dark soy sauce and the reserved marinade.

GARLIC MUSHROOMS

GARLIC AND MUSHROOMS MAKE A WONDERFUL COMBINATION. THEY MUST BE SERVED PIPING HOT, SO IF POSSIBLE USE A BALTI PAN OR CAST-IRON FRYING PAN AND DON'T STAND ON CEREMONY — SERVE STRAIGHT FROM THE PAN.

SERVES FOUR (as a starter)

INGREDIENTS
  2 tablespoons sunflower oil
  1 ounce butter
  5 scallions, thinly sliced
  3 garlic cloves, crushed
  1 pound white mushrooms
  1½ ounces fresh white bread crumbs
  1 tablespoon chopped fresh parsley
  2 tablespoons lemon juice
  salt and freshly ground black pepper

1 Heat the oil and butter in a balti pan, wok or cast-iron frying pan. Add the scallions and garlic and stir-fry over medium heat for 1–2 minutes.

2 Add the whole white mushrooms and fry over high heat for 4–5 minutes, stirring and tossing with a large wide spatula or wooden spoon, all the time.

3 Stir in the bread crumbs, parsley, lemon juice and seasoning. Stir-fry for a few minutes until the lemon juice has virtually evaporated and then serve.

ROAST GARLIC <u>WITH</u> CROÛTONS

YOUR GUESTS WILL BE ASTONISHED TO BE SERVED A WHOLE ROAST GARLIC FOR A STARTER. ROAST GARLIC HAS A HEAVENLY FLAVOR AND IS SO IRRESISTIBLE THAT THEY WILL EVEN FORGIVE YOU THE NEXT DAY!

SERVES FOUR

INGREDIENTS
  2 garlic bulbs
  3 tablespoons olive oil
  3 tablespoons water
  sprig of rosemary
  sprig of thyme
  1 bay leaf
  sea salt and freshly ground
    black pepper
To serve
  slices of Italian bread
  olive or sunflower oil, for frying
  6 ounces young goat cheese or soft
    cream cheese
  2 tablespoons chopped fresh herbs,
    e.g. marjoram, parsley and chives

3 Heat a little oil in a frying pan and fry the Italian bread on both sides until golden. Blend the cheese with the mixed herbs and place in a serving dish.

4 Cut each garlic bulb in half and open out slightly. Serve the garlic on small plates with the croûtons and soft cheese. Each garlic clove should be squeezed out of its papery shell, spread over a croûton and eaten with the cheese.

1 Preheat the oven to 375°F. Place the garlic bulbs in a small ovenproof dish and pour over the oil and water. Add the rosemary, thyme and bay leaf and sprinkle with sea salt and pepper. Cover with foil and bake in the oven for 30 minutes.

2 Remove the foil, baste the garlic heads with the juices from the dish and bake for a further 15–20 minutes until they feel soft when pressed.

LEEKS IN EGG AND LEMON SAUCE

THE COMBINATION OF EGGS AND LEMON IN SAUCES AND SOUPS IS COMMONLY FOUND IN RECIPES FROM GREECE, TURKEY AND THE MIDDLE EAST. THIS SAUCE HAS A DELICIOUS FRESH TASTE AND BRINGS OUT THE BEST IN THE LEEKS. BE SURE TO USE TENDER BABY LEEKS FOR THIS RECIPE.

SERVES FOUR

INGREDIENTS

1½ pounds baby leeks
1 tablespoon cornstarch
2 teaspoons sugar
2 egg yolks
juice of 1½ lemons
salt

1 Trim the leeks, slit them from top to bottom and rinse very well under cold water to remove any dirt.

2 Place the leeks in a large saucepan, preferably so they lie flat on the bottom, cover with water and add a little salt. Bring to boil, cover and simmer for 4–5 minutes until just tender.

3 Carefully remove the leeks using a slotted spoon, drain well and arrange in a shallow serving dish. Reserve 7 fluid ounces of the cooking liquid.

4 Blend the cornstarch with the cooled cooking liquid and place in a small saucepan. Bring to boil, stirring all the time, and cook over low heat until the sauce thickens slightly. Stir in the sugar and then remove the saucepan from the heat and allow to cool slightly.

5 Beat the egg yolks thoroughly with the lemon juice and stir gradually into the cooled sauce. Cook over very low heat, stirring all the time, until the sauce is fairly thick. Be careful not to overheat the sauce or it may curdle. As soon as the sauce has thickened remove the pan from the heat and continue stirring for a minute. Taste and add salt or sugar as necessary. Cool slightly.

6 Stir the cooled sauce with a wooden spoon. Pour the sauce over the leeks and then cover and chill well for at least 2 hours before serving.

LEEK SOUFFLÉ

SOME PEOPLE THINK OF A SOUFFLÉ AS A DINNER PARTY DISH, AND A RATHER TRICKY ONE AT THAT. HOWEVER, OTHERS FREQUENTLY SERVE THEM FOR FAMILY MEALS BECAUSE THEY ARE QUICK AND EASY TO MAKE, AND PROVE TO BE VERY POPULAR AND SATISFYING.

SERVES TWO TO THREE

INGREDIENTS

   1 tablespoon sunflower oil
   1½ ounces butter
   2 leeks, thinly sliced
   about 1¼ cups milk
   1 ounce all-purpose flour
   4 eggs, separated
   3 ounces Gruyère or Emmenthal
     cheese, grated
   salt and freshly ground black pepper

1 Preheat the oven to 350°F and butter a large soufflé dish. Heat the oil and ½ ounce of the butter in a small saucepan or flameproof casserole and fry the leeks over low heat for 4–5 minutes until soft but not brown, stirring occasionally.

2 Stir in the milk and bring to boil. Cover and simmer for 4–5 minutes until the leeks are tender. Put the liquid through a strainer into a measuring jug.

3 Melt the remaining butter in a saucepan, stir in the flour and cook for 1 minute. Remove pan from the heat. Make up the reserved liquid with milk to 1¼ cups. Gradually stir the milk into the pan to make a smooth sauce. Return to the heat and bring to a boil, stirring. When thickened, remove from the heat. Cool slightly and then beat in the egg yolks, cheese and the leeks.

4 Whisk the egg whites until stiff and, using a large metal spoon, fold into the leek and egg mixture. Pour into the prepared soufflé dish and bake in the oven for about 30 minutes until golden and puffy. Serve immediately.

TAGLIATELLE ᵂᴵᵀᴴ LEEKS ᴬᴺᴰ PROSCIUTTO

LEEKS ARE A VERY VERSATILE VEGETABLE. THEIR DELICATE, MILDLY ONIONY FLAVOR MAKES THEM IDEAL TO USE IN STIR-FRIES, RISOTTOS, EGG DISHES, SOUPS AND SAUCES. IF USING OLDER LEEKS, MAKE SURE THEY HAVE NOT DEVELOPED A WOODY CORE.

SERVES FOUR as a snack or light lunch

INGREDIENTS
  5 leeks
  1½ ounces butter or margarine
  8 ounces tagliatelle, preferably
    green and white
  4 teaspoons dry sherry
  2 tablespoons lemon juice
  2 teaspoons chopped fresh basil
  4–5 ounces prosciutto, torn into strips
  6 ounces ricotta cheese
  salt and freshly ground black pepper
  fresh basil leaves, to garnish
  Parmesan cheese, to serve

4 Stir the sherry, lemon juice, basil and seasoning into the leek mixture and cook for 1–2 minutes so that the flavors can blend together. Add the prosciutto and ricotta cheese, stir and cook for about 1–2 minutes until heated through.

5 Drain the pasta and place in a warmed serving dish. Pour the leek and prosciutto mixture on top and mix lightly together. Garnish each serving with basil leaves and serve with shavings of Parmesan cheese.

1 Trim the leeks and then cut a slit from top to bottom, rinse well under cold water and cut into thin slices.

2 Melt the butter or margarine in a saucepan or flameproof casserole, add the leeks and fry over low heat for 3–4 minutes until tender but not too soft.

3 Add the tagliatelle to a large saucepan of boiling water and cook according to the instructions on the packet (about 3–5 minutes for fresh pasta; 8 minutes for dried pasta).

BAKED LEEKS <u>WITH</u> CHEESE <u>AND</u> YOGURT TOPPING

LIKE ALL VEGETABLES, THE FRESHER LEEKS ARE, THE BETTER THEIR FLAVOR, AND THE FRESHEST LEEKS AVAILABLE SHOULD BE USED FOR THIS DISH. SMALL, YOUNG LEEKS ARE AROUND AT THE BEGINNING OF THE SEASON AND ARE PERFECT TO USE HERE.

SERVES FOUR

INGREDIENTS

   8 small leeks, about 1½ pounds
   2 small eggs or 1 large one, beaten
   5 ounces fresh goat cheese
   ⅓ cup plain yogurt
   2 ounces Parmesan cheese, grated
   1 ounce fresh white or brown bread
     crumbs
   salt and freshly ground black pepper

1 Preheat the oven to 350°F and butter a shallow ovenproof dish. Trim the leeks, cut a slit from top to bottom and rinse well under cold water.

2 Place the leeks in a saucepan of water, bring to the boil and simmer gently for 6–8 minutes until just tender. Remove and drain well using a slotted spoon, and arrange in the prepared dish.

3 Beat the eggs with the goat cheese, yogurt and half the Parmesan cheese, and season well with salt and pepper.

4 Pour the cheese and yogurt mixture over the leeks. Mix the bread crumbs and remaining Parmesan cheese together and sprinkle over the sauce. Bake in the oven for 35–40 minutes until the top is crisp and golden brown.

CHICKEN WITH SHALLOTS

SERVES FOUR

INGREDIENTS
1 small chicken, about 3 pounds, or 4
   chicken pieces
seasoned all-purpose flour, for coating
2 tablespoons sunflower oil
1 ounce butter
4 ounces unsmoked lean bacon,
   chopped
1¾ cups red wine
1 bay leaf
2 thyme sprigs
2 garlic cloves
9 ounces shallots
4 ounces white mushrooms,
   halved if large
2 teaspoons plain flour
salt and freshly ground black pepper

1 Preheat the oven to 350°F. Remove
any excess skin or fat from the chicken
and cut into four or eight pieces. Place a
little seasoned flour in a large plastic
bag, add the chicken pieces and shake
to coat evenly.

2 Heat the oil and half the butter in
large flameproof casserole and fry the
bacon for 3–4 minutes. Add the chicken
pieces and fry, in batches if necessary,
until lightly browned. Add the wine, bay
leaf and thyme and bring to a boil. Cover
and cook in the oven for 1 hour.

3 Peel the shallots and boil them in
salted water for 10 minutes. Heat the
remaining oil in a small frying pan and
fry the shallots for 3–4 minutes until
beginning to brown. Add the mushrooms
and fry for a further 2–3 minutes.

4 Stir the shallots and mushrooms into
the casserole with the chicken and cook
for a further 8–10 minutes. Using a fork
blend the flour with the remaining butter
to make a thick paste.

5 Transfer the chicken pieces, shallots
and mushrooms to a serving dish and
keep warm. Bring the liquid to a boil and
then add small pieces of the flour paste,
stirring vigorously after each addition.
When all the paste has been added and
the sauce is thick, either pour over the
chicken pieces or return the chicken to
the casserole and serve.

GLAZED SHALLOTS

SERVES FOUR

INGREDIENTS
12–14 ounces shallots
1 tablespoon olive oil
1 ounce butter
1 tablespoon sugar
about ¾ cup water
salt and freshly ground black pepper

1 Peel the shallots and break in two if
the onions are joined. Heat the oil and
butter in a heavy-based saucepan and
gently fry the shallots over moderate heat
for 5–6 minutes until patches of brown
begin to appear. Stir occasionally.

2 Sprinkle the shallots with the sugar
and cook, stirring, for 1 minute.

3 Add enough water to just cover the
shallots and then cover and simmer over
low heat for about 25–35 minutes until
tender. Add a little extra water if necessary, to avoid the pan boiling dry. When
the onions are completely tender, remove
the lid and continue simmering gently
until the liquid at the bottom of the pan
has reduced to a thin syrup. Stir occasionally.

4 Spoon the shallots into a serving dish
and pour over the syrup. Serve with roast
meat or a baked vegetable dish.

SHOOT AND STEM RECIPES

ASPARAGUS TART WITH RICOTTA

SERVES FOUR

INGREDIENTS
For the pastry
  3 ounces butter or margarine
  6 ounces all-purpose flour
  pinch of salt
For the filling
  8 ounces asparagus
  2 eggs, beaten
  8 ounces ricotta cheese
  2 tablespoons strained plain yogurt
  1½ ounces Parmesan cheese, grated
  salt and freshly ground black pepper

1 Preheat the oven to 400°F. Rub the butter or margarine into the flour and salt until the mixture resembles fine bread crumbs. Stir in enough cold water to form a smooth dough and knead lightly on a floured surface.

2 Roll out the pastry and line a 9-inch flan ring. Press firmly into the pan and prick all over with a fork. Bake in the oven for about 10 minutes until the pastry is pale but firm. Remove from the oven and reduce the temperature to 350°F.

3 To make the filling, trim the asparagus and cut 2 inches from the top and chop the remaining stalks into 1-inch pieces. Add the stalks to a saucepan of boiling water and after 1 minute add the tops. Simmer for 4–5 minutes until almost tender, then drain and refresh under cold water.

4 Beat together the eggs, ricotta, yogurt, Parmesan cheese and seasoning. Stir in the asparagus stalks and pour the mixture into the pastry case. Arrange the asparagus tips on top, pressing them down slightly into the ricotta mixture.

5 Bake in the oven for 35–40 minutes until golden. Serve warm or cold.

ASPARAGUS WITH TARRAGON HOLLANDAISE

THIS IS THE IDEAL STARTER FOR AN EARLY SUMMER DINNER PARTY WHEN THE NEW SEASON'S ASPARAGUS IS JUST IN AND AT ITS BEST. MAKING HOLLANDAISE SAUCE IN A BLENDER OR FOOD PROCESSOR IS INCREDIBLY EASY AND VIRTUALLY FOOLPROOF!

SERVES FOUR

INGREDIENTS
  1¼ pounds fresh asparagus
  salt
For the hollandaise sauce
  2 egg yolks
  1 tablespoon lemon juice
  4 ounces butter
  2 teaspoons finely chopped fresh
    tarragon
  salt and freshly ground black pepper

1 Prepare the asparagus, lay it in a steamer or in an asparagus steamer and place over a saucepan of rapidly boiling water. Cover and steam for 6–10 minutes until tender (the cooking time will depend on the thickness of the asparagus stems).

2 To make the hollandaise sauce, place the egg yolks, lemon juice and seasoning in a blender or food processor and process briefly. Melt the butter in a small pan until foaming and then, with the blender running, pour it on to the egg mixture in a slow, steady stream.

3 Stir in the tarragon by hand or process it (for a sauce speckled with green or a pale green sauce, respectively).

4 Arrange the asparagus on small plates and pour over some of the hollandaise sauce. Serve remaining sauce in a jug.

ASPARAGUS SOUP

HOME-MADE ASPARAGUS SOUP HAS A DELICATE FLAVOR, QUITE UNLIKE THAT FROM A CAN. THIS SOUP IS BEST MADE WITH YOUNG ASPARAGUS, WHICH IS TENDER AND BLENDS WELL. SERVE IT WITH WAFER-THIN SLICES OF BREAD.

SERVES FOUR

INGREDIENTS
    1 pound young asparagus
    1½ ounces butter
    6 shallots, sliced
    ½ ounce all-purpose flour
    2½ cups vegetable stock or water
    1 tablespoon lemon juice
    1 cup milk
    ½ cup light cream
    2 teaspoons chopped fresh chervil
    salt and freshly ground black pepper

1 Trim the stalks of the asparagus if necessary. Cut 1½ inches off the tops of half the asparagus and set aside for a garnish. Slice the remaining asparagus.

2 Melt 1 ounce of the butter in a large saucepan and gently fry the sliced shallots for 2–3 minutes until soft but not brown, stirring occasionally.

3 Add the sliced asparagus and fry over low heat for about 1 minute. Stir in the flour, cook for 1 minute. Stir in the stock or water, lemon juice and season to taste. Bring to a boil and then simmer, partially covered, for 15–20 minutes until the asparagus is very tender.

4 Cool slightly and then process the soup in a food processor or blender until smooth. Then press the puréed asparagus through a strainer placed over a clean saucepan. Add the milk by pouring and stirring it through the strainer with the asparagus so as to extract the maximum amount of asparagus purée.

5 Melt the remaining butter and fry the reserved asparagus tips gently for about 3–4 minutes to soften.

6 Heat the soup gently for 3–4 minutes. Stir in the cream and the asparagus tips. Heat gently and serve sprinkled with the chopped fresh chervil.

ROAST ASPARAGUS CRÊPES

Roast asparagus is delicious and good enough to eat just as it comes. However, for a really splendid starter, try this simple recipe. Either make six large or twice as many cocktail-size pancakes to use with smaller stems of asparagus.

SERVES SIX (as a starter)

INGREDIENTS
  1 pound fresh asparagus
  6–8 tablespoons olive oil
  6 ounces mascarpone cheese
  4 tablespoons light cream
  1 ounce Parmesan cheese, grated
  sea salt
For the pancakes
  6 ounces all-purpose flour
  2 eggs
  1½ cups milk
  vegetable oil, for frying
  pinch of salt

1 To make the pancake batter, mix the flour with the salt in a large bowl, food processor or blender, then add the eggs and milk and beat or process to make a smooth, fairly thin, batter.

2 Heat a little oil in a large frying pan and add a small amount of batter, swirling the pan to coat the base evenly. Cook over moderate heat for about 1 minute, then flip over and cook the other side until golden. Set aside and cook the rest of the pancakes in the same way; the mixture makes about six large or 12 smaller pancakes.

3 Preheat the oven to 350°F and lightly grease a large shallow ovenproof dish or roasting pan with some of the olive oil.

4 Trim the asparagus by placing on a board and cutting off the bases. Using a small sharp knife, peel away the woody ends, if necessary.

5 Arrange the asparagus in a single layer in the dish, trickle over the remaining olive oil, rolling the asparagus to coat each one thoroughly. Sprinkle with a little salt and then roast in the oven for about 8–12 minutes until tender (the cooking time depends on the stem thickness).

6 Blend the mascarpone cheese with the cream and Parmesan cheese and spread a generous tablespoonful over each of the pancakes, leaving a little extra for the topping. Preheat the broiler.

7 Divide the asparagus spears among the pancakes, roll up and arrange in a single layer in an ovenproof dish. Spoon over the remaining cheese mixture and then place under a moderate broiler for 4–5 minutes, until heated through and golden brown. Serve at once.

ARTICHOKES WITH GARLIC AND HERB BUTTER

IT IS FUN EATING ARTICHOKES AND EVEN MORE FUN TO SHARE ONE BETWEEN TWO PEOPLE. YOU CAN ALWAYS HAVE A SECOND ONE TO FOLLOW SO THAT YOU GET YOUR FAIR SHARE!

SERVES FOUR

INGREDIENTS
   2 artichokes
   salt
For the garlic and herb butter
   3 ounces butter
   1 garlic clove, crushed
   1 tablespoon mixed chopped fresh
     tarragon, marjoram and parsley

1 Wash the artichokes well in cold water. Using a sharp knife cut off the stalks level with the bases. Cut off the top ½ inch of leaves. Snip off the pointed ends of the remaining leaves with scissors.

2 Put the prepared artichokes in a large saucepan of lightly salted water. Bring to a boil, cover and cook for about 40–45 minutes or until a lower leaf comes away easily when gently pulled.

3 Drain upside down for a couple of minutes while making the sauce. Melt the butter over low heat, add the garlic and cook for 30 seconds. Remove from the heat, stir in the herbs and then pour into one or two small serving bowls.

4 Place the artichokes on serving plates and serve with the garlic and herb butter.

COOK'S TIP
To eat an artichoke, pull off each leaf and dip into the garlic and herb butter. Scrape off the soft fleshy base with your teeth. When the center is reached, pull out the hairy choke and discard it, as it is inedible. The base can be cut up and eaten with the remaining garlic butter.

STUFFED ARTICHOKES

THE AMOUNT OF STUFFING NEEDED FOR THIS DISH DEPENDS ON THE SIZE OF THE ARTICHOKES — IF THEY ARE SMALL YOU COULD SERVE ONE PER PERSON. TO INCREASE THE AMOUNT OF STUFFING, ADD EXTRA MOZZARELLA AND LEEK RATHER THAN BACON.

SERVES FOUR (as a starter)

INGREDIENTS
    2 artichokes, prepared
    lemon juice
For the stuffing
    1 ounce butter
    2–3 small leeks, sliced
    2–3 bacon strips, chopped (optional)
    3 ounces mozzarella cheese, cut into
        small cubes
    1–1½ ounces fresh brown or white
        bread crumbs
    1 teaspoon chopped fresh basil
    fresh basil leaves, to garnish
    salt and freshly ground black pepper

1 Place the artichokes in a large saucepan of salted water. Bring to a boil, cover and cook for 35–40 minutes or until a lower leaf comes away easily.

3 Drain the artichokes, upside down, and when cool enough to handle, cut in half from top to bottom using a sharp knife. Remove the inner leaves, pull out and discard the choke and then sprinkle the inside and base liberally with lemon juice to prevent discoloration.

4 Preheat the broiler. Spoon a little of the stuffing into each artichoke half and place them in a single layer in an oven-proof dish. Set under a moderately hot broiler and broiler for 5–6 minutes until the stuffing is golden brown. Serve on small plates garnished with basil leaves.

2 To make the stuffing, melt the butter in a saucepan and gently fry the leeks for 3–4 minutes. Add the bacon, if using, and continue frying until the leek is soft and the bacon lightly golden brown. Remove the pan from the heat and stir in the mozzarella cubes, bread crumbs, basil and seasoning to taste.

CELERY ROOT GRATIN

ALTHOUGH CELERY ROOT HAS A RATHER UNATTRACTIVE APPEARANCE WITH ITS HARD, KNOBBLY SKIN, IT IS A VEGETABLE THAT HAS A VERY DELICIOUS SWEET AND NUTTY FLAVOR. THIS IS ACCENTUATED IN THIS DISH BY THE ADDITION OF THE SWEET YET NUTTY EMMENTAL CHEESE.

SERVES FOUR

INGREDIENTS
1 pound celery root
juice of ½ lemon
1 ounce butter
1 small onion, finely chopped
2 tablespoons all-purpose flour
1¼ cups milk
1 ounce Emmental cheese, grated
1 tablespoon capers
salt and cayenne pepper

1 Preheat the oven to 375°F. Peel the celery root and cut into ¼-inch slices, immediately plunging them into a saucepan of cold water acidulated with the lemon juice.

2 Bring the water to a boil and simmer the celery root for 10–12 minutes until just tender. Drain and arrange the celery root in a shallow ovenproof dish.

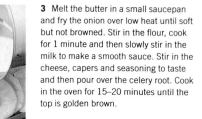

3 Melt the butter in a small saucepan and fry the onion over low heat until soft but not browned. Stir in the flour, cook for 1 minute and then slowly stir in the milk to make a smooth sauce. Stir in the cheese, capers and seasoning to taste and then pour over the celery root. Cook in the oven for 15–20 minutes until the top is golden brown.

VARIATION
For a less strongly flavored dish, alternate the layers of celery root with potato. Slice the potato, cook until almost tender, then drain well before assembling the dish.

CELERY ROOT AND BLUE CHEESE ROULADE

CELERY ROOT ADDS A DELICATE AND SUBTLE FLAVOR TO THIS ATTRACTIVE DISH. THE SPINACH ROULADE MAKES AN ATTRACTIVE CONTRAST TO THE CREAMY FILLING, BUT YOU COULD USE A PLAIN OR CHEESE ROULADE BASE INSTEAD. BE SURE TO ROLL UP THE ROULADE WHILE IT IS STILL WARM AND PLIABLE.

SERVES SIX

INGREDIENTS
  ½ ounce butter
  8 ounces cooked spinach, drained and
    chopped
  ⅔ cup light cream
  4 large eggs, separated
  ½ ounce Parmesan cheese, grated
  pinch of nutmeg
  salt and freshly ground black pepper
For the filling
  8 ounces celery root
  lemon juice
  3 ounces blue cheese
  4 ounces ricotta cheese
  freshly ground black pepper

1 Preheat the oven to 400°F and line a 13 x 9-inch jelly roll tin with non-stick baking parchment.

2 Melt the butter in a saucepan and add the spinach. Cook gently until all the liquid has evaporated, stirring frequently. Remove the pan from the heat and stir in the cream, egg yolks, Parmesan cheese, nutmeg and seasoning.

4 Bake in the oven for 10–15 minutes until the roulade is firm to the touch and lightly golden on top. Carefully turn out onto a sheet of wax paper and peel away the lining paper. Roll it up with the paper inside and leave to cool slightly.

5 To make the filling, peel and grate the celery root into a bowl and sprinkle well with lemon juice. Blend the blue cheese and ricotta cheese together and mix with the celery root and a little black pepper.

6 Unroll the roulade, spread with the filling and roll up again. Serve at once or wrap loosely and chill.

3 Whisk the egg whites until stiff, fold them gently into the spinach mixture and then spoon into the prepared pan. Spread the mixture evenly and use a metal spatula to smooth the surface.

BRAISED CELERY WITH GOAT CHEESE

THE SHARP FLAVOR OF THE CELERY IN THIS DISH IS PERFECTLY COMPLEMENTED BY THE MILD YET TANGY GOAT CHEESE. THIS RECIPE IS AN EXAMPLE OF QUICK AND EASY PREPARATION TO MAKE A DELICIOUS ACCOMPANIMENT TO GRILLED MEAT OR STUFFED PANCAKES.

SERVES FOUR

INGREDIENTS
  1 ounce butter
  1 head of celery, thinly sliced
  6 ounces mild medium-fat
    goat cheese
  3–4 tablespoons light cream
  salt and freshly ground black pepper

1 Preheat the oven to 350°F and lightly butter a medium-size shallow ovenproof dish.

2 Melt the butter in a heavy-based saucepan and fry the thinly sliced celery for 2–3 minutes, stirring frequently. Add 3–4 tablespoons of water to the pan, heat gently and then cover and simmer over low heat for 5–6 minutes, until the celery is nearly tender and the water has almost evaporated.

3 Remove the pan from the heat and stir in the goat cheese and cream. Taste and season with salt and pepper, and then turn into the prepared dish.

4 Cover the dish with buttered wax paper and cook in the oven for 10–12 minutes. Serve at once.

CELERY, AVOCADO AND WALNUT SALAD

THE CRUNCHINESS OF THE CELERY AND WALNUTS CONTRASTS PERFECTLY WITH THE SMOOTH AVOCADO. SERVE IT WITH A SOUR CREAM DRESSING AS SUGGESTED, OR SIMPLY DRESSED WITH A LITTLE OLIVE OIL AND FRESHLY SQUEEZED LEMON JUICE.

SERVES FOUR

INGREDIENTS
  3 bacon strips (optional)
  8 tender white celery stalks,
    very thinly sliced
  3 scallions, finely chopped
  2 ounces walnut halves
  1 ripe avocado
  lemon juice
For the dressing
  ½ cup sour cream
  1 tablespoon olive oil
  pinch of cayenne pepper

1 Dry-fry the bacon, if using, until golden and then chop into small pieces and place in a salad bowl with the celery, scallions and walnuts.

2 Halve the avocado and, using a very sharp knife, cut into thin slices. Peel away the skin from each slice and then sprinkle generously with lemon juice and add to the celery mixture.

3 Lightly beat the sour cream, olive oil and cayenne pepper together in a jug or small bowl. Either fold carefully into the salad or serve separately.

SPRING ROLLS

BAMBOO SHOOTS AND BEAN SPROUTS ARE PERFECT COMPANIONS IN THIS POPULAR SNACK, PROVIDING THE CONTRAST IN TEXTURE THAT IS THE PRINCIPLE ELEMENT IN CHINESE COOKING. THE BAMBOO SHOOTS RETAIN THEIR CRISPNESS, WHILE THE BEAN SPROUTS BECOME MORE CHEWY WHEN COOKED.

MAKES ABOUT TWENTY

INGREDIENTS
4 tablespoons vegetable oil
2 tablespoons dark soy sauce
2 tablespoons medium-dry sherry
about ½-inch piece fresh ginger,
    finely grated
8 ounces firm tofu, chopped finely
2 ounces rice vermicelli
4–5 shiitake mushrooms
4–5 scallions
7-ounce can bamboo shoots
1 garlic clove, crushed
1 carrot, grated
3 ounces bean sprouts, roughly
    chopped
1 tablespoon cornstarch, blended
    with 2 tablespoons water
about 20 x 6-inch spring roll wrappers
vegetable oil, for deep frying

1 Blend together 2 tablespoons of the oil, the soy sauce, sherry and ginger in a medium-size bowl. Add the tofu, stir well and set aside for 10–15 minutes.

2 Place the rice vermicelli in a large bowl, cover with boiling water and leave to stand for 10 minutes. Drain well and then chop roughly.

3 Wipe the mushrooms, remove the stalks and slice the caps thinly, halving them if the mushrooms are large.

4 Using a sharp knife, cut the scallions into diagonal slices, including all but the tips of the green parts.

5 Drain the bamboo shoots and rinse them very well under cold running water. Cut in half if they are large.

6 Heat 1 tablespoon of the remaining oil in a wok or large frying pan and cook the garlic for a few seconds. Add the scallions and stir-fry for 2–3 minutes. Add the mushrooms and stir-fry for a further 3–4 minutes. Transfer the vegetables to a plate, using a slotted spoon.

7 Heat the remaining oil in the wok. Drain the tofu, reserving the marinade, and then stir-fry for 4–5 minutes.

8 Add the bamboo shoots to the tofu together with the carrot, vermicelli, the mushroom and onion mixture and the reserved marinade, and stir well. Add the bean sprouts, stir well and then remove from the heat and cool.

9 Place a level tablespoon of mixture at one corner of a spring roll sheet. Brush the edges of the pastry with the cornstarch mixture and roll up, folding the left and right corners inward as you roll. Continue making spring rolls in this way, until all the mixture is used up.

10 Heat the oil in a large wok or deep-fryer and fry two or three rolls at a time for 3–4 minutes until golden, turning them so that they cook evenly. Drain on paper towels and keep warm. Serve with extra soy sauce.

SAMPHIRE WITH CHILLED FISH CURRY

EVEN IF YOU'RE A BIG CURRY FAN, DON'T BE TEMPTED TO ADD TOO MUCH CURRY PASTE TO THIS DISH.
YOU NEED ONLY THE MEREST HINT OF MILD CURRY PASTE SO THAT THE FLAVOR OF THE SAMPHIRE AND
FISH CAN STILL BE APPRECIATED.

SERVES FOUR

INGREDIENTS

6 ounces samphire
12 ounces fresh salmon steak or fillet
12 ounces sole fillet
fish stock or water
4 ounces large peeled shrimp
1 ounce butter
1 small onion, very finely chopped
2 teaspoons mild curry paste
1–2 teaspoons apricot jam
⅔ cup sour cream
sprig of mint, to garnish (optional)

1 Trim the samphire and blanch in boiling water for about 5 minutes until tender. Drain and set aside.

2 Place the salmon and sole in a large frying pan, cover with fish stock or water and bring to the boil. Reduce the heat, cover and cook for 6–8 minutes until the fish is tender.

COOK'S TIP
As the samphire has a fresh salty tang of the sea, there is not really any need to add extra salt to this recipe.

3 Transfer the fish to a plate and when cool enough to handle, break the salmon and sole into bite-size pieces, removing any skin and bones. Place in a mixing bowl with the shrimp.

4 Melt the butter in a saucepan and gently fry the onion for 3–4 minutes until soft but not brown. Add the curry paste, cook for 30 seconds, then remove from the heat. Stir in the jam. Allow to cool and then stir in the sour cream.

5 Pour the curry cream over the fish. Arrange the samphire around the edge of a serving plate and spoon the fish into the center. Garnish with a sprig of mint.

FENNEL AND MUSSEL PROVENÇAL

SERVES FOUR

INGREDIENTS
2 large fennel bulbs
4–4½ pounds fresh mussels in their
    shells, well scrubbed under cold
    water and beards removed
¾ cup water
sprig of thyme
1 ounce butter
4 shallots, finely chopped
1 garlic clove, crushed
1 cup white wine
2 teaspoons all-purpose flour
¾ cup light cream
1 tablespoon chopped fresh parsley
salt and freshly ground black pepper
sprig of dill, to garnish

1 Trim the fennel and cut into slices
¼ inch thick and then cut into ½-inch
sticks. Cook in a little salted water until
just tender and drain.

2 Discard any mussels that are
damaged or do not close. Put in a large
saucepan, add the water and thyme,
cover tightly, bring to the boil and cook
for about 5 minutes until the mussels
open, shaking occasionally.

3 Transfer the mussels to a plate and
discard any that are unopened. When
cool enough to handle, remove them
from their shells, reserving a few in their
shells for a garnish.

4 Melt the butter in a saucepan and fry
the shallots and garlic for 3–4 minutes
until softened but not browned. Add the
fennel, fry briefly for 30–60 seconds and
then stir in the wine and simmer gently
until the liquid is reduced by half.

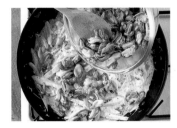

5 Blend the flour with a little extra wine
or water. Add the cream, parsley and
seasoning to the saucepan and heat
gently. Stir in the blended flour and the
mussels. Cook over low heat until the
sauce thickens. Season to taste and pour
into a warmed serving dish. Garnish with
dill and reserved mussels in their shells.

BRAISED FENNEL WITH TOMATOES

SERVES FOUR

INGREDIENTS
3 small fennel bulbs
2–3 tablespoons olive oil
5–6 shallots, sliced
2 garlic cloves, crushed
4 tomatoes, peeled and chopped
about ¾ cup dry white wine
1 tablespoon chopped fresh basil or
    ½ teaspoon dried
1½–2 ounces fresh white bread
    crumbs
salt and freshly ground black pepper

1 Preheat the oven to 300°F. Trim the
fennel bulbs and cut into slices about
½ inch thick.

2 Heat the olive oil in a large saucepan
and fry the shallots and garlic for about
4–5 minutes over moderate heat until
the shallots are slightly softened. Add the
tomatoes, stir-fry briefly and then stir in
⅔ cup of the wine, the basil and seasoning. Bring to a boil, add the fennel, then
cover and cook for 5 minutes.

3 Arrange the fennel in layers in an
ovenproof dish. Pour the tomato mixture
over and sprinkle the top with half the
bread crumbs. Bake in the oven for
about 1 hour. From time to time, press
down on the crumb crust with the back
of a spoon and sprinkle over another
layer of bread crumbs and a little more of
the wine. The crust slowly becomes gold-
en brown and very crunchy.

ROOT RECIPES

PATATAS BRAVAS

THIS IS A CLASSIC SPANISH TAPAS DISH OF DEEP-FRIED CUBES OF POTATO WITH A SPICY TOMATO SAUCE.

SERVES FOUR

INGREDIENTS
1½ pounds potatoes
oil, for deep frying
For the sauce
1 tablespoon olive oil
1 small onion, chopped
1 garlic clove, crushed
14 ounce can tomatoes
2 teaspoons Worcestershire
   sauce
1 teaspoon wine vinegar
about 1 teaspoon Tabasco sauce

1 Peel and cut the potatoes into small cubes and place in a large bowl of cold water to remove the excess starch.

2 Heat the oil in a medium-size frying pan and fry the onion and garlic for 3–4 minutes until the onion is soft and just beginning to brown.

3 Pour the tomatoes into a blender or food processor, process until smooth and then pour into the pan with the onion. Simmer, uncovered, over moderate heat for 8–10 minutes until the mixture is thick and reduced, stirring occasionally.

4 Heat the oil in a deep-fryer. Drain the potatoes and pat dry with paper towels. Fry the potatoes in the hot oil, in batches if necessary, until golden brown. Drain on paper towels.

5 Stir the Worcestershire sauce, vinegar and Tabasco sauce into the tomato mixture. Add the potatoes, stirring well so that all the potatoes are coated with the sauce. Spoon into individual serving dishes and serve at once.

POTATO DAUPHINOIS

SERVES FOUR

INGREDIENTS
1½ pounds potatoes, peeled and thinly
   sliced
1 garlic clove
1 ounce butter
1¼ cups light cream
¼ cup milk
salt and white pepper

1 Preheat the oven to 300°F. Place the potato slices in a bowl of cold water to remove the excess starch. Drain and pat dry with paper towels.

2 Cut the garlic in half and rub the cut side around the inside of a wide shallow ovenproof dish. Butter the dish generously. Blend the cream and milk in a jug.

3 Cover the bottom of the dish with a layer of potatoes. Dot a little butter over the potato layer, season with salt and pepper and then pour over a little of the cream and milk mixture.

4 Continue making layers, until all the ingredients have been used up, ending with a layer of cream.

5 Bake in the oven for about 1¼ hours. If the dish browns too quickly and seems to be drying out, cover with a lid or with a piece of foil. The potatoes are ready when they are very soft and the top is pale golden brown.

COOK'S TIP
For a slightly speedier version of this recipe, parboil the potato slices for 3–4 minutes. Drain well and assemble as above. Cook at 325°F for 45–50 minutes until potatoes are completely tender.

HASSELBACK POTATOES

A VERY UNUSUAL WAY WITH POTATOES. EACH POTATO HALF IS SLICED ALMOST TO THE BASE AND THEN ROASTED WITH OIL AND BUTTER. THE CRISPY POTATOES ARE THEN COATED IN AN ORANGE GLAZE AND RETURNED TO THE OVEN UNTIL DEEP GOLDEN BROWN AND CRUNCHY.

<u>SERVES FOUR TO SIX</u>

INGREDIENTS
   4 large potatoes
   1 ounce butter, melted
   3 tablespoons olive oil
   freshly ground black pepper
For the glaze
   juice of 1 orange
   grated rind of ½ orange
   1 tablespoon brown sugar

1 Preheat the oven to 375°F. Cut each potato in half lengthwise, place flat-side down and then cut down as if making very thin slices, but leaving the bottom ½ inch intact.

2 Place the potatoes in a large roasting dish. Using a pastry brush coat the potatoes generously with the melted butter and pour the olive oil over the bottom and around the potatoes.

3 Bake the potatoes in the oven for 40–50 minutes until they begin to brown. Baste occasionally during cooking.

4 Meanwhile, place the orange juice, orange rind and sugar in a small saucepan and heat gently, stirring until the sugar has dissolved. Simmer for 3–4 minutes until the glaze is fairly thick and then remove from the heat.

5 When the potatoes begin to brown, brush all over with the orange glaze and return to the oven to roast for a further 15 minutes or until the potatoes are a deep golden brown. Serve at once.

PUFFY CREAMED POTATOES

THIS ACCOMPANIMENT CONSISTS OF CREAMED POTATOES INCORPORATED INTO MINI YORKSHIRE PUDDINGS. SERVE THEM WITH ROAST DUCK OR BEEF, OR WITH A VEGETARIAN CASSEROLE. FOR A MEAL ON ITS OWN, SERVE TWO OR THREE PER PERSON AND ACCOMPANY WITH SALADS.

MAKES SIX

INGREDIENTS
    10 ounces potatoes
    whole milk and butter for mashing
    1 teaspoon chopped fresh parsley
    1 teaspoon chopped fresh tarragon
    3 ounces all-purpose flour
    1 egg
    about ½ cup milk
    oil or sunflower fat, for baking
    salt and freshly ground black pepper

1 Boil the potatoes until tender and mash with a little milk and butter. Stir in the chopped parsley and tarragon and season well to taste. Preheat the oven to 400°F.

2 Process the flour, egg, milk and a little salt in a food processor or blender to make a smooth batter.

3 Place about ½ teaspoon oil or a small pat of sunflower fat in each of six ramekin dishes and place in the oven on a baking sheet for 2–3 minutes until the oil or fat is very hot.

4 Working quickly, pour a small amount of batter (about 4 teaspoons) into each ramekin dish. Add a heaped tablespoon of mashed potatoes and then pour an equal amount of the remaining batter in each dish. Place in the oven and bake for 15–20 minutes until the puddings are puffy and golden brown.

5 Using a metal spatula, carefully ease the puddings out of the ramekin dishes and arrange on a large warm serving dish. Serve at once.

PARSNIP <u>AND</u> CHESTNUT CROQUETTES

THE SWEET NUTTY TASTE OF CHESTNUTS BLENDS PERFECTLY WITH THE SIMILARLY SWEET BUT EARTHY FLAVOR OF PARSNIPS. FRESH CHESTNUTS NEED TO BE PEELED BUT FROZEN CHESTNUTS ARE EASY TO USE AND ARE NEARLY AS GOOD AS FRESH FOR THIS RECIPE.

MAKES TEN TO TWELVE

INGREDIENTS

1 pound parsnips, cut roughly into
   small pieces
4 ounces frozen chestnuts
1 ounce butter
1 garlic clove, crushed
1 tablespoon chopped fresh cilantro
1 egg, beaten
1½–2 ounces fresh white bread
   crumbs
vegetable oil, for frying
salt and freshly ground black pepper
sprig of cilantro, to garnish

1 Place the parsnips in a saucepan with enough water to cover. Bring to a boil, cover and simmer for 15–20 minutes until completely tender.

2 Place the frozen chestnuts in a pan of water, bring to a boil and simmer for 8–10 minutes until very tender. Drain, place in a bowl and mash roughly.

3 Melt the butter in a small saucepan and cook the garlic for 30 seconds. Drain the parsnips and mash with the garlic butter. Stir in the chestnuts, chopped cilantro and season well.

4 Take about 1 tablespoon of mixture at a time and form into small croquettes, about 3 inches long. Dip each croquette into the beaten egg and then roll in the bread crumbs.

5 Heat a little oil in a frying pan and fry the croquettes for 3–4 minutes until golden, turning frequently so they brown evenly. Drain on paper towels and then serve at once, garnished with cilantro.

PARSNIP, EGGPLANT AND CASHEW BIRYANI

SERVES FOUR TO SIX

INGREDIENTS
    1 small eggplant, sliced
    10 ounces basmati rice
    3 parsnips
    3 onions
    2 garlic cloves
    1-inch piece fresh ginger, peeled
    about 4 tablespoons vegetable oil
    6 ounces unsalted cashew nuts
    1½ ounces golden raisins
    1 red bell pepper, seeded and sliced
    1 teaspoon ground cumin
    1 teaspoon ground coriander
    ½ teaspoon chili powder
    ½ cup plain yogurt
    1¼ cups vegetable or chicken stock
    1 ounce butter
    salt and freshly ground black pepper
    sprigs of cilantro, to garnish
    2 hard-boiled eggs, quartered

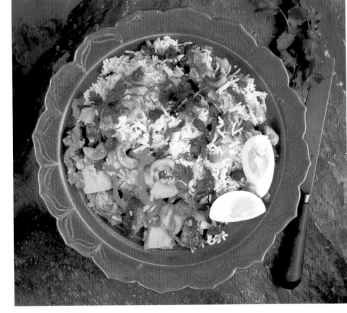

1 Sprinkle the eggplant with salt and leave for 30 minutes. Rinse, pat dry and cut into bite-size pieces. Soak the rice in a bowl of cold water for 40 minutes. Peel and core the parsnips. Cut into ½-inch pieces. Roughly chop 1 onion and put in a food processor or blender with the garlic and ginger. Add 2–3 tablespoons water and process to a paste.

2 Finely slice the remaining onions. Heat 3 tablespoons of the oil in a large flameproof casserole and fry gently for 10–15 minutes until deep golden brown. Remove and drain. Add 1½ ounces of the cashew nuts to the pan, stir-fry for 2 minutes. Add the golden raisins and fry until they swell. Remove and drain.

3 Add the eggplant and pepper to the pan and stir-fry for 4–5 minutes. Drain on paper towels. Fry the parsnips for 4–5 minutes. Stir in the remaining cashew nuts and fry for 1 minute. Transfer to the plate with the eggplants.

4 Add the remaining 1 tablespoon of oil to the pan. Add the onion paste. Cook, stirring over moderate heat for 4–5 minutes until the mixture turns golden. Stir in the cumin, cilantro and chili powder. Cook, stirring, for 1 minute, then reduce the heat and add the yogurt.

5 Bring the mixture slowly to a boil and stir in the stock, parsnips, eggplant and peppers. Season, cover and simmer for 30–40 minutes until the parsnips are tender and then transfer to an ovenproof casserole.

6 Preheat the oven to 300°F. Drain the rice and add to 1¼ cups of salted boiling water. Cook gently for 5–6 minutes until it is tender but slightly undercooked.

7 Drain the rice and pile it in a mound on top of the parsnips. Make a hole from the top to the base using the handle of a wooden spoon. Scatter the reserved fried onions, cashew nuts and golden raisins over the rice and dot with butter. Cover with a double layer of foil and then secure in place with a lid.

8 Cook in the oven for 35–40 minutes. To serve, spoon the mixture onto a warmed serving dish and garnish with cilantro sprigs and quartered eggs.

MEDITERRANEAN CHICKEN <u>WITH</u> TURNIPS

TURNIPS ARE POPULAR IN ALL PARTS OF THE MEDITERREAN, COOKED WITH TOMATOES AND SPINACH IN SIMPLE VEGETARIAN DISHES, OR TEAMED WITH FISH OR POULTRY FOR A MORE SUBSTANTIAL MEAL. THIS RECIPE COMES FROM THE EASTERN MEDITERRANEAN.

SERVES FOUR

INGREDIENTS
2 tablespoons sunflower oil
8 chicken thighs or 4 chicken pieces
4 small turnips
2 onions, chopped
2 garlic cloves, crushed
6 tomatoes, peeled and chopped
1 cup tomato juice
1 cup chicken stock
½ cup white wine
1 teaspoon paprika
good pinch of cayenne pepper
20 black olives, pitted
½ lemon, cut into wedges
salt and freshly ground black pepper
fresh parsley, to garnish
couscous, to serve

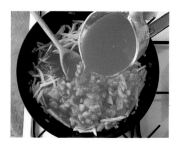

1 Preheat the oven to 325°F. Heat 1 tablespoon of the oil in a large frying pan and fry the chicken pieces until lightly browned. Peel the turnips and cut into julienne strips.

2 Transfer the chicken to a large casserole. Add the remaining oil to the pan and fry the onions and garlic for 4–5 minutes until lightly golden brown, stirring occasionally.

3 Add the turnip and stir-fry for about 2–3 minutes. Add the tomatoes, tomato juice, stock, wine, paprika, cayenne and seasoning. Bring to a boil. Pour over the chicken. Stir in the olives and lemon.

4 Cover tightly and cook in the oven for 1–1¼ hours until the chicken is tender.

5 Garnish with fresh parsley and serve on a bed of couscous.

RUTABAGA CRISPS

TENDER SLICES OF RUTABAGA WITH A CRUNCHY BREADCRUMB COATING PROVIDE A FEAST FOR THE SENSES. THE SLIGHTLY PEPPERY FLAVOR OF RUTABAGA IS COMPLEMENTED BY THE SPICY BREADCRUMB MIXTURE.

SERVES FOUR

INGREDIENTS
1 small rutabaga
2 ounces fresh brown or white
   bread crumbs
1 tablespoon all-purpose flour
½ teaspoon paprika
½ teaspoon ground coriander
½ teaspoon ground cumin
pinch of cayenne pepper
1 egg, beaten
salt and freshly ground black pepper
oil, for deep frying
mango chutney, to serve

1 Peel the rutabaga, cut in half and slice thinly. Cook in boiling water for 3–5 minutes until just tender. Drain well.

2 Mix together the bread crumbs, flour, paprika, coriander, cumin, cayenne pepper and seasoning. Dip the rutabaga slices first in the egg and then in the breadcrumb mixture.

3 Heat the oil in a deep fryer or wok and fry the rutabaga discs, in batches if necessary, for 4–5 minutes until golden on the outside and soft inside. Drain on paper towels and serve with mango chutney.

COOK'S TIP
Fry the discs until the rutabaga is tender, so that the crunchiness of the breadcrumb coating contrasts with the soft vegetable.

GLAZED CARROTS WITH CIDER

THIS RECIPE IS EXTREMELY SIMPLE TO MAKE. THE CARROTS ARE COOKED IN THE MINIMUM OF LIQUID TO BRING OUT THE BEST OF THEIR FLAVOR, AND THE CIDER ADDS A PLEASANT SHARPNESS.

SERVES FOUR

INGREDIENTS
1 pound young carrots
1 ounce butter
1 tablespoon brown sugar
½ cup cider
4 tablespoons vegetable stock or water
1 teaspoon French mustard
1 tablespoon finely chopped fresh
   parsley

1 Trim the tops and bottoms off the carrots. Peel or scrape them. Using a sharp knife cut the carrots into julienne.

2 Melt the butter in a saucepan, add the carrots and sauté for 4–5 minutes, stirring frequently. Sprinkle over the sugar and cook, stirring for 1 minute or until the sugar has dissolved.

3 Add the cider and stock or water, bring to a boil and stir in the French mustard. Partially cover the pan and simmer for about 10–12 minutes until the carrots are just tender. Remove the lid and continue cooking until the liquid has reduced to a thick sauce.

4 Remove the saucepan from the heat, stir in the parsley and then spoon into a warmed serving dish. Serve as an accompaniment to broiled meat or fish or with a vegetarian dish.

COOK'S TIP
If the carrots are cooked before the liquid in the saucepan has reduced, transfer the carrots to a serving dish and rapidly boil the liquid until thick. Pour over the carrots and sprinkle with parsley.

CARROT, APPLE AND ORANGE COLESLAW

THIS DISH IS AS DELICIOUS AS IT IS EASY TO MAKE. THE GARLIC AND HERB DRESSING ADDS THE NECESSARY CONTRAST TO THE SWEETNESS OF THE SALAD.

SERVES FOUR

INGREDIENTS
12 ounces young carrots,
   finely grated
2 eating apples
1 tablespoon lemon juice
1 large orange
For the dressing
3 tablespoons olive oil
4 tablespoons sunflower oil
3 tablespoons lemon juice
1 garlic clove, crushed
4 tablespoons plain yogurt
1 tablespoon chopped mixed fresh
   herbs: tarragon, parsley, chives
salt and freshly ground black pepper

1 Place the carrots in a large serving bowl. Quarter the apples, remove the core and then slice thinly. Sprinkle with the lemon juice to prevent them discoloring and then add to the carrots.

2 Using a sharp knife, remove the peel and pith from the oranges and then separate into segments.

3 To make the dressing, place all the ingredients in a jar with a tight-fitting lid and shake vigorously to blend.

4 Just before serving, pour the dressing over the salad and toss well together.

CARROT AND CILANTRO SOUP

NEARLY ALL ROOT VEGETABLES MAKE EXCELLENT SOUPS AS THEY PURÉE WELL AND HAVE AN EARTHY FLAVOR WHICH COMPLEMENTS THE SHARPER FLAVORS OF HERBS AND SPICES. CARROTS ARE PARTICULARLY VERSATILE AND THIS SIMPLE SOUP IS ELEGANT IN BOTH FLAVOR AND APPEARANCE.

SERVES FOUR TO SIX

INGREDIENTS

  1 pound carrots, preferably young and
    tender
  1 tablespoon sunflower oil
  1½ ounces butter
  1 onion, chopped
  1 celery stalk, sliced plus 2–3 pale
    leafy celery tops
  2 small potatoes, chopped
  4 cups chicken stock
  2–3 teaspoons ground coriander
  1 tablespoon chopped fresh cilantro
  ⅞ cup milk
  salt and freshly ground black pepper

1 Trim the carrots, peel if necessary and cut into chunks. Heat the oil and 1 ounce of the butter in a large flame-proof casserole or heavy-based saucepan and fry the onion over a gentle heat for 3–4 minutes until slightly softened but not browned.

2 Cut the celery stalk into slices. Add the celery and potato to the onion in the pan, cook for a few minutes and then add the carrots. Fry over low heat for 3–4 minutes, stirring frequently, and then cover. Reduce the heat even further and sweat for about 10 minutes. Shake the pan or stir occasionally so the vegetables do not stick to the bottom.

3 Add the stock, bring to a boil and then partially cover and simmer for a further 8–10 minutes until the carrots and pota-to are tender.

4 Remove 6–8 tiny celery leaves for a garnish and finely chop the remaining celery tops (about 1 tablespoon once chopped). Melt the remaining butter in a small saucepan and fry the ground coriander for about 1 minute, stirring constantly.

5 Reduce the heat and add the chopped celery and fresh cilantro and fry for about 1 minute. Set aside.

6 Process the soup in a food processor or blender and pour into a clean saucepan. Stir in the milk, coriander/cilantro mixture and seasoning. Heat gently, taste and adjust the seasoning. Serve garnished with the reserved celery.

COOK'S TIP
For a more piquant flavor, add a little lemon juice just before serving.

BORSCHT

THIS CLASSIC SOUP WAS THE STAPLE DIET OF PRE-REVOLUTION RUSSIAN PEASANTS FOR HUNDREDS OF YEARS. THERE ARE MANY VARIATIONS AND IT IS RARE TO FIND TWO RECIPES THE SAME.

SERVES SIX

INGREDIENTS

  12 ounces whole, uncooked beetroot
  1 tablespoon sunflower oil
  4 ounces lean bacon, chopped
  1 large onion
  1 large carrot, cut into julienne strips
  3 celery stalks, thinly sliced
  6¼ cups chicken stock
  about 8 ounces tomatoes, peeled,
    seeded and sliced
  about 2 tablespoons lemon juice
    or wine vinegar
  2 tablespoons chopped dill
  4 ounces white cabbage, thinly sliced
  ⅔ cup sour cream
  salt and freshly ground black pepper

1 Peel the beets, slice and then cut into very thin strips.

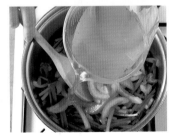

2 Heat the oil in a large, heavy-based saucepan and fry the bacon over low heat for 3–4 minutes. Add the onion, fry for 2–3 minutes and then add the carrot, celery and beets. Cook gently for 4–5 minutes, stirring frequently, until the oil has been absorbed.

3 Add the stock, tomatoes, lemon juice or vinegar, half of the dill and seasoning. Bring to the boil and simmer for about 30–40 minutes until the vegetables are completely tender.

4 Add the cabbage and simmer for 5 minutes until tender. Adjust the seasoning and serve sprinkled with remaining dill and the sour cream.

ARTICHOKE RÖSTI

SERVES FOUR TO SIX

INGREDIENTS
 1 pound Jerusalem artichokes
 juice of 1 lemon
 1 pound potatoes
 about 2 ounces butter
 salt

1 Peel the Jerusalem artichokes and place in a saucepan of water together with the lemon juice and a pinch of salt. Bring to a boil and cook for about 5 minutes until barely tender.

2 Peel the potatoes and place in a separate pan of salted water. Bring to a boil and cook until barely tender – they will take slightly longer than the artichokes.

3 Drain and cool both the artichokes and potatoes, and then grate them into a bowl. Mix them with your fingers, without breaking them up too much.

4 Melt the butter in a large heavy-based frying pan. Add the artichoke mixture, spreading it out with the back of a spoon. Cook gently for about 10 minutes.

5 Invert the "cake" onto a plate and slide back into the pan. Cook for about 10 minutes until golden. Serve at once.

ARTICHOKE TIMBALES WITH SPINACH SAUCE

SERVES SIX

INGREDIENTS
 2 pounds Jerusalem artichokes
 juice of 1 lemon
 1 ounce butter
 1 tablespoon oil
 1 onion, finely chopped
 1 garlic clove, crushed
 2 ounces fresh white bread crumbs
 1 egg
 4–5 tablespoons vegetable stock
  or milk
 1 tablespoon chopped fresh parsley
 1 teaspoon finely chopped sage
 salt and freshly ground black pepper
For the sauce
 8 ounces fresh spinach, prepared
 ½ ounce butter
 2 shallots, finely chopped
 ⅔ cup light cream
 ¾ cup vegetable stock
 salt and freshly ground black pepper

1 Preheat the oven to 350°F. Grease six ⅔-cup ramekin dishes, and then place a circle of wax paper in the bottom of each.

2 Peel the artichokes and put in a saucepan with the lemon juice and water to cover. Bring to a boil and simmer for about 10 minutes until tender. Drain and mash with the butter.

3 Heat the oil in a small frying pan and fry the onion and garlic until soft. Place in a food processor or blender with the bread crumbs, egg, stock, parsley, sage and seasoning. Process to a smooth purée, add the artichokes and process again briefly using the pulse button.

4 Put the mixture in the prepared dishes. Smooth the tops. Cover with wax paper, place in a roasting pan half-filled with boiling water and bake for 35–40 minutes.

5 To make the sauce, cook the spinach without water, in a large covered saucepan, for 2–3 minutes. Shake the pan occasionally. Strain and press out the excess liquid.

6 Melt the butter in a small saucepan and fry the shallots gently until slightly softened but not browned. Place in a food processor or blender and process to make a smooth purée. Pour back into the pan, add the cream and seasoning, and keep warm over very low heat. Do not allow the mixture to boil.

7 Allow the timbales to stand for a few minutes after cooking and then turn out onto warmed serving plates. Spoon the warm sauce over them and serve.

COOK'S TIP
When puréeing the artichokes in a food processor or blender, use the pulse button and process for a very short time. The mixture will become cloying if it is over-processed.

YAM FRITTERS

YAMS HAVE A SLIGHTLY DRIER FLAVOR THAN POTATOES AND ARE PARTICULARLY GOOD WHEN MIXED WITH SPICES AND THEN FRIED. THE FRITTERS CAN ALSO BE MOLDED INTO SMALL BALLS AND DEEP-FRIED. THIS IS A FAVORITE AFRICAN WAY OF SERVING YAMS.

MAKES ABOUT 18–20

INGREDIENTS
1½ pounds yams
milk, for mashing
2 small eggs, beaten
3 tablespoons chopped tomato flesh
3 tablespoons finely chopped
   scallions
1 green chili, seeded and finely sliced
flour, for shaping
1½ ounces white bread crumbs
vegetable oil, for shallow frying
salt and freshly ground black pepper

1 Peel the yams and cut into chunks. Place in a saucepan of salted water and boil for 20–30 minutes until tender. Drain and mash with a little milk and about 3 tablespoons of the beaten eggs.

2 Add the chopped tomato, scallions, chili and seasoning and stir well.

3 Using floured hands shape the yam and vegetable mixture into round fritters, about 3 inches in diameter.

4 Dip each in the remaining beaten egg and then coat evenly with the bread crumbs. Heat a little oil in a large frying pan and fry the yam fritters for about 4–5 minutes until golden brown. Turn the fritters over once during cooking. Drain well on paper towels and serve.

EDDO, CARROT AND PARSNIP MEDLEY

EDDO (TARO), LIKE YAMS, IS WIDELY EATEN IN AFRICA AND THE CARIBBEAN, OFTEN AS A PURÉE. HERE, IT IS ROASTED AND COMBINED WITH MORE COMMON ROOT VEGETABLES TO MAKE A COLORFUL DISPLAY.

SERVES FOUR TO SIX

INGREDIENTS
1 pound eddoes or taros
12 ounces parsnips
1 pound carrots
1 ounce butter
3 tablespoons sunflower oil
For the dressing
2 tablespoons fresh orange juice
2 tablespoons brown sugar
2 teaspoons soft green peppercorns
salt
fresh parsley, to garnish

1 Preheat the oven to 400°F. Peel the eddoes and cut into pieces about 2 x ¾ inches, and place in a large bowl.

2 Peel the parsnips, halve lengthwise and remove the inner core if necessary. Cut into the same size pieces as the eddo and add to the bowl. Blanch in boiling water for 2 minutes and then drain. Peel or scrub the carrots, and halve or quarter them according to their size.

3 Place the butter and sunflower oil in a roasting pan and heat in the oven for 3–4 minutes. Add the vegetables, turning them in the oil to coat evenly. Roast in the oven for 30 minutes.

4 Meanwhile, blend the orange juice, sugar and soft green peppercorns in a small bowl. Remove the roasting pan from the oven and allow to cool for a minute or so and then carefully pour the mixture over the vegetables, stirring to coat them all. (If the liquid is poured on immediately, the hot oil will spit.)

5 Return the tin to the oven and cook for a further 20 minutes until the vegetables are crisp and golden. Transfer to a warmed serving plate and sprinkle with salt. Garnish with parsley to serve.

SWEET POTATO CHIPS WITH ROCK CORNISH HENS

SERVES FOUR

INGREDIENTS
   4 Rock Cornish Hens, about
      10–12 ounces each
   ¾–1 cup chicken stock
   ¾ cup white wine
   2 tablespoons lemon juice
   1 tablespoon chopped fresh tarragon
      or 2 teaspoons dried
   1 ounce butter
   2 teaspoons all-purpose flour
   salt and freshly ground black pepper
For the stuffing
   1 sweet potato, about 8 ounces
   1 tablespoon lemon juice
   1 ounce butter or margarine
   2 shallots, finely chopped
   1 ounce slivered almonds
   2 ounces ready-to-eat apricots,
      chopped
   1 ounce fresh brown or white
      bread crumbs
   1 teaspoon chopped fresh thyme
   salt and freshly ground black pepper
For the sweet potato chips
   1 pound sweet potatoes
   juice of ½ lemon
   flour, for coating
   good pinch of cayenne pepper
   good pinch of ground coriander
   good pinch of ground cumin
   oil, for deep frying
   salt

1 Preheat the oven to 350°F and prepare the stuffing. Peel the sweet potato
and cook in boiling water with the lemon
juice until tender. Drain and mash with
half of the butter.

2 Melt the remaining butter in a small
frying pan and fry the shallots for 2–3
minutes until softened. Add the almonds
and continue frying until both the
almonds and shallots are flecked with
brown. Stir into the mashed potato
together with the apricots, bread
crumbs, thyme and seasoning to taste.

3 Loosely stuff the hens with the mixture and place them in a roasting pan.
Mix together the stock, white wine and
lemon juice in a small saucepan and
bring to a boil. Pour over the hens.

4 Sprinkle each with tarragon and
seasoning and use half the butter to dot
evenly over each bird.

5 Cover loosely with foil and roast in the
oven for 35–45 minutes, basting often
with the juices.

6 To prepare the sweet potato chips,
peel and thinly slice the potatoes and
place in a bowl of water with the lemon
juice. Mix the flour, cayenne pepper,
ground coriander, ground cumin and salt
on a plate.

7 Ten minutes before the hens are
ready, heat the oil in a deep-fryer or wok.
Dry the potato slices with paper towels
and dip into the seasoned flour. Fry the
slices, in batches, for 2–3 minutes until
golden. Drain well on paper towels and
keep warm.

8 When the hens are cooked and the
juices run clear, increase the oven temperature to 425°F. Cook uncovered for 5
minutes or until well browned. Transfer
to a serving plate and arrange the sweet
potato chips around the edge.

9 Pour the cooking juices into a
saucepan and heat gently. Mix the
remaining butter and flour to a paste and
add small pieces to the stock, whisking
well between each addition. Pour the
sauce into a jug and serve with the Rock
Cornish hens and potato chips.

CASSAVA AND VEGETABLE KEBABS

THIS IS AN ATTRACTIVE AND DELICIOUS ASSORTMENT OF AFRICAN VEGETABLES, MARINATED IN A SPICY GARLIC SAUCE. IF CASSAVA IS UNAVAILABLE, USE SWEET POTATO OR YAM INSTEAD.

SERVES FOUR

INGREDIENTS

    6 ounces cassava
    1 onion, cut into wedges
    1 eggplant, cut into bite-size pieces
    1 zucchini, sliced
    1 ripe plantain, sliced
    1 red pepper or ½ red bell pepper,
      ½ green bell pepper, sliced
    16 cherry tomatoes
For the marinade
    4 tablespoons lemon juice
    4 tablespoons olive oil
    3–4 tablespoons soy sauce
    1 tablespoon tomato paste
    1 green chili, seeded and finely
      chopped
    ½ onion, grated
    2 garlic cloves, crushed
    1 teaspoon mixed spice
    pinch dried thyme
    rice or couscous, to serve

1 Peel the cassava and cut into bite-size pieces. Place in a bowl, cover with boiling water and leave to blanch for 5 minutes. Drain well.

2 Place all the vegetables, including the cassava, in a large bowl.

3 Blend together all the marinade ingredients and pour over the prepared vegetables. Set aside for 1–2 hours.

4 Preheat the broiler and thread all the vegetables and cherry tomatoes onto eight skewers.

5 Broil the vegetables under low heat for about 15 minutes until tender and browned, turning frequently and basting occasionally with the marinade.

6 Meanwhile, pour the remaining marinade into a small saucepan and simmer for 10 minutes until slightly reduced.

7 Arrange the vegetable kebabs on a serving plate and strain the sauce into a small jug. Serve with rice or couscous.

PAN-FRIED SWEET POTATOES WITH BACON

THIS IS A COMFORTING DISH TO EAT ON A COLD WINTER'S EVENING. BACON AND ONION COUNTERACT THE SWEETNESS OF THE POTATO, AND THE CAYENNE PEPPER GIVES THE NECESSARY EXTRA "BITE."

SERVES FOUR

INGREDIENTS
1½–2 pounds sweet potatoes
juice of 1 lemon
1 tablespoon all-purpose flour
a good pinch of cayenne pepper
about 3 tablespoons sunflower oil
1 large onion, chopped
4 ounces lean bacon, chopped
2 ounces fresh brown or white bread
   crumbs
salt

1 Peel the sweet potatoes and cut into chunks about 1½ inches square. Place in a pan of boiling water with the lemon juice and a little salt and simmer for 8–10 minutes until cooked but not soft.

2 Mix together the flour, cayenne pepper and a pinch of salt. Drain the potatoes and then dust with the seasoned flour, coating the pieces well.

3 Heat 1 tablespoon of the oil in a large frying pan and fry the onion for about 2 minutes. Add the bacon and fry over low heat for 6–8 minutes until the onion and bacon are golden. Transfer to a plate using a slotted spoon.

4 Add the bread crumbs and fry, stirring, for about 1–2 minutes until golden. Add to the plate with the bacon.

5 Heat the remaining oil in the pan and fry the potatoes for 5–6 minutes, turning occasionally, until evenly browned. Stir in the breadcrumb and bacon mixture and cook for 1 minute. Serve at once.

SALSIFY GRATIN

THE SPINACH IN THIS RECIPE ADDS COLOR AND MAKES IT GO FURTHER. HOWEVER, IF YOU CAN OBTAIN SALSIFY EASILY AND HAVE THE PATIENCE TO PEEL A LOT OF IT, INCREASE THE QUANTITY AND LEAVE OUT THE SPINACH. FOR VEGETARIANS USE VEGETABLE INSTEAD OF CHICKEN STOCK.

SERVES FOUR

INGREDIENTS

1 pound salsify, cut into
  2-inch lengths
juice of 1½ lemons
1 pound spinach, prepared
⅔ cup chicken stock
1¼ cups light cream
salt and freshly ground black pepper

3 Cook the spinach in a large saucepan over moderate heat for 2–3 minutes until the leaves have wilted, shaking the pan occasionally. Place the stock, cream and seasoning in a small saucepan and heat through very gently, stirring.

4 Arrange the salsify and spinach in layers in the prepared dish. Pour over the stock and cream mixture and bake in the oven for about 1 hour until the top is golden brown and bubbling.

1 Trim away the tops and bottoms of the salsify and peel or scrape away the outer skin. Place each peeled root immediately in water with lemon juice added, to prevent discoloration.

2 Preheat the oven to 325°F and butter an ovenproof dish. Place the salsify in a saucepan of boiling water with the lemon juice. Simmer for about 10 minutes until the salsify is just tender, and then drain.

GREENS RECIPES

BROCCOLI AND CHICKEN LASAGNE

SERVES SIX

INGREDIENTS

    1 pound broccoli, broken into florets
    1 pound chicken breasts, skinned and
      boned
    1 tablespoon sunflower oil
    1 ounce butter
    1 onion, finely chopped
    1 garlic clove, chopped
    2½ cups passata or creamed strained
      tomatoes
    ½ teaspoon thyme
    ½ teaspoon oregano
    about 12 sheets precooked lasagne
    10 ounces fromage frais
    3 ounces Parmesan cheese, grated
    8 ounces mozzarella cheese,
      thinly sliced
    salt and freshly ground black pepper

1 Preheat the oven to 350°F and butter a large shallow ovenproof dish. Steam or boil the broccoli until nearly tender. Strain and set aside.

2 Cut the chicken into thin strips. Heat the oil and butter in a frying pan and fry the chicken for a few minutes until lightly browned. Transfer to a plate using a slotted spoon and set aside.

3 Add the onion and garlic to the pan and fry for 3–4 minutes until the onion has softened and is lightly golden brown. Stir in the passata or creamed tomatoes, thyme, oregano and seasoning, and cook for about 3–4 minutes over moderate heat until the sauce is slightly thickened, stirring regularly.

4 Spoon half the tomato sauce into the prepared dish. Add a layer of lasagne and then half the chicken and half the broccoli. Dot with half the fromage frais and sprinkle with half the Parmesan cheese. Put another layer of lasagne on top and spoon over the remaining tomato sauce, chicken, broccoli and fromage frais. End with a layer of lasagne.

5 Arrange the mozzarella cheese slices on top and sprinkle with the remaining Parmesan cheese. Bake in the oven for 30–35 minutes until the top is golden.

BROCCOLI CRUMBLE

SERVES FOUR

INGREDIENTS

    1 ounce butter or margarine
    2 leeks, thinly sliced
    1 ounce all-purpose flour
    ⅔ cup milk
    ½ cup water
    8 ounces broccoli, broken into florets
    1 ounce Parmesan cheese
    salt and freshly ground black pepper
For the topping
    4 ounces all-purpose flour
    1 teaspoon dried basil
    3 ounces butter or margarine
    2 ounces fresh brown or white
      bread crumbs
    pinch of salt

1 Preheat the oven to 375°F. Melt the butter in a flameproof casserole or saucepan and fry the leeks for 2–3 minutes until softened. Stir in the flour and then gradually add the milk and water. Bring to a boil, add the broccoli, season and simmer, half-covered, over low heat for 5 minutes.

2 Stir in the Parmesan cheese, season with salt and pepper and pour into a medium ovenproof dish.

3 To make the topping, mix the flour with the basil and salt. Rub in the butter or margarine and then stir in the bread crumbs. Sprinkle over the broccoli and then bake in the oven for 20–25 minutes until the topping is golden.

SPINACH AND CANNELLINI BEANS

THIS HEARTY DISH CAN BE MADE WITH ALMOST ANY DRIED BEAN OR PEA, SUCH AS BLACK-EYED PEAS, HARICOTS OR CHICK-PEAS. IT IS A GOOD DISH TO SERVE ON A COLD EVENING.

SERVES FOUR

INGREDIENTS
8 ounces cannellini beans,
   soaked overnight
3 tablespoons olive oil
1 slice white bread
1 onion, chopped
3–4 tomatoes, peeled and chopped
a good pinch of paprika
1 pound spinach
1 garlic clove, halved
salt and freshly ground black pepper

5 Add the onion and tomato mixture to the spinach, mix well and stir in the cannellini beans. Place the garlic and fried bread in a food processor and process until smooth. Stir into the spinach and bean mixture. Add ⅔ cup cold water and then cover and simmer gently for 20–30 minutes, adding more water if necessary.

1 Drain the beans, place in a saucepan and cover with water. Bring to a boil and boil rapidly for 10 minutes. Cover and simmer for about 1 hour until the beans are tender. Drain.

2 Heat 2 tablespoons of the oil in a frying pan and fry the bread until golden brown. Transfer to a plate.

3 Fry the onion in the remaining oil over low heat until soft but not brown, then add the tomatoes and continue cooking over low heat.

4 Heat the remaining oil in a large pan, stir in the paprika and then add the spinach. Cover and cook for a few minutes until the spinach has wilted.

SPINACH IN FILO WITH THREE CHEESES

A GOOD CHOICE TO SERVE WHEN VEGETARIANS AND MEAT EATERS ARE GATHERED FOR A MEAL, AS WHATEVER THEIR PREFERENCE, EVERYONE SEEMS PARTIAL TO THIS TASTY DISH.

SERVES FOUR

INGREDIENTS
    1 pound spinach
    1 tablespoon sunflower oil
    ½ ounce butter
    1 small onion, finely chopped
    6 ounces ricotta cheese
    4 ounces feta cheese, cut into
        small cubes
    3 ounces Gruyère or Emmenthal
        cheese, grated
    1 tablespoon fresh chopped chervil
    1 teaspoon fresh chopped marjoram
    salt and freshly ground black pepper
    5 large or 10 small sheets filo pastry
    1½–2 ounces butter, melted

1 Preheat the oven to 375°F. Cook the spinach in a large saucepan over moderate heat for 3–4 minutes until the leaves have wilted, shaking the saucepan occasionally. Strain and press out the excess liquid.

2 Heat the oil and butter in a saucepan and fry the onion for 3–4 minutes until softened. Remove from the heat and add half of the spinach. Combine using a metal spoon, breaking up the spinach.

3 Add the ricotta cheese and stir until evenly combined. Stir in the remaining spinach, again chopping it into the mixture with a metal spoon. Fold in the feta and Gruyère or Emmenthal cheeses, chervil, marjoram and seasoning.

4 Lay a sheet of filo pastry measuring about 12 inches square on a work surface. (If you have small filo sheets, lay them side by side, overlapping by about 1 inch in the middle.) Brush with melted butter and cover with a second sheet; brush this with butter and build up five layers of pastry in this way.

5 Spread the filling over the pastry, leaving a 1-inch border. Fold the two shorter sides inward and then roll up.

6 Place the roll, seam side down, on a greased baking sheet and brush with the remaining butter. Bake in the oven for about 30 minutes until golden brown.

SPINACH RAVIOLI

HOME-MADE RAVIOLI IS TIME-CONSUMING, YET IT IS WORTH THE EFFORT AS EVEN THE BEST SHOP-BOUGHT PASTA NEVER TASTES QUITE AS FRESH. TO COMPLEMENT THIS EFFORT, MAKE THE FILLING EXACTLY TO YOUR LIKING, TASTING IT FOR THE RIGHT BALANCE OF SPINACH AND CHEESE.

SERVES FOUR

INGREDIENTS
8 ounces fresh spinach
1½ ounces butter
1 small onion, finely chopped
1 ounce Parmesan cheese, grated
1½ ounces Dolcellate cheese,
    crumbled
1 tablespoon chopped fresh parsley
salt and freshly ground black pepper
For the pasta dough
    12 ounces unbleached all-purpose
        flour
    ¾ teaspoon salt
    2 eggs
    1 tablespoon olive oil
    shavings of Parmesan cheese, to serve

1 To make the pasta dough, mix together the flour and salt in a large bowl or food processor. Add the eggs, olive oil and about 3 tablespoons of cold water or enough to make a pliable dough. If working by hand, mix the ingredients together and then knead the dough for about 15 minutes until very smooth. Or, process for about 1½ minutes in a food processor. Place the dough in a plastic bag and chill for at least 1 hour (or overnight if more convenient).

2 Cook the spinach in a large, covered saucepan for 3–4 minutes, until the leaves have wilted. Strain and press out the excess liquid. Set aside to cool a little and then chop finely.

3 Melt half the butter in a small saucepan and fry the onion over low heat for about 5–6 minutes until soft. Place in a bowl with the chopped spinach, the Parmesan and Dolcellate cheeses, and seasoning. Mix well.

4 Grease a ravioli sheet. Roll out half or a quarter of the pasta dough to a thickness of about ⅛ inch. Lay the dough over the ravioli sheet, pressing it well into each of the squares.

5 Spoon a little spinach mixture into each cavity, then roll out a second piece of dough and lay it on top. Press a rolling pin evenly over the top of the sheet to seal the edges and then cut the ravioli into squares using a pastry cutter.

6 Place the ravioli in a large saucepan of boiling water and simmer for about 4–5 minutes until cooked through but *al dente*. Drain well and then toss with the remaining butter and the parsley.

7 Divide between four serving plates and serve scattered with shavings of Parmesan cheese.

COOK'S TIP
For a small ravioli sheet of 32 holes, divide the dough into quarters. Roll the dough out until it covers the sheet comfortably – it takes some time but the pasta needs to be thin otherwise the ravioli will be too stodgy. For a large ravioli sheet of 64 holes, divide the dough in half.

CAULIFLOWER, SHRIMP AND BROCCOLI TEMPURA

ALL SORTS OF VEGETABLES ARE DELICIOUS DEEP-FRIED JAPANESE-STYLE (TEMPURA). FIRM VEGETABLES, SUCH AS CAULIFLOWER AND BROCCOLI, ARE BEST BLANCHED BEFORE FRYING BUT SNOW PEAS, RED AND GREEN BELL PEPPER SLICES, AND MUSHROOMS CAN SIMPLY BE DIPPED IN THE BATTER AND FRIED.

SERVES FOUR

INGREDIENTS
½ cauliflower
10 ounces broccoli
8 raw shrimp
8 white mushrooms (optional)
sunflower or vegetable oil, for
  deep frying
lemon wedges and sprigs of cilantro,
  to garnish
soy sauce, to serve
For the batter
4 ounces all-purpose flour
pinch of salt
2 eggs, separated
¾ cup ice water
2 tablespoons sunflower or vegetable
  oil

1 Cut the cauliflower and broccoli into medium-size florets. Blanch all the florets for 1–2 minutes. Drain. Refresh under cold running water. Set aside. Peel the shrimp, but leave their tails intact. Set aside.

2 To make the batter, place the flour and salt in a bowl, blend together the egg yolks and water and stir into the flour, beating well to make a smooth batter.

3 Beat in the oil and then whisk the egg whites until stiff and fold into the batter.

4 Heat the oil for deep frying to 375°F. Coat a few of the vegetables and prawns in the batter and then fry for 2–3 minutes until lightly golden and puffy. Transfer to a plate lined with paper towels and keep warm while frying the remaining tempura.

5 Arrange the tempura on individual plates, garnish with lemon and cilantro and serve with little bowls of soy sauce.

COOK'S TIP
Try cooking other vegetables in this way, such as eggplant and zucchini, or even the young delicate leaves of cauliflower, or celery leaves.

CAULIFLOWER AND MUSHROOM GOUGÈRE

THIS IS AN ALL-ROUND FAVORITE VEGETARIAN DISH. WHEN COOKING THIS DISH FOR MEAT LOVERS, CHOPPED ROAST HAM OR FRIED BACON CAN BE ADDED.

SERVES FOUR TO SIX

INGREDIENTS
1¼ cups water
4 ounces butter or margarine
5 ounces all-purpose flour
4 eggs
4 ounces Gruyère or Cheddar cheese, finely diced
1 teaspoon French mustard
salt and freshly ground black pepper
For the filling
14-ounce can tomatoes
1 tablespoon sunflower oil
½ ounce butter or margarine
1 onion, chopped
4 ounces white mushrooms, halved if large
1 small cauliflower, broken into small florets
sprig of thyme
salt and freshly ground black pepper

1 Preheat the oven to 400°F and butter a large oval ovenproof dish. Place the water and butter together in a large saucepan and heat until the butter has melted. Remove from the heat and add all the flour at once. Beat well with a wooden spoon for about 30 seconds until smooth. Allow to cool slightly.

2 Beat in the eggs, one at a time, and continue beating until the mixture is thick and glossy. Stir in the cheese and mustard and season with salt and pepper. Spread the mixture around the sides of the ovenproof dish, leaving a hollow in the center for the filling.

3 To make the filling, purée the tomatoes in a blender or food processor and then pour into a measuring jug. Add enough water to make up to 1¼ cups of liquid.

4 Heat the oil and butter in a flameproof casserole and fry the onion for about 3–4 minutes until softened but not browned. Add the mushrooms and cook for 2–3 minutes until they begin to be flecked with brown. Add the cauliflower florets and stir-fry for 1 minute.

5 Add the tomato liquid, thyme and seasoning. Cook, uncovered, over low heat for about 5 minutes until the cauliflower is only just tender.

6 Spoon the mixture into the hollow in the ovenproof dish, adding all the liquid. Bake in the oven for about 35–40 minutes, until the outer pastry is well risen and golden brown.

COOK'S TIP
For a variation, ham or bacon can be added. Use about 4–5 ounces thickly sliced roast ham and add to the sauce at the end of step 5.

BALTI-STYLE CAULIFLOWER WITH TOMATOES

BALTI IS A TYPE OF MEAT AND VEGETABLE COOKING FROM PAKISTAN AND NORTHERN INDIA. IT CAN REFER BOTH TO THE PAN USED FOR COOKING, WHICH IS LIKE A LITTLE WOK, AND THE SPICES USED. IN THE ABSENCE OF A GENUINE BALTI PAN, USE EITHER A WOK OR A HEAVY FRYING PAN.

SERVES FOUR

INGREDIENTS

2 tablespoons vegetable oil
1 onion, chopped
2 garlic cloves, crushed
1 cauliflower, broken into florets
1 teaspoon ground coriander
1 teaspoon ground cumin
1 teaspoon ground fennel seeds
½ teaspoon garam masala
pinch of ground ginger
½ teaspoon chili powder
4 plum tomatoes, peeled, seeded
  and quartered
6 fluid ounces water
6 ounces fresh spinach, roughly
  chopped
1–2 tablespoons lemon juice
salt and freshly ground black pepper

1 Heat the oil in a balti pan, wok, or large frying pan. Add the onion and garlic and stir-fry for 2–3 minutes over high heat until the onion begins to brown. Add the cauliflower florets and stir-fry for a further 2–3 minutes until the cauliflower is flecked with brown.

2 Add the coriander, cumin, fennel seeds, garam masala, ginger and chili powder and cook over high heat for 1 minute, stirring all the time; then add the tomatoes, water and salt and pepper. Bring to a boil and then reduce the heat, cover and simmer for 5–6 minutes until the cauliflower is just tender.

3 Stir in the chopped spinach, cover and cook for 1 minute until the spinach is tender. Add enough lemon juice to sharpen the flavor and adjust the seasoning to taste.

4 Serve straight from the pan, with an Indian meal or with chicken or meat.

HOT BROCCOLI TARTLETS

APART FROM THE UBIQUITOUS QUICHE, VEGETABLE TARTS ARE NOT VERY COMMON IN NORTH AMERICA. HOWEVER, IN FRANCE YOU CAN FIND A WHOLE VARIETY OF SAVORY TARTLETS, FILLED WITH ONIONS, LEEKS, MUSHROOMS AND BROCCOLI.

MAKES EIGHT TO TEN

INGREDIENTS
    1 tablespoon oil
    1 leek, finely sliced
    6 ounces broccoli, broken into florets
    ½ ounce butter
    ½ ounce all-purpose flour
    ⅔ cup milk
    2 ounces Cheddar cheese, grated
    fresh chervil, to garnish
For the pastry
    6 ounces all-purpose flour
    3 ounces butter
    1 egg
    pinch of salt

1 To make the pastry, place the flour and salt in a large bowl and rub in the butter and egg to make a dough. Add a little cold water if necessary, knead lightly, then cover with plastic wrap and leave to rest in the fridge for 1 hour.

2 Preheat the oven to 375°F. Let the dough return to room temperature for 10 minutes and then roll out on a lightly floured surface and line 8–10 deep muffin pans. Prick the bases with a fork and bake in the oven for about 10–15 minutes until the pastry is firm and lightly golden. Increase the oven temperature to 400°F.

3 Heat the oil in a small saucepan and sauté the leek for 4–5 minutes until soft. Add the broccoli, stir-fry for about 1 minute and then add a little water. Cover and steam for 3–4 minutes until the broccoli is just tender.

4 Melt the butter in a separate saucepan, stir in the flour and cook for a minute, stirring all the time. Slowly add the milk and stir to make a smooth sauce. Add half of the cheese and season with salt and pepper.

5 Spoon a little broccoli and leek into each tartlet case and then spoon over the sauce. Sprinkle each tartlet with the remaining cheese and then bake in the oven for about 10 minutes until golden.

6 Serve the tartlets as part of a buffet or as a starter, garnished with chervil.

CHARD PASTIES

CHARD, LIKE SPINACH, GOES PARTICULARLY WELL IN PASTIES. UNLIKE SOME GREEN VEGETABLES, IT CAN SURVIVE A LITTLE EXTRA COOKING AND IS SUBSTANTIAL ENOUGH TO BE THE PRINCIPAL INGREDIENT.

SERVES FOUR

INGREDIENTS
   1½ pounds chard
   1 ounce butter or margarine
   1 onion, finely chopped
   3 ounces lean bacon, chopped
   2 ounces Gruyère cheese, grated
   1 ounce fresh brown or white
     bread crumbs
   6 tablespoons light cream
   salt and freshly ground black pepper
For the pastry
   10 ounces all-purpose flour
   5 ounces butter or margarine
   pinch of salt
   beaten egg for glazing

1 To make the pastry, place the flour and salt in a mixing bowl and rub in the butter or margarine. Add a little cold water and mix to a soft dough. Knead lightly on a floured surface. Cover with plastic wrap and chill for 30 minutes.

2 Trim the stalks of the chard and then chop both the leaves and stalk. Place in a heavy-based pan, cover and cook over low heat for 6–8 minutes until the stalks are tender and the leaves wilted. Shake the pan occasionally. Strain and press out the excess liquid, then place in a mixing bowl and leave to cool.

3 Melt the butter in a small frying pan and fry the onion and bacon for about 4–5 minutes until the onion is lightly golden and the bacon browned.

4 Add the onion and bacon to the chard and stir in the cheese, bread crumbs, cream and seasoning to taste. Preheat the oven to 400°F.

5 Divide the pastry into four and roll out into rounds. Spoon the filling onto the center of each and dampen the edges with water. Bring the sides together over the filling and press together to seal. Brush with beaten egg and then put on an oiled baking sheet. Bake for about 15–20 minutes until the pastry is golden.

CRUNCHY CABBAGE SALAD <u>WITH</u> PESTO MAYONNAISE

BOTH THE PESTO AND THE MAYONNAISE CAN BE MADE FOR THIS DISH. HOWEVER, IF TIME IS SHORT, YOU CAN BUY THEM BOTH READY-PREPARED AND IT WILL TASTE JUST AS GOOD.

SERVES FOUR TO SIX

INGREDIENTS
    1 small or ½ medium white cabbage
    3–4 carrots, grated
    4 scallions, finely sliced
    1–1½ ounces pine nuts
    1 tablespoon chopped fresh mixed
      herbs; parsley, basil and chervil
For the pesto dressing
    1 egg yolk
    about 2 teaspoons lemon juice
    ⅝ cup sunflower oil
    2 teaspoons pesto
    4 tablespoons plain yogurt
    salt and freshly ground black pepper

1 To make the mayonnaise, place the egg yolk in a blender or food processor and process with the lemon juice. With the machine running, very slowly add the oil, pouring it more quickly as the mayonnaise emulsifies. Season to taste with salt and pepper and a little more lemon juice if necessary. Alternately, make by hand using a balloon whisk.

2 Spoon 5 tablespoons of mayonnaise into a bowl and stir in the pesto and yogurt, beating well to make a fairly thin dressing. (The remaining mayonnaise will keep for about 3–4 weeks in a screw-top jar in the fridge.)

3 Using a food processor or a sharp knife, thinly slice the cabbage and place in a large salad bowl.

4 Add the carrots and scallions, together with the herbs and pine nuts, mixing thoroughly with your hands. Stir the pesto dressing into the salad or serve separately in a small dish if preferred.

PASTA <u>WITH</u> SAVOY CABBAGE <u>AND</u> GRUYÈRE

THIS IS AN INEXPENSIVE AND SIMPLE DISH WITH A SURPRISING TEXTURE AND FLAVOR. THE CABBAGE IS COOKED SO THAT IT HAS PLENTY OF "BITE" TO IT, CONTRASTING WITH THE SOFTNESS OF THE PASTA.

SERVES FOUR

INGREDIENTS
  1 ounce butter
  1 small Savoy or green cabbage,
    thinly sliced
  1 small onion, chopped
  12 ounces pasta, e.g. tagliatelle,
    fettucine, penne, etc.
  1 tablespoon chopped fresh parsley
  ⅔ cup light cream
  2 ounces Gruyère or Cheddar cheese,
    grated
  about 1¼ cups hot vegetable or
    chicken stock
  salt and freshly ground black pepper

1 Preheat the oven to 350°F and butter a large casserole. Place the cabbage in a mixing bowl.

2 Melt the butter in a small frying pan and fry the onion until softened. Stir into the cabbage in the bowl.

3 Cook the pasta according to the instructions, until *al dente*.

4 Drain well and stir into the bowl with the cabbage and onion. Add the parsley and mix well and then pour into the prepared casserole.

5 Beat together the cream and Gruyère or Cheddar cheese and then stir in the hot stock. Season well and pour over the cabbage and pasta, so that it comes about halfway up the casserole. If necessary, add a little more stock.

6 Cover tightly and cook in the oven for 30–35 minutes, until the cabbage is tender and the stock is bubbling. Remove the lid for the last 5 minutes of the cooking time to brown the top.

KALE WITH PARMESAN AND GARLIC

KALE IS A ROBUST, FULL-BODIED TYPE OF CABBAGE. IT HAS A VERY PRONOUNCED FLAVOR AND IS GOOD WHEN COOKED WITH OTHER STRONG-FLAVORED INGREDIENTS SUCH AS ONIONS, GARLIC AND PARMESAN CHEESE. IT DOES NOT NEED LONG COOKING AS THE LEAVES ARE QUITE TENDER.

SERVES FOUR

INGREDIENTS

3 tablespoons olive oil
2 garlic cloves, crushed
4 scallions, sliced
12 ounces curly kale, thinly sliced,
   tough stalk removed
2 ounces Parmesan cheese, grated
salt and freshly ground black pepper
shavings of Parmesan cheese,
   to garnish

1 Heat the olive oil in a large saucepan or wok and fry the garlic gently for a few seconds. Add the scallions, stir-fry for 2 minutes and then add the kale.

2 Stir-fry for a few minutes so that the kale is coated in oil, and then add about ¼ cup water. Bring to a boil, cover and simmer until the kale is tender. Stir occasionally during cooking and do not allow the pan to boil dry.

3 Bring the liquid to the boil and allow the excess to evaporate and then stir in the Parmesan cheese. Serve at once with extra shavings of cheese, if liked.

KOHLRABI STUFFED WITH PEPPERS

IF YOU HAVEN'T SAMPLED KOHLRABI, OR HAVE ONLY EATEN IT IN STEWS WHERE ITS FLAVOR IS LOST, THIS DISH IS RECOMMENDED. THE SLIGHTLY SHARP FLAVOR OF THE PEPPERS IS AN EXCELLENT FOIL TO THE MORE EARTHY FLAVOR OF THE KOHLRABI.

SERVES FOUR

INGREDIENTS
    4 small kohlrabi, about 6–8 ounces
        each
    about 1⅔ cups hot vegetable stock
    1 tablespoon olive or sunflower oil
    1 onion, chopped
    1 small red bell pepper, seeded and
        sliced
    1 small green bell pepper, seeded
        and sliced
    salt and freshly ground black pepper
    flat leaf parsley, to garnish (optional)

1 Preheat the oven to 350°F. Trim and remove the ends of the kohlrabi, and arrange in the bottom of a medium-size ovenproof dish.

2 Pour over the stock to come about halfway up the vegetables. Cover and braise in the oven for about 30 minutes until tender. Transfer to a plate and allow to cool, reserving the stock.

3 Heat the oil in a frying pan and fry the onion for 3–4 minutes over low heat, stirring occasionally. Add the peppers and cook for a further 2–3 minutes, until the onion is lightly browned.

4 Add the reserved vegetable stock, and a little seasoning and simmer, uncovered, over moderate heat until the stock has almost evaporated.

5 Scoop out the flesh from the kohlrabis and roughly chop. Stir the flesh into the onion and pepper mixture, taste and adjust the seasoning. Arrange the shells in a shallow ovenproof dish.

6 Spoon the filling into the kohlrabi shells. Place in the oven for 5–10 minutes to heat through and then serve, garnished with flat leaf parsley, if liked.

STIR-FRIED BRUSSELS SPROUTS

INGREDIENTS
   1 pound Brussels sprouts
   1 tablespoon sunflower oil
   6–8 scallions, cut into 1-inch lengths
   2 slices fresh ginger
   1½ ounces slivered almonds
   ⅔–¾ cup vegetable or chicken stock
   salt

1 Remove any large outer leaves and trim the bases of the Brussels sprouts. Cut into slices about ⅓ inch thick.

2 Heat the oil in a wok or heavy frying pan and fry the scallions and the ginger for 2–3 minutes, stirring frequently. Add the almonds and stir-fry over moderate heat until both the onions and almonds begin to brown.

3 Remove and discard the ginger, reduce the heat and stir in the Brussels sprouts. Stir-fry for a few minutes and then pour in the stock and cook over low heat for 5–6 minutes or until the sprouts are nearly tender.

4 Add a little salt, if necessary, and then increase the heat to boil off the excess liquid. Spoon into a warmed serving dish and serve immediately.

BRUSSELS SPROUT GRATIN

INGREDIENTS
   ⅔ cup heavy or whipping cream
   ⅔ cup milk
   1 ounce Parmesan cheese, grated
   1½ pounds Brussels sprouts, thinly
     sliced
   ½ ounce butter
   1 garlic clove, finely chopped
   salt and freshly ground black pepper

1 Preheat the oven to 300°F and butter a shallow ovenproof dish. Blend together the cream, milk, Parmesan cheese and seasoning.

2 Place a layer of Brussels sprouts in the bottom of the prepared dish, sprinkle with a little garlic and pour over about a quarter of the cream mixture. Add another layer of sprouts and continue building layers in this way, ending with the remaining cream and milk

3 Cover loosely with wax paper and bake for 1–1¼ hours. Halfway through cooking, remove the paper and press the sprouts under the liquid in the dish. Return to the oven to brown.

CHINESE CABBAGE WITH LIME DRESSING

FOR THIS THAI RECIPE, THE COCONUT DRESSING IS TRADITIONALLY MADE USING FISH SAUCE, BUT VEGETARIANS COULD USE MUSHROOM SAUCE INSTEAD. BEWARE, THIS IS A FIERY DISH!

SERVES FOUR

INGREDIENTS
    6 scallions
    ½ Chinese cabbage, finely shredded
    2 tablespoons oil
    3 fresh red chilies, cut into thin strips
    4 garlic cloves, thinly sliced
    1 tablespoon crushed peanuts
For the dressing
    1–2 tablespoons fish sauce
    2 tablespoons lime juice
    1 cup coconut milk

1 To make the dressing, blend together the fish sauce and lime juice, and then stir in the coconut milk.

2 Cut the scallions diagonally into slices, including all but the very tips of the green parts.

3 Using a large sharp knife, cut the Chinese cabbage into very fine shreds.

4 Heat the oil in a wok and stir-fry the chilies for 2–3 minutes until crisp. Transfer to a plate using a slotted spoon.

5 Stir-fry the garlic for 30–60 seconds until golden brown and transfer to the plate with the chilies.

6 Stir-fry the white parts of the scallions for about 2–3 minutes and then add the green parts and stir-fry for a further 1 minute. Add to the plate with the chilies and garlic.

7 Bring a large pan of salted water to the boil and add the cabbage; stir twice and then drain immediately.

8 Place the warmed cabbage in a large bowl, add the coconut dressing and stir well. Spoon into a large serving bowl and sprinkle with the crushed peanuts and the stir-fried chili mixture. Serve either warm or cold.

COOK'S TIP
Coconut milk is available in cans from large supermarkets and Chinese stores. Alternately, creamed coconut is available in packets. To use creamed coconut, place about 4 ounces in a jug and pour over 1 cup boiling water. Stir well until dissolved.

DOLMADES

DOLMADES ARE STUFFED VINE LEAVES, A TRADITIONAL GREEK DISH. IF YOU CAN'T OBTAIN FRESH VINE LEAVES, USE A PACKET OF BRINED VINE LEAVES. SOAK THE LEAVES IN HOT WATER FOR 20 MINUTES THEN RINSE AND DRY WELL ON PAPER TOWELS BEFORE USE.

MAKES 20–24

INGREDIENTS

20–30 fresh young vine leaves
2 tablespoons olive oil
1 large onion, finely chopped
1 garlic clove, crushed
8 ounces cooked long grain rice,
  or mixed white and wild rice
about 3 tablespoons pine nuts
1 tablespoon slivered almonds
1½ ounces golden raisins
15ml/ 1 tablespoon snipped chives
1 tablespoon finely chopped
  fresh mint
juice of ½ lemon
⅔ cup white wine
hot vegetable stock
salt and freshly ground black pepper
sprig of mint, to garnish
Greek yogurt, to serve

1 Bring a large pan of water to a boil and cook the vine leaves for about 2–3 minutes. They will darken and go limp after about 1 minute and simmering for a further minute or so ensures they are pliable. If using leaves from a packet, place them in a large bowl, cover with boiling water and leave for a few minutes until the leaves can be easily separated. Rinse them under cold water and drain on paper towels.

2 Heat the oil in a small frying pan and fry the onion and garlic for 3–4 minutes over low heat until soft.

3 Spoon the onion and garlic mixture into a bowl and add the cooked rice,

4 Stir in 2 tablespoons of the pine nuts, the almonds, golden raisins, chives, mint, lemon juice and seasoning and mix well.

5 Lay a vine leaf on a clean work surface, veined side uppermost. Place a spoonful of filling near the stem, fold the lower part of the leaf over it and roll up, folding in the sides as you go. Continue stuffing the vine leaves in the same way.

6 Line the bottom of a deep frying pan with four large vine leaves. Place the stuffed vine leaves close together in the pan, seam side down, in a single layer.

7 Add the wine and enough stock to just cover the vine leaves. Place a plate directly over the leaves, then cover and simmer gently for 30 minutes, checking to make sure the pan does not boil dry.

8 Chill the vine leaves garnished with the remaining pine nuts and a sprig of mint and serve with a little yogurt.

BEAN, PEA AND SEED RECIPES

LAMB AND FAVA BEAN COUSCOUS

SERVES FOUR

INGREDIENTS

2–3 tablespoons vegetable oil
12 ounces lean lamb, cut into cubes
3 skinless chicken pieces, cut into
    large chunks
1 large onion, chopped
2 garlic cloves, crushed
3 carrots, cut into 1½-inch lengths
1 small parsnip, cut into chunks
4 tomatoes, skinned and chopped
1⅔ cups chicken stock
1 cinnamon stick
½ teaspoon ground ginger
sprig of thyme
1 small red or green bell pepper,
    seeded and sliced
8 ounces shelled fava beans
1–2 teaspoons Tabasco or chili sauce
salt and freshly ground black pepper
For the couscous
8 ounces couscous
1 tablespoon olive oil
pinch of salt

1 Heat the oil in a large flameproof casserole and fry the cubes of lamb until evenly browned. Drain and transfer to a plate. Add the chicken pieces and cook until brown. Drain and put on the plate.

2 Heat a further 1 tablespoon oil and fry the onion and garlic over low heat for 4–5 minutes until softened. Add the carrots and parsnip, stir-fry for a few minutes and then add the tomatoes, stock, cinnamon stick, ginger, thyme and seasoning, together with the meat. Bring to a boil, stirring occasionally, and then reduce the heat, cover and simmer gently for about 45–60 minutes until the meat is cooked and very tender.

3 Meanwhile, in a large bowl rub the olive oil and salt into the couscous. Stir in boiling water to cover and leave to soak for at least 10 minutes.

4 Add the pepper and fava beans to the stew and simmer for 10 minutes until the vegetables are cooked.

5 Place the soaked couscous in a colander and make five or six "holes" in the grain using the handle of a wooden spoon. Set the couscous over the stew, cover and steam for 10 minutes.

6 Just before serving, ladle about ⅔ cup of the cooking liquid into a small pan. Add a little Tabasco sauce and heat gently. Taste and add more Tabasco sauce, if liked, for a hotter and spicier sauce, and then pour into a warmed serving jug.

7 Spoon the couscous onto a large warmed serving plate and pour the stew over. Serve with the hot sauce.

FAVA BEANS À LA PAYSANNE

SERVES FOUR

INGREDIENTS

1 tablespoon olive oil
1 onion, finely chopped
3 ounces lean ham in a thick slice,
    finely diced
12 ounces shelled fava beans
2 Bibb lettuces, chopped
⅓ cup chicken or vegetable stock
¼ cup light cream
salt and freshly ground black pepper
sprigs of mint or chervil, to garnish

1 Heat the oil in a saucepan. Fry the onion and ham until soft. Add the beans and lettuce. Cover, cook gently for 6–8 minutes, stirring occasionally.

2 Stir in the stock, cream and seasoning and cook over very low heat for 20–30 minutes. Stir occasionally, taking care not to break up the beans.

3 Turn into a warmed serving dish and garnish with a sprig of mint or chervil. Serve with broiled meat or an omelet.

COOK'S TIP
Larger fava beans sometimes have a tough outer skin. It is a good idea to cook them briefly, peel off the outer skin and use the tender green centers.

PEAS WITH BABY ONIONS AND CREAM

IDEALLY, USE FRESH PEAS AND FRESH BABY ONIONS. FROZEN PEAS ARE AN ACCEPTABLE SUBSTITUTE IF FRESH ONES AREN'T AVAILABLE, BUT FROZEN ONIONS TEND TO BE INSIPID AND ARE NOT WORTH USING. ALTERNATELY, USE THE WHITE PART OF SCALLIONS.

SERVES FOUR

INGREDIENTS

6 ounces baby onions
½ ounce butter
2 pounds fresh peas (about 12 ounces shelled or frozen)
⅔ cup heavy cream
½ ounce all-purpose flour
2 teaspoons chopped fresh parsley
1–2 tablespoons lemon juice (optional)
salt and freshly ground black pepper

1 Peel the onions and halve them if necessary. Melt the butter in a flame-proof casserole and fry the onions for 5–6 minutes over moderate heat, until they begin to be flecked with brown.

3 Using a small whisk, blend the cream with the flour. Remove the pan from the heat and stir in the combined cream and flour, parsley and seasoning to taste.

4 Cook over low heat for about 3–4 minutes, until the sauce is thick. Taste and adjust the seasoning; add a little lemon juice to sharpen, if liked.

2 Add the peas and stir-fry for a few minutes. Add ¼ cup water and bring to a boil. Partially cover and simmer for about 10 minutes until both the peas and onions are tender. There should be a thin layer of water on the bottom of the pan – add a little more water if necessary or if there is too much liquid, remove the lid and increase the heat until the liquid is reduced.

SNOW PEAS WITH CHICKEN AND CILANTRO

SNOW PEAS ARE SO DELICATE AND FRESH-TASTING THAT IT SEEMS A CRIME TO DO ANYTHING AT ALL WITH THEM, BARRING FLASH COOKING AND SERVING THEM HOT OR COLD WITH A LITTLE BUTTER OR A VINAIGRETTE DRESSING. THEY ARE EXCELLENT IN STIR-FRIES, ADDING COLOR AND TEXTURE.

SERVES FOUR

INGREDIENTS
4 boned and skinned chicken breasts
8 ounces snow peas
3 tablespoons vegetable oil, plus
   oil for deep frying
3 garlic cloves, finely chopped
1-inch piece fresh ginger, freshly
   grated
5–6 scallions, cut into 1½-inch
   lengths
2 teaspoons sesame oil
For the marinade
1 teaspoon cornstarch
1 tablespoon light soy sauce
1 tablespoon medium dry sherry
1 tablespoon vegetable oil
For the sauce
1 teaspoon cornstarch
2–3 teaspoons dark soy sauce
½ cup chicken stock
2 tablespoons oyster sauce
boiled rice, to serve

1 Cut the chicken into strips about ½ x 1½ inches. To make the marinade, blend together the cornstarch and soy sauce. Stir in the sherry and oil. Pour over the chicken, turning the pieces over to coat evenly, and leave for 30 minutes.

2 Trim the snow peas and plunge into a pan of boiling salted water. Bring back to the boil and then drain and refresh them under cold running water.

3 To make the sauce, mix together the cornstarch, soy sauce, stock and oyster sauce and set aside.

4 Heat the oil in a deep fryer. Drain the chicken strips and fry, in batches if necessary, for about 30 seconds to brown. Drain and transfer to a plate using a slotted spoon.

5 Heat 1 tablespoon of the vegetable oil in a wok and add the garlic and ginger. Stir-fry for 30 seconds. Add the snow peas and stir-fry for 1–2 minutes. Transfer to a plate and keep warm.

6 Heat the remaining vegetable oil in the wok, add the scallions and stir-fry for 1–2 minutes. Add the chicken and stir-fry for 2 minutes. Pour in the sauce, reduce the heat and cook until it thickens and the chicken is cooked through.

7 Stir in the sesame oil, and pour over the snow peas. Serve with boiled rice.

GREEN BEAN SALAD

ALTHOUGH BEAN SALADS ARE DELICIOUS SERVED WITH A SIMPLE VINAIGRETTE DRESSING, THIS DISH IS A LITTLE MORE ELABORATE. IT DOES, HOWEVER, ENHANCE THE FRESH FLAVOR OF THE BEANS.

SERVES FOUR

INGREDIENTS

1 pound green beans
1 tablespoon olive oil
1 ounce butter
½ garlic clove, crushed
2 ounces fresh white bread crumbs
1 tablespoon chopped fresh parsley
1 egg, hard-boiled and finely chopped
For the dressing
2 tablespoons olive oil
2 tablespoons sunflower oil
2 teaspoons white wine vinegar
½ garlic clove, crushed
¼ teaspoon Dijon mustard
pinch of sugar
pinch of salt

3 Heat the oil and butter in a frying pan and fry the garlic for 1 minute. Stir in the bread crumbs and fry over moderate heat for about 3–4 minutes until golden brown, stirring frequently.

4 Remove the pan from the heat and stir in the parsley and then the egg. Sprinkle the breadcrumb mixture over the green beans. Serve warm or at room temperature.

1 Trim the green beans and cook in boiling salted water for 5–6 minutes until tender. Drain the beans and refresh them under cold running water and place in a serving bowl.

2 Make the salad dressing by blending the oils, vinegar, garlic, mustard, sugar and salt thoroughly together. Pour over the beans and toss to mix.

COOK'S TIP

For a more substantial salad, boil about 1 pound scrubbed new potatoes until tender, cool and then cut them into bite-size chunks. Stir into the green beans and then add the dressing.

GREEN BEANS WITH BACON AND CREAM

SERVES FOUR

INGREDIENTS

    12 ounces green beans
    2–3 ounces bacon, chopped
    1 ounce butter or margarine
    1 tablespoon all-purpose flour
    1½ cups milk and light cream, mixed
    salt and freshly ground black pepper

1 Preheat the oven to 375°F. Trim the beans and cook in lightly salted boiling water for about 5 minutes until just tender. Drain and place them in an oven-proof dish.

2 Dry-fry the bacon until crisp, chop into small pieces and stir into the beans.

3 Melt the butter or margarine in a saucepan, stir in the flour and then add the milk and cream to make a smooth sauce. Season well with salt and pepper.

4 Pour the sauce over the beans and carefully mix it in. Cover lightly with a piece of foil and bake in the oven for 15–20 minutes until hot.

WAX BEANS WITH GARLIC

DELICATE AND FRESH TASTING FLAGEOLET BEANS AND GARLIC ADD A DISTINCT FRENCH FLAVOR TO THIS SIMPLE SIDE DISH. SERVE TO ACCOMPANY ROAST LAMB OR VEAL.

<u>SERVES FOUR</u>

INGREDIENTS

    8 ounces flageolet beans
    1 tablespoon olive oil
    1 ounce butter
    1 onion, finely chopped
    1–2 garlic cloves, crushed
    3–4 tomatoes, peeled and chopped
    12 ounces wax beans, prepared and
      sliced
    ⅔ cup white wine
    ⅔ cup vegetable stock
    2 tablespoons chopped fresh parsley
    salt and freshly ground black pepper

1 Place the flageolet beans in a large saucepan of water, bring to a boil and simmer for ¾–1 hour until tender. Drain.

2 Heat the oil and butter in a large frying pan and sauté the onion and garlic for 3–4 minutes until soft. Add the chopped tomatoes and continue cooking over low heat until they are soft.

3 Stir the flageolet beans into the onion and tomato mixture, then add the wax beans, wine, stock, and a little salt. Stir well. Cover and simmer for 5–10 minutes until the wax beans are tender.

4 Increase the heat to reduce the liquid, then stir in the parsley and season with a little more salt, if necessary, and pepper.

INDIAN–STYLE OKRA

WHEN OKRA (BHINDI) IS SERVED IN INDIAN RESTAURANTS IT IS OFTEN FLAT AND SOGGY BECAUSE IT HAS BEEN OVERCOOKED OR LEFT STANDING. HOWEVER, WHEN YOU MAKE THIS DISH YOURSELF, YOU WILL REALIZE HOW DELICIOUS OKRA CAN BE.

SERVES FOUR

INGREDIENTS

12 ounces okra
2 small onions
2 garlic cloves, crushed
½-inch piece fresh ginger
1 green chili, seeded
2 teaspoons ground cumin
2 teaspoons ground coriander
2 tablespoons vegetable oil
juice 1 lemon

3 Reduce the heat and add the garlic and ginger mixture. Cook for about 2–3 minutes, stirring frequently, and then add the okra, lemon juice and 7 tablespoons water. Stir well, cover tightly and simmer over low heat for about 10 minutes until tender. Transfer to a serving dish, sprinkle with the fried onion rings and serve at once.

1 Trim the okra and cut into ½-inch lengths. Roughly chop one of the onions and place in a food processor or blender with the garlic, ginger, chili and 6 tablespoons water. Process to a paste. Add the cumin and coriander and blend again.

2 Thinly slice the remaining onion into rings and fry in the oil for 6–8 minutes until golden brown. Transfer to a plate using a slotted spoon.

CORN AND CHEESE PASTIES

THESE TASTY PASTIES ARE REALLY SIMPLE TO MAKE AND IRRESISTIBLE — WHY NOT MAKE DOUBLE THE AMOUNT, AS THEY'LL GO LIKE HOTCAKES.

MAKES 18–20

INGREDIENTS
    9 ounces corn
    4 ounces feta cheese
    1 egg, beaten
    2 tablespoons heavy or whipping
      cream
    ½ ounce Parmesan cheese, grated
    3 scallions, chopped
    8–10 small sheets filo pastry
    4 ounces butter, melted
    freshly ground black pepper

1 Preheat the oven to 375°F and butter two muffin pans.

2 If using fresh corn, strip the kernels from the cob using a sharp knife and simmer in a little salted water for 3–5 minutes until tender. For canned corn, drain and rinse well under cold running water.

.3 Crumble the feta cheese into a bowl and stir in the corn. Add the egg, cream, Parmesan cheese, scallions and ground black pepper, and stir well.

4 Take one sheet of pastry and cut it in half to make a square. (Keep the remaining pastry covered with a damp cloth to prevent it drying out.) Brush with melted butter and then fold into four, to make a smaller square (about 3 inches).

5 Place a heaped teaspoon of mixture in the center of each pastry square and then squeeze the pastry around the filling to make a "money bag" casing.

6 Continue making pasties until all the mixture is used up. Brush the outside of each "bag" with any remaining butter and then bake in the oven for about 20–25 minutes until golden. Serve hot.

CORN AND SCALLOP CHOWDER

FRESH HOME-GROWN CORN IS IDEAL FOR THIS CHOWDER, ALTHOUGH CANNED OR FROZEN CORN ALSO WORKS WELL. THIS SOUP IS ALMOST A MEAL IN ITSELF AND MAKES A PERFECT LUNCH DISH.

SERVES FOUR TO SIX

INGREDIENTS

2 ears of corn or 7 ounces frozen or
    canned corn
2½ cups milk
½ ounce butter or margarine
1 small leek or onion, chopped
1 small garlic clove, crushed
1½ ounces smoked lean bacon,
    finely chopped
1 small green bell pepper, seeded
    and diced
1 celery stalk, chopped
1 medium potato, diced
1 tablespoon all-purpose flour
1¼ cups chicken or vegetable stock
4 scallops
4 ounces cooked fresh mussels
pinch of paprika
⅔ cup light cream (optional)
salt and freshly ground black pepper

1 Using a sharp knife, slice down the ears of the corn to remove the kernels. Place half of the kernels in a food processor or blender and process with a little of the milk.

2 Melt the butter or margarine in a large saucepan and gently fry the leek or onion, garlic and bacon for 4–5 minutes until the leek is soft but not browned. Add the green bell pepper, celery and potato and sweat over low heat for a further 3–4 minutes, stirring frequently.

3 Stir in the flour and cook for about 1–2 minutes until the mixture is golden and frothy. Gradually stir in the milk and corn mixture, stock, the remaining milk and corn kernels and seasoning.

4 Bring to a boil and then reduce the heat to a gentle simmer, and cook, partially covered, for 15–20 minutes until the vegetables are tender.

5 Pull the corals away from the scallops and slice the white flesh into ¼-inch slices. Stir the scallops into the soup, cook for 4 minutes and then stir in the corals, mussels and paprika. Allow to heat through for a few minutes and then stir in the cream, if using. Adjust the seasoning to taste and serve.

SQUASH RECIPES

SQUASH RISOTTO

SERVES FOUR

INGREDIENTS
  1 pumpkin, about 2–2¼ pounds
  2 tablespoons olive oil
  1 onion, chopped
  1–2 garlic cloves, crushed
  4 ounces lean bacon, chopped
  4 ounces arborio rice
  2½–3 cups chicken stock
  1½ ounces Parmesan cheese, grated
  1 tablespoon chopped fresh parsley
  salt and freshly ground black pepper

1 Halve or quarter the pumpkin, remove the seeds and skin, and then cut into chunks about ½–¾ inches in size.

2 Heat the oil in a flameproof casserole and fry the onion and garlic for about 3–4 minutes, stirring frequently. Add the bacon and continue frying until both the onion and bacon are lightly golden.

3 Add the pumpkin, stir-fry for a few minutes. Add the rice and cook for about 2 minutes, stirring all the time.

4 Pour in about half of the stock and season. Stir well and then half cover and simmer gently for about 20 minutes, stirring occasionally. As the liquid is absorbed, add more stock and stir to prevent the mixture sticking to the bottom.

5 When the pumpkin and rice are nearly tender, add a little more stock. Cook uncovered for 5–10 minutes. Stir in the Parmesan cheese and parsley and serve.

PUMPKIN SOUP

THE SWEET FLAVOR OF PUMPKIN IS GOOD IN SOUPS, TEAMING WELL WITH OTHER MORE SAVORY INGREDIENTS SUCH AS ONIONS AND POTATOES TO MAKE A WARM AND COMFORTING DISH.

SERVES FOUR TO SIX

INGREDIENTS
  1 tablespoon sunflower oil
  1 ounce butter
  1 large onion, sliced
  1½-pound pumpkin, cut into
    large chunks
  1 pound potatoes, sliced
  2½ cups vegetable stock
  good pinch of nutmeg
  1 teaspoon chopped fresh tarragon
  2½ cups milk
  about 1–2 teaspoons lemon juice
  salt and freshly ground black pepper

1 Heat the oil and butter in a heavy-based saucepan and fry the onion for 4–5 minutes over low heat until soft but not browned, stirring frequently.

2 Add the pumpkin and potato, stir well and then cover and sweat over low heat for about 10 minutes until the vegetables are almost tender, stirring occasionally to prevent them from sticking to the pan.

3 Stir in the stock, nutmeg, tarragon and seasoning. Bring to a boil and then simmer for about 10 minutes until the vegetables are completely tender.

4 Allow to cool slightly, then pour into a food processor or blender and process until smooth. Pour back into a clean saucepan and add the milk. Heat gently and then taste, adding the lemon juice and extra seasoning if necessary. Serve piping hot with country brown bread.

BAKED ZUCCHINI

WHEN VERY SMALL AND VERY FRESH ZUCCHINI ARE USED FOR THIS RECIPE IT IS WONDERFUL, BOTH SIMPLE AND DELICIOUS. THE CREAMY YET TANGY GOAT CHEESE CONTRASTS WELL WITH THE VERY DELICATE FLAVOR OF THE YOUNG ZUCCHINI.

SERVES FOUR

INGREDIENTS

8 small zucchini, about 1 pound total weight
1 tablespoon olive oil, plus extra for greasing
3–4 ounces goat cheese, cut into thin strips
small bunch fresh mint, finely chopped
freshly ground black pepper

1 Preheat the oven to 350°F. Cut out eight rectangles of foil large enough to encase each zucchini and brush each with a little oil.

2 Trim the zucchini and cut a thin slit along the length of each.

3 Insert pieces of goat cheese in the slits. Add a little mint and sprinkle over the olive oil and black pepper.

4 Wrap each zucchini in the foil rectangles, place on a baking sheet and bake for about 25 minutes until tender.

COOK'S TIP
Almost any cheese could be used in this recipe. Mild cheeses, however, such as a mild cheddar or mozzarella, will best allow the flavor of the zucchini to be appreciated.

ZUCCHINI ITALIAN-STYLE

IF YOU GROW YOUR OWN ZUCCHINI AND HAVE HUGE QUANTITIES TO USE UP, THIS IS A QUICK AND EASY RECIPE. ITS SIMPLICITY BELIES ITS EXCELLENCE.

SERVES FOUR

INGREDIENTS

1 tablespoon virgin olive oil
1 tablespoon sunflower oil
1 large onion, chopped
1 garlic clove, crushed
4–5 medium zucchini, cut into ½-inch slices
⅔ cup chicken or vegetable stock
½ teaspoon chopped fresh oregano
salt and freshly ground black pepper
chopped fresh parsley, to garnish

3 Stir in the stock, oregano and seasoning and simmer gently for 8–10 minutes, until the liquid has almost evaporated. Spoon the zucchini into a serving dish, sprinkle with parsley and serve.

1 Heat the oils in a large frying pan and fry the onion and garlic over moderate heat for 5–6 minutes until the onion has softened and is beginning to brown.

2 Add the zucchini and fry for about 4 minutes until they just begin to be flecked with brown. Stir frequently.

MARROWS WITH GNOCCHI

A SIMPLE WAY WITH MARROW, THIS DISH MAKES AN EXCELLENT ACCOMPANIMENT TO BROILED MEAT BUT IT IS ALSO GOOD WITH A VEGETARIAN DISH, OR SIMPLY SERVED WITH GRILLED TOMATOES.

SERVES FOUR

INGREDIENTS

1 small marrow, cut into
  bite-size chunks
2 ounces butter
14-ounce packet gnocchi
½ garlic clove, crushed
salt and freshly ground black pepper
chopped fresh basil, to garnish

1 Preheat the oven to 350°F and butter a large ovenproof dish. Place the marrow, more or less in a single layer, in the dish. Dot all over with the remaining butter.

2 Place a double piece of buttered wax paper over the top. Cover with an ovenproof plate or lid so that it presses the marrow down, and then place a heavy, ovenproof weight on top of that. (Use a couple of old-fashioned scale weights.)

3 Put in the oven to bake for about 15 minutes, by which time the marrow should just be tender.

4 Cook the gnocchi in a large saucepan of boiling salted water for 2–3 minutes, or according to the instructions on the packet. Drain well.

5 Stir the garlic and gnocchi into the marrow. Season and then place the wax paper over the marrow and return to the oven for 5 minutes (the weights are not necessary).

6 Just before serving, sprinkle the top with a little chopped fresh basil.

BAKED MARROW IN PARSLEY SAUCE

*THIS IS A REALLY GLORIOUS WAY WITH A SIMPLE AND MODEST VEGETABLE. TRY TO FIND A SMALL, FIRM
AND UNBLEMISHED MARROW FOR THIS RECIPE, AS THE FLAVOR WILL BE SWEET, FRESH AND DELICATE.*

SERVES FOUR

INGREDIENTS
    1 small young marrow, about 2 pounds
    2 tablespoons olive oil
    ½ ounce butter
    1 onion, chopped
    1 tablespoon all-purpose flour
    1¼ cups milk and light cream mixed
    2 tablespoons chopped fresh parsley
    salt and freshly ground black pepper

1 Preheat the oven to 350°F and cut the
marrow into pieces measuring about
2 x 1 inches.

2 Heat the oil and butter in a flameproof
casserole and fry the onion over a gentle
heat until very soft.

3 Add the marrow and sauté for
1–2 minutes and then stir in the flour.
Cook for a few minutes and then stir in
the milk and cream mixture.

4 Add the parsley and seasoning, stir
well and then cover and cook in the oven
for 30–35 minutes. If liked, remove the
lid for the final 5 minutes of cooking to
brown the top. Alternately, serve the
marrow in its rich pale sauce.

COOK'S TIP
Chopped fresh basil or a mixture of basil
and chervil also tastes good in this dish.

CUCUMBER AND TROUT MOUSSE

THIS IS A VERY LIGHT, REFRESHING MOUSSE, MAKING THE MOST OF THE CLEAN TASTE OF CUCUMBER.
SERVE IT AS A STARTER OR FOR A LIGHT LUNCH WITH A GREEN SALAD.

SERVES SIX

INGREDIENTS
1 small cucumber
3 smoked trout fillets, about 5 ounces
  total weight
4 ounces ricotta cheese
1 tablespoon powdered gelatin
⅔ cup vegetable stock
12–14 pimiento stuffed olives, sliced
2 tablespoons lemon juice
1 teaspoon finely chopped fresh
  tarragon
⅔ cup heavy or whipping cream
2 egg whites
salt and freshly ground black pepper
peeled shrimp and lemon wedges,
  to garnish
For the topping
1 tablespoon powdered gelatin
6 tablespoons vegetable stock

1 Lightly oil six ramekin dishes. To prepare the topping, take one quarter of the cucumber and slice thinly . Sprinkle the gelatin over the stock, leave to soak for a few minutes and then place over a saucepan of simmering water and stir until completely dissolved.

2 Spoon a little of the gelatin mixture into each dish and arrange two or three cucumber slices on top. Put in the fridge to set. Pour over the remaining gelatin mixture and return to the fridge to set.

3 To make the mousse, peel and very finely dice the remaining cucumber and put in a bowl. Flake the fish, discarding the skin and any bones and add to the cucumber. Beat in the ricotta cheese.

4 Sprinkle the gelatin over 2 tablespoons of water in a bowl and leave to soak for a few minutes. Place over a saucepan of simmering water and stir until dissolved.

5 Heat the stock. Stir in the dissolved gelatin and leave until cool but not set. Pour over the trout and stir in the olives, lemon juice, tarragon and seasoning.

6 Lightly whip the cream and whisk the egg whites until stiff. Fold the cream into the trout mixture, followed by the egg whites. Spoon the mousse into the ramekin dishes, leveling the surface. Cover and chill for 1–2 hours and then unmold onto serving plates

7 Garnish with any remaining cucumber slices together with a few peeled shrimp and some lemon wedges.

LOOFAH AND EGGPLANT RATATOUILLE

LOOFAHS HAVE A SIMILAR FLAVOR TO ZUCCHINI AND CONSEQUENTLY TASTE EXCELLENT WITH EGGPLANT AND TOMATOES. THE CILANTRO ADDS AN EXTRA EXOTIC TOUCH.

SERVES FOUR

INGREDIENTS

1 large or 2 medium eggplants
1 pound young loofahs or
   sponge gourds
1 large red bell pepper, cut into
   large chunks
8 ounces cherry tomatoes
8 ounces shallots, peeled
2 teaspoons ground coriander
4 tablespoons olive oil
2 garlic cloves, finely chopped
a few cilantro leaves
salt and freshly ground black pepper

1 Cut the eggplants into thick chunks and sprinkle the pieces with salt. Set aside in a colander for about 45 minutes and then rinse well under cold running water and pat dry.

2 Preheat the oven to 425°F. Slice the loofahs into ¾-inch pieces. Place the eggplant, loofah and pepper pieces, together with the tomatoes and shallots in a roasting pan which is large enough to take all the vegetables in a single layer.

3 Sprinkle with the ground coriander and olive oil and then scatter the chopped garlic and cilantro leaves on top. Season to taste.

4 Roast for about 25 minutes, stirring the vegetables occasionally, until the loofah is golden brown and the peppers are beginning to char at the edges.

CHOCOLATE ZUCCHINI CAKE

THE RECIPE FOR THIS MOIST CHOCOLATE CAKE COMES FROM AMERICA. PERHAPS AN UNLIKELY COMBINATION, IT IS A DELICIOUS VARIATION WELL WORTH TRYING.

SERVES FOUR TO SIX

INGREDIENTS

4 ounces margarine
½ cup sunflower oil
4 ounces caster sugar
8 ounces soft brown sugar
3 eggs, beaten
½ cup milk
12 ounces all-purpose flour
2 teaspoons baking powder
4 tablespoons cocoa powder
½ teaspoon ground allspice
1 pound zucchini, peeled and grated
1 teaspoon vanilla extract
8 ounces semisweet chocolate dots

1 Preheat the oven to 375°F and line a 9 x 13-inch baking pan with wax paper.

2 Cream the margarine, oil and sugars together until light and fluffy, then gradually beat in the eggs and milk.

3 Sift the flour, baking powder, cocoa powder and ground allspice together and fold gently into the mixture.

4 Stir in the grated zucchini and vanilla extract and spoon the mixture into the prepared pan. Smooth the top using a metal spatula and sprinkle the chocolate dots over the top.

5 Bake in the oven for 35–45 minutes until the cake is firm and a knife comes out clean. Cut into squares while still warm and then leave to cool.

PUMPKIN AND HAM FRITTATA

A FRITTATA IS AN ITALIAN VERSION OF THE SPANISH TORTILLA, A SUBSTANTIAL OMELET MADE OF EGGS AND VEGETABLES. IT IS CUT LIKE A CAKE AND CAN BE EATEN HOT, COLD OR WARM.

SERVES FOUR

INGREDIENTS

2 tablespoons sunflower oil
1 large onion, chopped
1 pound pumpkin, chopped into bite-size pieces
7 fluid ounces chicken stock
4 ounces smoked ham, chopped
6 eggs
2 teaspoons chopped fresh marjoram
salt and freshly ground black pepper

1 Preheat the oven to 375°F and oil a large shallow ovenproof dish. Heat the oil in a large frying pan and fry the onion for 3–4 minutes until softened.

2 Add the pumpkin and fry over a brisk heat for 3–4 minutes, stirring frequently. Stir in the stock, cover and simmer over low heat for 5–6 minutes until the pumpkin is slightly tender. Add the ham.

3 Pour the mixture into the prepared dish. Beat the eggs with the marjoram and a little seasoning. Pour into the dish and then bake for 20–25 minutes until the frittata is firm and lightly golden.

FRUIT RECIPES

EGGPLANT AND ZUCCHINI BAKE

SERVES FOUR TO SIX

INGREDIENTS
- 1 large eggplant
- 2 tablespoons olive oil
- 1 large onion, chopped
- 1–2 garlic cloves, crushed
- 2 pounds tomatoes, peeled and chopped
- a handful of basil leaves, shredded or 1 teaspoon dried basil
- 1 tablespoon chopped fresh parsley
- 2 zucchini, sliced lengthwise
- all-purpose flour, for coating
- 5–6 tablespoons sunflower oil
- 12 ounces mozzarella, sliced
- 1 ounce Parmesan cheese, grated

1 Slice the eggplant, sprinkle with salt and set aside for 45–60 minutes.

2 Heat the olive oil in a large frying pan. Fry the onion and garlic for 3–4 minutes until softened. Stir in the tomatoes, half the basil, the parsley and seasoning. Bring to a boil. Reduce the heat and cook, stirring, for 25–35 minutes until thickened. Mash the tomatoes to a pulp.

3 Rinse and dry the eggplant. Dust the eggplant and zucchini with flour.

4 Heat the sunflower oil in another frying pan and fry the eggplant and zucchini until golden brown. Set aside.

5 Preheat the oven to 350°F. Butter an ovenproof dish. Put a layer of eggplant and then zucchini in the dish, pour over half the sauce and scatter with half the mozzarella. Sprinkle over most of the remaining basil and a little parsley. Repeat the layers, ending with mozzarella. Sprinkle the Parmesan cheese and remaining herbs on top and bake for 30–35 minutes. Serve at once.

EGGPLANT WITH TZATZIKI

SERVES FOUR

INGREDIENTS
- 2 medium-sized eggplants
- oil, for deep frying
- salt

For the batter
- 3 ounces all-purpose flour
- 1 egg
- ½–⅔ cup milk, or ½ milk, ½ water
- pinch of salt

For the tzatziki
- ½ cucumber, peeled and diced
- ⅔ cup plain yogurt
- 1 garlic clove, crushed
- 1 tablespoon chopped fresh mint

1 To make the tzatziki, place the cucumber in a colander, sprinkle with salt and leave for 30 minutes. Rinse, drain well and pat dry on kitchen paper. Mix the yogurt, garlic, mint and cucumber in a bowl. Cover and chill. Slice the eggplant lengthwise. Sprinkle with salt. Leave for 1 hour.

2 To make the batter, sift the flour and salt into a large bowl add the egg and milk and beat until smooth.

3 Rinse the eggplant slices and pat dry. Heat ½ inch of oil in a large frying pan. Dip the eggplant slices in the batter and fry them for 3–4 minutes until golden, turning once. Drain on paper towels and serve with the tzatziki.

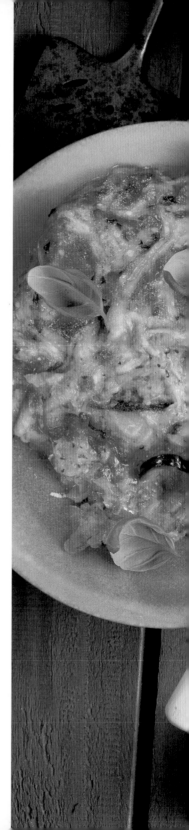

GAZPACHO

GAZPACHO IS A CLASSIC SPANISH SOUP. IT IS POPULAR ALL OVER SPAIN BUT NOWHERE MORE SO THAN IN ANDALUCIA, WHERE THERE ARE HUNDREDS OF VARIATIONS. IT IS A COLD SOUP OF TOMATOES, TOMATO JUICE, GREEN BELL PEPPER AND GARLIC, WHICH IS SERVED WITH A SELECTION OF GARNISHES.

SERVES FOUR

INGREDIENTS

3–3½ pounds ripe tomatoes
1 green bell pepper, seeded and
   roughly chopped
2 garlic cloves, crushed
2 slices white bread, crusts removed
4 tablespoons olive oil
4 tablespoons tarragon wine vinegar
⅔ cup tomato juice
good pinch of sugar
salt and freshly ground black pepper
ice cubes, to serve
For the garnishes
2 tablespoons sunflower oil
2–3 slices white bread, diced
1 small cucumber, peeled and
   finely diced
1 small onion, finely chopped
1 red bell pepper, seeded and finely diced
1 green bell pepper, seeded and finely
   diced
2 hard-boiled eggs, chopped

1 Skin the tomatoes, then quarter them and remove the cores.

2 Place the pepper in a food processor and process for a few seconds. Add the tomatoes, garlic, bread, olive oil and vinegar and process again. Add the tomato juice, sugar, seasoning and a little extra tomato juice or cold water and process. The consistency should be thick but not too stodgy.

3 Pour into a bowl and chill for at least 2 hours but no more than 12 hours, otherwise the textures deteriorate.

4 To prepare the bread cubes to use as a garnish, heat the oil in a frying pan and fry them until golden brown. Drain well.

5 Place each garnish in a separate small dish, or alternately arrange them in rows on a large plate.

6 Just before serving, stir a few ice cubes into the soup and then spoon into serving bowls. Serve with the garnishes.

TOMATO <u>AND</u> BASIL TART

IN FRANCE, PATISSERIES DISPLAY MOUTH-WATERING SAVORY TARTS IN THEIR WINDOWS. THIS IS A VERY SIMPLE YET EXTREMELY TASTY TART MADE WITH RICH PIECRUST PASTRY, FILLED WITH SLICES OF MOZZARELLA CHEESE AND TOMATOES AND TOPPED WITH OLIVE OIL AND BASIL LEAVES.

SERVES FOUR

INGREDIENTS
    5 ounces young mozzarella,
       thinly sliced
    4 large tomatoes, thickly sliced
    about 10 basil leaves
    2 tablespoons olive oil
    2 garlic cloves, thinly sliced
    sea salt and freshly ground
       black pepper
For the pastry
    4 ounces all-purpose flour
    pinch of salt
    2 ounces butter or margarine
    1 egg yolk

1 To prepare the pastry, mix together the flour and salt, then rub in the butter or margarine and egg yolk. Add enough cold water to make a smooth dough and knead lightly on a floured surface. Place in a plastic bag and chill for about 1 hour.

2 Preheat the oven to 375°F. Remove pastry from the fridge and allow about 10 minutes for it to return to room temperature and then roll out into an 8-inch round. Press into the bottom of an 8-inch flan dish or pan. Prick all over with a fork and then bake in the oven for about 10 minutes until firm but not brown. Allow to cool slightly. Reduce the oven temperature to 350°F.

3 Arrange the mozzarella slices over the pastry base. On top, arrange a single layer of the sliced tomatoes, overlapping them slightly. Dip the basil leaves in olive oil and arrange them on the tomatoes.

4 Scatter the garlic on top, drizzle with the remaining olive oil and season with a little salt and a good sprinkling of black pepper. Bake for 40–45 minutes, until the tomatoes are well cooked. Serve hot.

ITALIAN ROAST PEPPERS

SIMPLE AND EFFECTIVE, THIS DISH WILL DELIGHT ANYONE WHO LIKES PEPPERS. IT CAN BE EATEN EITHER AS A STARTER SERVED WITH ITALIAN BREAD, OR AS A LIGHT LUNCH WITH COUSCOUS OR RICE.

SERVES FOUR

INGREDIENTS
  4 small red bell peppers, halved,
    cored and seeded
  2–3 tablespoons capers, chopped
  10–12 black olives, pitted
    and chopped
  2 garlic cloves, finely chopped
  2–3 ounces mozzarella, grated
  1–1½ ounces fresh white bread
    crumbs
  ½ cup white wine
  3 tablespoons olive oil
  1 teaspoon finely chopped fresh mint
  1 teaspoon chopped fresh parsley
  freshly ground black pepper

1 Preheat the oven to 350°F and butter a shallow ovenproof dish. Place the peppers tightly together in the dish and sprinkle over the chopped capers, black olives, garlic, mozzarella and bread crumbs.

2 Pour over the wine and olive oil and then sprinkle with the mint, parsley and freshly ground black pepper.

3 Bake for 30–40 minutes until the topping is crisp and golden brown.

SWEET PEPPER CHOUX WITH ANCHOVIES

THE RATATOUILLE VEGETABLES IN THIS DISH ARE ROASTED INSTEAD OF STEWED, AND HAVE A WONDERFUL AROMATIC FLAVOR. ANY COMBINATION OF RED, GREEN OR YELLOW BELL PEPPERS CAN BE USED. FOR VEGETARIANS, OMIT THE ANCHOVIES.

SERVES SIX

INGREDIENTS

1¼ cups water
4 ounces butter or margarine
5 ounces all-purpose flour
4 eggs
4 ounces Gruyère or Cheddar cheese, finely diced
1 teaspoon Dijon mustard
salt

For the filling

3 bell peppers; red, yellow and green
1 large onion, cut into eighths or sixteenths
3 tomatoes, peeled and quartered
1 zucchini, sliced
6 basil leaves, torn in strips
1 garlic clove, crushed
2 tablespoons olive oil
about 18 black olives, pitted
3 tablespoons red wine
¾ cup passata or puréed canned tomatoes
2-ounce can anchovy fillets, drained
salt and freshly ground black pepper

1 Preheat the oven to 475°F and grease six individual ovenproof dishes. To prepare the filling, halve the peppers, discard the seeds and core and cut into 1-inch chunks.

2 Place the peppers, onion, tomatoes and zucchini in a roasting pan. Add the basil, garlic and olive oil, stirring so the vegetables are well coated. Sprinkle with salt and pepper and then roast for about 25–30 minutes until the vegetables are just beginning to blacken at the edges.

3 Reduce the oven temperature to 400°F. To make the choux pastry, put the water and butter or margarine together in a large saucepan, heat until the butter melts. Remove from the heat and add all the flour immediately. Beat well with a wooden spoon for about 30 seconds until smooth. Allow to cool slightly.

4 Beat in the eggs, one at a time, and then continue beating until the mixture is thick and glossy. Stir in the cheese and mustard, then season with salt and pepper. Spoon the mixture around the sides of the prepared dishes.

5 Spoon the vegetables into a large mixing bowl, together with any juices or scrapings from the bottom of the pan. Add the olives and stir in the wine and passata or puréed tomatoes. (Or, you can stir these into the roasting pan but allow the pan to cool slightly otherwise the liquid will boil and evaporate.)

6 Divide the pepper mixture between the six dishes and arrange the drained anchovy fillets on top. Bake in the oven for about 25–35 minutes until the choux pastry is puffy and golden. Serve hot with a fresh green salad.

EGGS FLAMENCO

A VARIATION OF THE POPULAR BASQUE DISH PIPERADE, THE EGGS ARE COOKED WHOLE INSTEAD OF BEATING THEM BEFORE ADDING TO THE PEPPER MIXTURE. THE RECIPE IS KNOWN AS CHAKCHOUKA IN NORTH AFRICA AND MAKES A GOOD LUNCH OR SUPPER DISH.

SERVES FOUR

INGREDIENTS
2 red bell peppers, seeded
1 green bell pepper, seeded
2 tablespoons olive oil
1 large onion, finely sliced
2 garlic cloves, crushed
5–6 tomatoes, peeled and chopped
½ cup puréed canned tomatoes or
   tomato juice
good pinch of dried basil
4 eggs
8 teaspoons light cream
pinch of cayenne pepper (optional)
salt and freshly ground black pepper

1 Preheat the oven to 350°F. Thinly slice the red and green peppers. Heat the olive oil in a large frying pan. Fry the onion and garlic gently for about 5 minutes, stirring, until softened.

2 Add the peppers to the onions and fry for 10 minutes. Stir in the tomatoes and tomato purée or juice, the basil and seasoning. Cook gently for a further 10 minutes until the peppers are soft.

3 Spoon the mixture into four ovenproof dishes, preferably earthenware. Make a hole in the centre and break an egg into each. Spoon 2 teaspoons cream over the yolk of each egg and sprinkle with a little black pepper or cayenne, as preferred.

4 Bake in the oven for 12–15 minutes until the white of the egg is lightly set. Serve at once with chunks of crusty warm Italian bread.

SPINACH AND PEPPER PIZZA

MAKES TWO 12-inch PIZZAS

INGREDIENTS

- 1 pound fresh spinach
- 4 tablespoons light cream
- 1 ounce Parmesan cheese, grated
- 1 tablespoon olive oil
- 1 large onion, chopped
- 1 garlic clove, crushed
- ½ green bell pepper, seeded and thinly sliced
- ½ red bell pepper, seeded and thinly sliced
- 6–8 fluid ounces passata sauce or puréed tomatoes
- 2 ounces black olives, pitted and chopped
- 1 tablespoon chopped fresh basil
- 6 ounces mozzarella cheese, grated
- 6 ounces Cheddar cheese, grated
- salt

For the dough

- 1 ounce fresh yeast or 1 tablespoon dried yeast and 1 teaspoon sugar
- 12 ounces unbleached all-purpose flour
- 2 tablespoons olive oil
- 1 teaspoon salt
- about ⅞ cup warm water

1 To make the dough, cream together the fresh yeast and ⅔ cup of the water and set aside until frothy. If using dried yeast, stir the sugar into ⅔ cup water, sprinkle over the yeast and leave until frothy.

2 Place the flour and salt in a large bowl, make a well in the center and pour in the olive oil and yeast mixture. Add the remaining water, mix to make a stiff but pliable dough. Knead on a lightly floured surface for about 10 minutes until smooth and elastic.

3 Shape the dough into a ball and place in a lightly oiled bowl, cover with plastic wrap and leave in a warm place for about 1 hour until it has doubled in size.

4 To prepare the topping, cook the spinach over moderate heat for 4–5 minutes until the leaves have wilted. Strain and press out the excess liquid. Place in a bowl and mix with the cream, Parmesan cheese and salt to taste.

5 Heat the oil in a frying pan and fry the onion and garlic over moderate heat for 3–4 minutes until the onion has slightly softened. Add the peppers and continue cooking until the onion is lightly golden, stirring regularly.

6 Preheat the oven to 425°F. Knead the dough briefly on a lightly floured surface. Divide the dough and roll out into two 12-inch rounds.

7 Spread each base with the passata sauce or puréed tomatoes. Add the onions and peppers and then spread over the spinach mixture. Scatter the olives and basil leaves and sprinkle with the mozzarella and Cheddar cheeses.

8 Bake in the oven for 15–20 minutes, or until the crust is lightly browned and the top is beginning to turn golden. Allow to cool slightly before serving.

ENCHILADAS WITH HOT CHILI SAUCE

IN MEXICO, CHILIES APPEAR IN ALMOST EVERY SAVORY DISH, EITHER IN THE FORM OF CHILI POWDER OR CHOPPED, SLICED OR WHOLE. BY MEXICAN STANDARDS, THIS IS A LOW-HEAT VERSION OF THE POPULAR CHICKEN ENCHILADAS. IF YOU LIKE YOUR FOOD HOT, ADD EXTRA CHILIES TO THE SAUCE.

SERVES FOUR

INGREDIENTS
8 wheat tortillas
6 ounces Cheddar cheese, grated
1 onion, finely chopped
12 ounces cooked chicken, cut into
   small chunks
1¼ cups sour cream
1 avocado, sliced and tossed in lemon
   juice, to garnish
For the salsa picante
1–2 green chilies
1 tablespoon vegetable oil
1 onion, chopped
1 garlic clove, crushed
14 ounce-can chopped tomatoes
2 tablespoons tomato paste
salt and freshly ground black pepper

3 Preheat the oven to 350°F and butter a shallow ovenproof dish. Take one tortilla and sprinkle with a good pinch of cheese and chopped onion, about 1½ ounces of chicken and 1 tablespoon of salsa picante. Pour over 1 tablespoon of sour cream, roll up and place, seam side down, in the dish. Make seven more enchiladas.

4 Pour the remaining salsa over the top and sprinkle with the remaining cheese and onion. Bake in the oven for about 25–30 minutes until the top is golden. Serve with the remaining sour cream either poured over, or in a separate jug, and garnish with the sliced avocado.

1 To make the salsa picante, cut the chilies in half lengthwise and carefully remove the cores and seeds. Slice the chilies very finely. Heat the oil in a frying pan and fry the onion and garlic for about 3–4 minutes until softened. Add the tomatoes, tomato paste and chilies. Simmer gently, uncovered, for about 12–15 minutes, stirring frequently.

2 Pour the sauce into a food processor or blender, and process until smooth. Return to the heat and cook very gently, uncovered, for a further 15 minutes. Season to taste then set aside.

HOT SOUR CHICK-PEAS

THIS DISH, KHATTE CHOLE, IS EATEN AS A SNACK ALL OVER INDIA, SOLD BY ITINERANT STREET VENDORS. THE HEAT OF THE CHILIES IS DAMPENED PARTLY BY THE CILANTRO, WHILE THE LEMON JUICE ADDS A WONDERFUL SOURNESS.

SERVES FOUR

INGREDIENTS

12 ounces chick-peas, soaked
   overnight
4 tablespoons vegetable oil
2 medium onions, very finely chopped
8 ounces tomatoes, peeled and finely
   chopped
1 tablespoon ground coriander
1 tablespoon ground cumin
1 teaspoon ground fenugreek
1 teaspoon ground cinnamon
1–2 hot green chilies, seeded
   and finely sliced
about 1-inch piece fresh ginger,
   grated
4 tablespoons lemon juice
1 tablespoon chopped fresh cilantro
salt

1 Drain the chick-peas and place them in a large saucepan, cover with water and bring to a boil. Cover and simmer for 1–1¼ hours until tender, making sure the chick-peas do not boil dry. Drain, reserving the cooking liquid.

2 Heat the oil in a large flameproof casserole. Reserve about 2 tablespoons of the chopped onions and fry the remainder in the casserole over moderate heat for 4–5 minutes, stirring frequently, until tinged with brown.

3 Add the tomatoes and continue cooking over moderately low heat for 5–6 minutes until soft. Stir frequently, mashing the tomatoes to a pulp.

4 Stir in the coriander, cumin, fenugreek and cinnamon. Cook for 30 seconds and then add the chick-peas and 12 fluid ounces of the reserved cooking liquid. Season with salt, cover and simmer very gently for about 15–20 minutes, stirring occasionally and adding more cooking liquid if the mixture becomes too dry.

5 Meanwhile, mix the reserved onion with the chili, ginger and lemon juice.

6 Just before serving, stir the onion and chili mixture and the cilantro into the chick-peas, and adjust the seasoning.

GUACAMOLE

THIS IS QUITE A FIERY VERSION OF A POPULAR MEXICAN DISH, ALTHOUGH PROBABLY NOWHERE NEAR AS HOT AS YOU WOULD BE SERVED IN MEXICO, WHERE IT SEEMS HEAT KNOWS NO BOUNDS!

SERVES FOUR

INGREDIENTS

2 ripe avocados, peeled and pitted
2 tomatoes, peeled, seeded and finely
chopped
6 scallions, finely chopped
1–2 chilies, seeded and finely
chopped
2 tablespoons fresh lime or lemon
juice
1 tablespoon chopped fresh cilantro
salt and freshly ground black pepper
coriander sprig, to garnish

1 Put the avocado halves into a bowl and mash roughly with a large fork.

2 Add the remaining ingredients. Mix well and season according to taste. Serve garnished with fresh cilantro.

PLANTAIN APPETIZER

PLANTAINS ARE A TYPE OF COOKING BANANA WITH A LOWER SUGAR CONTENT THAN DESSERT BANANAS. THEY ARE UNSUITABLE FOR EATING RAW AND CAN BE USED IN A WIDE RANGE OF DISHES. THIS DELICIOUS ASSORTMENT OF SWEET AND SAVORY PLANTAINS IS A POPULAR DISH IN AFRICA.

SERVES FOUR

INGREDIENTS
2 green plantains
3 tablespoons vegetable oil
1 small onion, very thinly sliced
1 yellow plantain
½ garlic clove, crushed
salt and cayenne pepper
vegetable oil, for frying

1 Peel one of the green plantains and cut into wafer-thin rounds, preferably using a swivel-headed potato peeler.

2 Heat about 1 tablespoon of the oil in a large frying pan and fry the plantain slices for 2–3 minutes until golden, turning occasionally. Transfer to a plate lined with paper towels and keep warm.

3 Coarsely grate the other green plantain and mix with the onion.

4 Heat 1 tablespoon of the remaining oil in the pan and fry the plantain and onion mixture for 2–3 minutes until golden, turning occasionally. Transfer to the plate with the plantain slices.

5 Peel the yellow plantain, cut into small chunks. Sprinkle with cayenne pepper. Heat the remaining oil and fry the yellow plantain and garlic for 4–5 minutes until brown. Drain and sprinkle with salt.

SALAD VEGETABLE RECIPES

CHICKEN LIVERS AND GREEN SALAD

SERVES FOUR

INGREDIENTS
a selection of fresh salad leaves
4 scallions, finely sliced
1 tablespoon roughly chopped
Italian parsley
4 ounces unsmoked lean bacon,
chopped
1 pound chicken livers
seasoned all-purpose flour, for dusting
1 tablespoon sunflower oil
1 ounce butter or margarine
salt and freshly ground black pepper
sprigs of fresh parsley, to garnish
For the dressing
⅓ cup sunflower oil
2–3 tablespoons lemon juice
1 teaspoon French mustard
1 small garlic clove, crushed
salt and freshly ground black pepper

1 To make the dressing, place the oil, lemon juice, mustard, garlic and seasoning in a screw-top jar and shake vigorously to mix.

2 Place the salad leaves in a large bowl with the scallions and parsley. Pour over the dressing, toss briefly and then arrange on four individual serving plates.

3 Dry-fry the bacon in a frying pan until golden brown. Transfer to a plate using a slotted spoon and keep warm.

4 Trim the chicken livers, pat dry on paper towels and then dust them thoroughly with the seasoned flour.

5 Heat the oil and butter in a frying pan and fry the livers over a fairly high heat for about 8 minutes, turning occasionally until cooked to your preference, either cooked through or slightly pink inside.

6 Arrange the chicken livers on the salad leaves and scatter the crisp bacon pieces over the top.

CAESAR SALAD

A CLASSIC SALAD WITH AN EGG YOLK DRESSING, THIS MUST BE MADE USING ROMAINE LETTUCE. THE ORIGINS OF ITS NAME ARE A MYSTERY. SOME PEOPLE SAY IT WAS INVENTED BY AN ITALIAN, CAESAR CARDINI, IN MEXICO, AND OTHERS THAT IT COMES FROM CALIFORNIA.

SERVES FOUR

INGREDIENTS
4–5 tablespoons olive oil
1 garlic clove, crushed
3 ounces stale white bread,
cut into cubes
1 romaine lettuce
8 anchovies, chopped
1½ ounces shavings of Parmesan
cheese
For the dressing
2 egg yolks
½ teaspoon French mustard
¼ cup olive oil
¼ cup sunflower oil
1 tablespoon white wine vinegar
a pinch of salt

1 Place the garlic in the oil and set aside for about 30 minutes for the garlic flavor to infuse into the oil.

2 To make the dressing, place the egg yolks, French mustard, olive oil, sunflower oil, vinegar and salt in a screw-top jar and shake well.

3 To make the croûtons, strain the garlic oil into a frying pan and discard the garlic. When hot, fry the bread until golden and then drain on paper towels.

4 Arrange the lettuce leaves in a salad bowl. Pour over the dressing and gently fold in the anchovies and croûtons. Scatter with Parmesan shavings.

RADICCHIO PIZZA

THIS UNUSUAL PIZZA TOPPING CONSISTS OF CHOPPED RADICCHIO WITH LEEKS, TOMATOES AND PARMESAN AND MOZZARELLA CHEESES. THE BASE IS A SCONE DOUGH, MAKING THIS A QUICK AND EASY SUPPER DISH TO PREPARE. SERVE WITH A CRISP GREEN SALAD.

SERVES TWO

INGREDIENTS
14-ounce can chopped tomatoes
2 garlic cloves, crushed
pinch of dried basil
1½ tablespoons olive oil, plus extra
   for dipping
2 leeks, sliced
3½ ounces radicchio, roughly chopped
¾ ounces Parmesan cheese, grated
4 ounces mozzarella cheese, sliced
10–12 black olives, pitted
basil leaves, to garnish
salt and freshly ground black pepper
For the dough
8 ounces self-rising flour
½ teaspoon salt
2 ounces butter or margarine
about ½ cup milk

1 Preheat the oven to 425°F and grease a baking sheet. Mix the flour and salt in a bowl, rub in the butter or margarine and gradually stir in the milk and water and mix to a soft dough.

4 Heat the olive oil in a large frying pan and fry the leeks and remaining garlic for 4–5 minutes until slightly softened. Add the radicchio and cook, stirring continuously for a few minutes, and then cover and simmer gently for about 5–10 minutes. Stir in the Parmesan cheese and season with salt and pepper.

5 Cover the dough base with the tomato mixture and then spoon the leek and radicchio mixture on top. Arrange the mozzarella slices on top and scatter over the black olives. Dip a few basil leaves in olive oil, arrange on top and then bake the pizza for 15–20 minutes until the scone base and top are golden brown.

2 Roll the dough out on a lightly floured surface to make a 10–11-inch round. Place on the baking sheet.

3 Purée the tomatoes and then pour into a small saucepan. Stir in one of the crushed garlic cloves, together with the dried basil and seasoning, and simmer over moderate heat until the mixture is thick and reduced by about half.

WARM DUCK SALAD WITH ORANGE

THE DISTINCT, SHARP FLAVOR OF RADICCHIO, FRISÉE AND FRESH ORANGES COMPLEMENTS THE RICH TASTE OF THE DUCK TO MAKE THIS A SUPERB DISH. IT IS GOOD SERVED WITH STEAMED NEW POTATOES FOR AN ELEGANT MAIN COURSE.

SERVES FOUR

INGREDIENTS
  2 boneless duck breasts
  salt
  2 oranges
  frisée, radicchio and lamb's lettuce
  2 tablespoons medium dry sherry
  2–3 teaspoons dark soy sauce

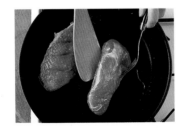

1 Rub the skin of the duck breasts with salt and then slash the skin several times with a sharp knife.

2 Heat a heavy cast-iron frying pan and fry the duck breasts, skin side down at first, for 20–25 minutes, turning once, until the skin is well browned and the flesh is cooked to your preference. Transfer to a plate to cool slightly and pour off the excess fat from the pan.

3 Peel the oranges. Separate the oranges into segments and use a knife to remove all the pith, catching the juice in a small bowl. Arrange the lettuces in a shallow serving bowl.

4 Heat the duck juices in the pan and stir in 3 tablespoons of the reserved orange juice. Bring to a boil, add the sherry and then just enough soy sauce to give the sauce a piquant, spicy flavor.

5 Cut the duck into thick slices and arrange over the salad. Pour over the warm dressing and serve.

BAKED CHICORY WITH PROSCIUTTO

ALTHOUGH CHICORY IS SOMETIMES TOO HARSHLY FLAVORED FOR SOME PEOPLE'S TASTES, SIMMERING IT BEFORE BRAISING ELIMINATES ANY BITTERNESS SO THAT THE FLAVOR IS PLEASANTLY MILD.

SERVES FOUR

INGREDIENTS
   4 heads of chicory
   1 ounce butter
   1 cup vegetable or chicken stock
   4 slices prosciutto
   3 ounces mascarpone cheese
   2 ounces Emmenthal or Cheddar
     cheese, sliced
   salt and freshly ground black pepper

4 Remove the chicory using a slotted spoon. Lay out the prosciutto slices and place one piece of chicory on each of the slices. Roll up and place, side by side, in a single layer in the prepared dish.

5 Simmer the stock until it is reduced by about half and then remove from the heat. Stir in the mascarpone cheese and pour the sauce over the chicory. Lay the slices of Emmenthal or Cheddar cheese over the top and bake in the oven for about 15 minutes until the top is golden and the sauce is bubbling.

1 Preheat the oven to 350°F. Grease an ovenproof dish. Trim the chicory and remove the central core.

2 Melt the butter in a large saucepan and gently sauté the chicory over a moderate heat for 4–5 minutes, turning occasionally, until the outer leaves begin to turn transparent.

3 Add the stock and a little seasoning, bring to a boil and then cover and simmer gently for 5–6 minutes until the chicory is almost tender.

A R U G U L A <u>A N D</u> G R I L L E D G O A T C H E E S E S A L A D

GOAT CHEESE CAN BE BOUGHT IN MANY DIFFERENT FORMS. FOR THIS RECIPE, LOOK OUT FOR CYLINDER-SHAPED GOAT CHEESE FROM A DELICATESSEN OR FOR SMALL ROLLS THAT CAN BE CUT INTO PIECES WEIGHING ABOUT 2 OUNCES.

SERVES FOUR

INGREDIENTS
  about 1 tablespoon olive oil
  about 1 tablespoon vegetable oil
  4 slices Italian bread
  3 tablespoons walnut oil
  1 tablespoon lemon juice
  8-ounce cylinder-shape goat cheese
  generous handful of arugula leaves
  about 4 ounces frisée
For the sauce
  3 tablespoons apricot jam
  4 tablespoons white wine
  2 teaspoons Dijon mustard

1 Heat the olive and vegetable oils in a frying pan and fry the slices of Italian bread on one side only, until lightly golden brown. Transfer to a plate lined with paper towels.

4 Preheat the broiler a few minutes before serving the salad. Cut the goat cheese into 2-ounce rounds and place each piece on a croûton, untoasted side up. Place under the broiler and cook for 3–4 minutes until the cheese melts.

5 Toss the arugula and frisée in the walnut oil dressing and arrange attractively on four individual serving plates. When the croûtons are ready, arrange on each plate and pour over a little of the apricot sauce.

2 To make the sauce, heat the jam in a small saucepan until warm but not boiling. Push through a strainer, into a clean pan, to remove the pieces of fruit, and then stir in the white wine and mustard. Heat gently and then keep warm until ready to serve.

3 Blend the walnut oil and lemon juice and season with a little salt and pepper.

STIR-FRIED CHINESE LEAVES <u>WITH</u> SCALLOPS

A SPEEDY STIR-FRY MADE USING SALAD VEGETABLES AND SCALLOPS. BOTH THE CHINESE RADISH AND CHINESE LEAVES HAVE A PLEASANT CRUNCHY "BITE," AND THE CHINESE LEAVES CARRY THE SAUCE.

SERVES FOUR

INGREDIENTS
10 prepared scallops
4–5 tablespoons vegetable oil
3 garlic cloves, finely chopped
½-inch piece fresh ginger, finely sliced
4–5 scallions, cut lengthwise into
   1-inch pieces
2 tablespoons medium dry sherry
½ Chinese radish (daikon), cut into
   ½-inch slices
1 Chinese cabbage, chopped
   lengthwise into thin strips
For the marinade
1 teaspoon cornstarch
1 egg white, lightly beaten
pinch of white pepper
For the sauce
1 teaspoon cornstarch
3 tablespoons oyster sauce

6 Heat another 2 tablespoons of oil in the wok, add the remaining garlic, ginger and scallions and stir-fry for 1 minute. Add the corals, stir-fry briefly and transfer to a dish.

1 Rinse the scallops and separate the corals from the white meat. Cut each scallop into 2–3 pieces and slice the corals. Place them on two dishes.

2 For the marinade, blend together the cornstarch, egg white and white pepper. Pour half over the scallops and the rest over the corals. Leave for 10 minutes

3 To make the sauce, blend the cornstarch with 4 tablespoons of water and the oyster sauce and set aside.

4 Heat about 2 tablespoons of the oil in a wok, add half of the garlic and let it sizzle, and then add half the ginger and half of the scallions. Stir-fry for about 30 seconds and then stir in the scallops (not the corals).

5 Stir-fry for ½–1 minute until the scallops start to become opaque and then reduce the heat and add 1 tablespoon of the sherry. Cook briefly and then spoon the scallops and the cooking liquid into a bowl and set aside.

7 Heat the remaining oil and add the daikon. Stir-fry for about 30 seconds and then stir in the cabbage. Stir-fry for about 30 seconds and then add the oyster sauce mixture and about 4 tablespoons of water. Allow the cabbage to simmer briefly and then stir in the scallops and corals, together with all their liquid and cook briefly to heat through.

RADISH, MANGO AND APPLE SALAD

RADISH IS AVAILABLE ALL YEAR THROUGH AND THIS SALAD CAN BE SERVED ANY TIME OF YEAR, WITH ITS CLEAN, CRISP TASTES AND MELLOW FLAVORS. SERVE WITH SMOKED FISH, SUCH AS ROLLS OF SMOKED SALMON OR WITH CONTINENTAL HAM OR SALAMI.

SERVES FOUR

INGREDIENTS
   10–15 radishes
   1 eating apple, peeled cored and
     thinly sliced
   2 celery stalks, thinly sliced
   1 small ripe mango, peeled and cut
     into small chunks
For the dressing
   ½ cup sour cream
   2 teaspoons creamed horseradish
   1 tablespoon chopped fresh dill
   salt and fresh ground black pepper
   sprig of dill, to garnish

3 Cut through the mango lengthwise either side of the pit. Make even criss-cross cuts through each side section. Take each one and bend it back to separate the cubes. Remove the mango cubes with a small knife and add to the bowl. Pour the dressing over the vegetables and fruit and stir gently so that all the ingredients are coated in the dressing. When ready to serve, spoon the salad into an attractive salad bowl and garnish with a sprig of dill.

1 To prepare the dressing, blend together the sour cream, horseradish and dill in a small jug or bowl and season with a little salt and pepper.

2 Remove the ends of the radishes and then slice them thinly. Add to a bowl together with the thinly sliced apple and celery.

WATERCRESS SOUP

INGREDIENTS
1 tablespoon sunflower oil
½ ounce butter
1 medium onion, finely chopped
1 medium potato, diced
about 6 ounces watercress
1⅔ cups chicken or vegetable stock
1⅔ cups milk
lemon juice
salt and freshly ground black pepper
sour cream, to serve (optional)

1 Heat the oil and butter in a large saucepan and fry the onion over low heat until soft but not browned. Add the potato, fry gently for 2–3 minutes and then cover and sweat for 5 minutes over low heat, stirring occasionally.

2 Strip the watercress leaves from the stalks and roughly chop the stalks.

3 Add the stock and milk to the pan, stir in the chopped stalks and season with salt and pepper. Bring to a boil and then simmer gently, partially covered, for 10–12 minutes until the potatoes are tender. Add all but a few of the watercress leaves and simmer for 2 minutes.

4 Process the soup in a food processor or blender, and then pour into a clean saucepan and heat gently with the reserved watercress leaves. Taste when hot and add a little lemon juice and adjust the seasoning.

5 Pour the soup into warmed soup dishes and swirl in a little sour cream, if using, just before serving.

COOK'S TIP
Provided you leave out the cream, this is a low calorie but nutritious soup, which, served with crusty bread, makes a satisfying meal.

WATERCRESS AND TWO-FISH TERRINE

THIS IS A PRETTY, DELICATE DISH, IDEAL FOR A SUMMER BUFFET PARTY OR PICNIC. SERVE WITH LEMON MAYONNAISE OR SOUR CREAM, AND A WATERCRESS AND GREEN SALAD.

INGREDIENTS
12-ounce monkfish, filleted
6-ounce sole, filleted
1 egg and 1 egg white
3–4 tablespoons lemon juice
1½–2 ounces fresh white bread
   crumbs
1¼ cups heavy or whipping cream
3 ounces smoked salmon
6 ounces watercress, roughly chopped
salt and freshly ground black pepper

1 Preheat the oven to 350°F and line a 6¼-cup loaf pan with wax paper.

2 Cut the fish into rough chunks, discarding the skin and bones. Put the fish into a food processor.

3 Process briefly and add the egg and egg white, lemon juice, bread crumbs and cream. Process to a paste. Put the mixture into a bowl. Take 5 tablespoons of the mixture and process with the smoked salmon. Transfer to a separate bowl. Take 5 tablespoons of the white fish mixture and process with the watercress.

4 Spoon half of the white fish mixture into the base of the prepared loaf pan and smooth the surface with a metal spatula.

5 Spread over the watercress mixture, then the smoked salmon mixture and finally spread over the remaining white fish mixture and smooth the top.

6 Lay a piece of buttered non-stick baking paper on top of the mixture and then cover with foil. Place the loaf tin in a roasting pan, half-filled with boiling water and cook in the oven for 1¼–1½ hours. Toward the end of the cooking time the terrine will begin to rise, which indicates that it is ready.

7 Allow to cool in the pan and then turn onto a serving plate and peel away the wax paper. Chill for 1–2 hours.

MUSHROOM RECIPES

CREAM OF MUSHROOM SOUP

A GOOD MUSHROOM SOUP MAKES THE MOST OF THE SUBTLE AND SOMETIMES RATHER ELUSIVE FLAVOR OF MUSHROOMS. WHITE MUSHROOMS ARE USED HERE FOR THEIR PALE COLOR; CREMINI OR, BETTER STILL, FIELD MUSHROOMS GIVE A FULLER FLAVOR BUT TURN THE SOUP BROWN.

SERVES FOUR

INGREDIENTS
10 ounces white mushrooms
1 tablespoon sunflower oil
1½ ounces butter
1 small onion, finely chopped
1 tablespoon all-purpose flour
1¾ cups vegetable stock
1¾ cups milk
pinch of dried basil
2–3 tablespoons light cream
  (optional)
fresh basil leaves, to garnish
salt and freshly ground black pepper

1 Separate the mushroom caps from the stalks. Finely slice the caps and finely chop the stalks.

2 Heat the oil and half the butter in a heavy-based saucepan and add the onion, mushroom stalks and ½–¾ of the sliced mushroom caps. Fry for about 1–2 minutes, stirring frequently, and then cover and sweat over low heat for 6–7 minutes, stirring occasionally.

3 Stir in the flour and cook for about 1 minute. Gradually add the stock and milk, to make a smooth thin sauce. Add the basil, and season with salt and pepper. Bring to a boil and then simmer, partly covered, for 15 minutes.

4 Cool slightly and then pour the soup into a food processor or blender and process until smooth. Melt the rest of the butter in a frying pan and fry the remaining mushrooms gently for 3–4 minutes until they are just tender.

5 Pour the soup into a clean saucepan and stir in the sliced mushrooms. Heat until very hot and adjust the seasoning. Add a little cream, if using. Serve sprinkled with fresh basil leaves.

SOUFFLÉ OMELET WITH MUSHROOM SAUCE

A SOUFFLÉ OMELET INVOLVES A LITTLE MORE PREPARATION THAN AN ORDINARY OMELET BUT THE RESULT IS LIGHT AND SPRINGY TO TOUCH. THIS DISH MAKES A DELICIOUS LIGHT LUNCH.

SERVES ONE

INGREDIENTS
2 eggs, separated
½ ounce butter
sprig of parsley or cilantro
For the mushroom sauce
½ ounce butter
3 ounces white mushrooms,
  thinly sliced
1 tablespoon all-purpose flour
½ cup milk
1 teaspoon chopped fresh parsley
  (optional)
salt and freshly ground black pepper

1 To make the mushroom sauce, melt the butter in a saucepan or frying pan and fry the sliced mushrooms for 4–5 minutes until tender.

2 Stir in the flour and then gradually add the milk, stirring all the time, to make a smooth sauce. Add the parsley, if using, and season with salt and pepper. Keep warm to one side.

3 Beat the egg yolks with 1 tablespoon of water and season with a little salt and pepper. Whisk the egg whites until stiff and then fold into the egg yolks using a metal spoon. Preheat the broiler.

4 Melt the butter in a large frying pan and pour the egg mixture into the pan. Cook over a gentle heat for 2–4 minutes. Place the frying pan under the broiler and cook for a further 3–4 minutes until the top is golden brown.

5 Slide the omelet onto a warmed serving plate, pour over the mushroom sauce and fold the omelet in half. Serve garnished with a sprig of parsley or fresh cilantro leaves.

STUFFED MUSHROOMS

THIS IS A CLASSIC MUSHROOM DISH, STRONGLY FLAVORED WITH GARLIC. IF YOU PREFER A MORE SUBTLE GARLIC FLAVOR, BRIEFLY FRY THE GARLIC FIRST.

SERVES FOUR

INGREDIENTS
 1 pound large flat mushrooms
 butter, for greasing
 3 tablespoons finely chopped fresh
   parsley
 1½–2 ounces fresh white bread crumbs
 2 garlic cloves, minced or very
   finely chopped
 about 5 tablespoons olive oil
 salt and freshly ground black pepper
 sprig Italian parsley, to garnish

1 Preheat the oven to 350°F. Cut off the mushroom stalks and reserve on one side.

2 Arrange the mushroom caps in a buttered shallow dish, gill sides upward.

3 Finely chop the mushroom stalks and mix with the parsley, bread crumbs, garlic, 2 tablespoons of the olive oil and seasoning to taste, and then pile a little of the mixture into each mushroom.

4 Add the remaining oil to the dish and cover the mushrooms with buttered wax paper. Bake for about 15–20 minutes, removing the paper for the last 5 minutes to brown the tops. Garnish with a sprig of Italian parsley.

COOK'S TIP
The cooking time for the mushrooms depends on their size and thickness. If they are fairly thin, cook for slightly less time. They should be tender but not too soft when cooked. If preferred, the garlic may be cooked before adding to the bread crumb mixture. Heat about 1 tablespoon of oil in a frying pan and fry the garlic very briefly and then stir into the breadcrumb mixture.

BOEUF EN CROÛTE

A DUXELLES FILLING OF FINELY CHOPPED MUSHROOMS, SHALLOTS, GARLIC AND PARSLEY IS THE CLASSIC FILLING FOR BOEUF EN CROÛTE. THESE INDIVIDUAL VERSIONS ARE GOOD SERVED WITH BOILED OR STEAMED NEW POTATOES AND A GREEN VEGETABLE.

SERVES FOUR

INGREDIENTS
    4 fillet steaks, about 4–5 ounces each
    a little Dijon mustard
    1 ounce butter
    10 ounces puff pastry
    1 ounce fresh white bread crumbs
    beaten egg, for glazing
    salt and freshly ground black pepper
    sprigs of parsley or chervil, to garnish
For the duxelles filling
    4 shallots, finely chopped
    1–2 garlic cloves, crushed
    8–10 ounces flat mushrooms, finely
       chopped
    1 tablespoon finely chopped parsley

1 Preheat the oven to 425°F. Rub a little mustard over each of the steaks and season with pepper. Melt the butter in a heavy-based frying pan and fry the steaks for about 1–2 minutes each side, so that they are browned on the outside but still red in the center. Transfer to a plate to cool.

4 Cut the pastry into four and roll out each piece very thinly to a 7-inch square. Cut the corners from each square and spread a spoonful of the mushroom mixture in the center. Top with a steak and sprinkle with a spoonful of fresh bread crumbs.

5 Bring the sides of the pastry up to the center and seal with water. Place seam side down on a baking sheet.

6 Decorate with pastry trimmings and brush each with beaten egg. Bake for about 20 minutes, until golden brown.

2 To make the filling, add the shallots and garlic to the pan and fry briefly. Stir in the finely chopped mushrooms.

3 Fry over fairly high heat for about 3–4 minutes, stirring, until the juices run. Lower the heat and cook gently for 4–5 minutes until the mixture is dry. Add the parsley and seasoning and cool.

GNOCCHI <u>WITH</u> OYSTER MUSHROOMS

GNOCCHI MAKES AN UNUSUAL AND PLEASANT ALTERNATIVE TO PASTA. IT IS BLAND ON ITS OWN BUT BRINGS OUT THE OYSTER MUSHROOM FLAVOR IN THIS DISH AND ITS SOFT TEXTURE CONTRASTS WITH THE FIRMNESS OF THE MUSHROOMS.

SERVES FOUR (as a snack)

INGREDIENTS
8 ounces oyster mushrooms
1 tablespoon olive oil
1 ounce butter, plus extra to serve
1 medium onion, finely chopped
1 garlic clove, crushed
4 plum tomatoes, peeled and chopped
3–4 tablespoons vegetable stock or water
11-ounce packet plain potato gnocchi
2 teaspoons chopped fresh parsley
Parmesan cheese, cut in shavings, to serve

1 Trim the mushrooms and cut into halves or quarters, if they are large. Heat the oil in a large frying pan and fry the onion and garlic over low heat for about 4–5 minutes until softened but not browned, stirring frequently.

2 Increase the heat, add the mushrooms to the pan and sauté for about 3–4 minutes, stirring constantly.

3 Stir in the chopped tomatoes, stock or water and seasoning and then cover and simmer for about 8 minutes until the tomatoes are very soft and reduced to a pulp. Stir occasionally.

4 Cook the gnocchi in a large pan of salted boiling water for 2–3 minutes (or according to the instructions on the packet) and then drain well. Place in a large warmed serving bowl and stir in the butter and chopped parsley.

5 Pour the mushroom and tomato mixture over the top, stir briefly and sprinkle with the Parmesan cheese.

COOK'S TIP
If the mushrooms are very large, the stalks are likely to be tough, therefore they should be discarded. Always tear rather than cut oyster mushrooms.

SEAFOOD <u>AND</u> OYSTER MUSHROOM STARTER

THIS DISH IS A REMARKABLY QUICK TO PREPARE. IT CAN BE MADE INTO A MORE SUBSTANTIAL DISH BY STIRRING 10–12 OUNCES OF COOKED PASTA SHELLS INTO THE SAUCE AT THE END.

SERVES FOUR

INGREDIENTS
1 tablespoon olive oil
½ ounce butter
1 garlic clove, crushed
6 ounces oyster mushrooms, halved or quartered
4–6 ounces peeled shrimp
4 ounces cooked mussels, optional
juice of ½ lemon
1 tablespoon medium dry sherry
⅔ cup heavy cream
salt and freshly ground black pepper

1 Heat the oil and butter in a frying pan and sauté the garlic for a few minutes, then add the mushrooms. Cook over moderate heat for 4–5 minutes until soft, stirring from time to time.

2 Reduce the heat and stir in the shrimp, mussels and lemon juice. Cook for 1 minute, stirring continuously. Stir in the sherry and cook for 1 minute.

3 Add the cream and cook gently until heated through but not boiling. Taste and adjust the seasoning and then spoon into warmed serving dishes. Serve immediately with chunks of Italian bread.

TAGLIATELLE FUNGI

THE MUSHROOM SAUCE IS QUICK TO MAKE AND THE PASTA COOKS VERY QUICKLY; BOTH NEED TO BE COOKED AS NEAR TO SERVING AS POSSIBLE SO CAREFUL COORDINATION IS REQUIRED. PUT THE PASTA IN TO COOK WHEN THE MASCARPONE CHEESE IS ADDED TO THE SAUCE.

SERVES FOUR (as a snack or starter)

INGREDIENTS
    about 2 ounces butter
    8–12 ounces chanterelles or other
        wild mushrooms
    1 tablespoon all-purpose flour
    ⅔ cup milk
    6 tablespoons crème fraiche or sour
        cream
    1 tablespoon chopped fresh parsley
    10 ounces fresh tagliatelle
    olive oil
    salt and freshly ground black pepper

3 Add the crème fraiche or sour cream, parsley, mushrooms and seasoning and stir well. Cook gently to heat through and then keep warm while cooking the pasta.

4 Cook the pasta in a large saucepan of boiling water for 4–5 minutes (or according to the instructions on the packet). Drain well, toss in a little olive oil and then turn onto a warmed serving plate. Pour the mushroom sauce over and serve immediately.

COOK'S TIP
Chanterelles are a little tricky to wash, as they are so delicate. However, since these are woodland mushrooms, it's important to clean them thoroughly. Hold each one by the stalk and let cold water run under the gills to dislodge hidden dirt. Shake gently to dry.

1 Melt 1½ ounces of the butter in a frying pan and fry the mushrooms for about 2–3 minutes over low heat until the juices begin to run, then increase the heat and cook until the liquid has almost evaporated. Transfer the mushrooms to a bowl using a slotted spoon.

2 Stir in the flour, adding a little more butter if necessary, and cook for about 1 minute, and then gradually stir in the milk to make a smooth sauce.

SHIITAKE FRIED RICE

SHIITAKE MUSHROOMS HAVE A STRONG MEATY MUSHROOMY AROMA AND FLAVOR. THIS IS A VERY EASY RECIPE TO MAKE, AND ALTHOUGH IT IS A SIDE DISH IT CAN ALMOST BE A MEAL IN ITSELF.

SERVES FOUR

INGREDIENTS
2 eggs
3 tablespoons vegetable oil
12 ounces shiitake mushrooms
8 scallions, sliced diagonally
1 garlic clove, crushed
½ green bell pepper, chopped
1 ounce butter
12 ounces cooked long grain rice
1 tablespoon medium dry sherry
2 tablespoons dark soy sauce
1 tablespoon chopped fresh cilantro
salt

1 Beat the eggs with 1 tablespoon of cold water and season with a little salt.

2 Heat 1 tablespoon of the oil in a wok or large frying pan, pour in the eggs and cook to make a large omelet. Lift the sides of the omelet and tilt the wok so that the uncooked egg can run underneath and be cooked. Roll up the omelet and slice thinly.

3 Remove and discard the mushroom stalks if tough and slice the caps thinly, halving them if they are large.

4 Heat 1 tablespoon of the remaining oil in the wok and stir-fry the scallions and garlic for 3–4 minutes until softened but not brown. Transfer them to a plate using a slotted spoon.

5 Add the pepper, stir-fry for about 2–3 minutes, then add the butter and the remaining 1 tablespoon of oil. As the butter begins to sizzle, add the mushrooms and stir-fry over moderate heat for 3–4 minutes until soft.

6 Loosen the rice grains as much as possible. Pour the sherry over the mushrooms and then stir in the rice.

7 Heat the rice over moderate heat, stirring all the time to prevent the rice sticking. If the rice seems very dry, add a little more oil. Stir in the reserved onions and omelet slices, the soy sauce and cilantro. Cook for a few minutes until heated through and serve.

COOK'S TIP
Unlike risotto, for which rice is cooked along with the other ingredients, Chinese fried rice is always made using cooked rice. If you use 6–8 ounces uncooked long grain, you will get about 16–20 ounces of cooked rice, enough for four people.

WILD MUSHROOMS IN BRIOCHE

SERVES FOUR

INGREDIENTS
    4 small brioches
    olive oil, for glazing
    4 teaspoons lemon juice
    sprigs of parsley, to garnish
For the mushroom filling
    1 ounce butter
    2 shallots
    1 garlic clove, crushed
    6–8 ounces assorted wild mushrooms,
      halved if large
    3 tablespoons white wine
    3 tablespoons double cream
    1 teaspoon chopped fresh basil
    1 teaspoon chopped fresh parsley
    salt and freshly ground black pepper

1 Preheat the oven to 350°F. Using a serrated or grapefruit knife, cut a circle out of the top of the brioche and reserve. Scoop out the bread inside to make a small cavity.

2 Place the brioches and the tops on a baking sheet and brush inside and out with olive oil. Bake for 7–10 minutes until golden and crisp. Squeeze 1 teaspoon of lemon juice inside each brioche.

3 To make the filling, melt the butter in a frying pan and fry the shallots and garlic for 2–3 minutes until softened.

4 Add the mushrooms and cook gently for about 4–5 minutes, stirring.

5 When the juices begin to run, reduce the heat and continue cooking for about 3–4 minutes, stirring occasionally, until the pan is fairly dry.

6 Stir in the wine. Cook for a few more minutes and then stir in the cream, basil, parsley and seasoning to taste.

7 Pile the mushroom mixture into the brioche shells and return to the oven and reheat for about 5–6 minutes. Serve as a starter, garnished with a sprig of parsley.

WILD MUSHROOMS WITH PANCAKES

SERVES SIX (as a starter)

INGREDIENTS
    8–10 ounces assorted wild
      mushrooms
    2 ounces butter
    1–2 garlic cloves
    splash of brandy (optional)
    freshly ground black pepper
    sour cream, to serve
For the pancakes
    4 ounces self-rising flour
    ¾ ounce buckwheat flour
    ½ teaspoon baking powder
    pinch of salt
    2 eggs
    about 1 cup milk
    oil, for frying

1 To make the pancakes, mix together the flours, baking powder and salt in a large bowl or food processor. Add the eggs and milk and beat or process to make a smooth batter, about the consistency of light cream.

2 Grease a large griddle or frying pan with a little oil and when hot, pour small amounts of batter (about 1–2 tablespoons per pancake) onto the griddle, well spaced apart.

3 Fry for a few minutes until bubbles begin to appear on the surface and the underside is golden, and then flip over. Cook for about 1 minute until golden. Keep warm, wrapped in a clean dish towel. (Makes about 18–20 pancakes.)

4 If the mushrooms are large, cut them in half. Melt the butter in a frying pan and add the garlic and mushrooms. Fry over moderate heat for a few minutes until the juices begin to run and then increase the heat and cook, stirring frequently, until nearly all the juices have evaporated. Stir in the brandy, if using, and season with a little black pepper.

5 Arrange the warm pancakes on a serving plate and spoon over a little sour cream. Top with the hot mushrooms and serve immediately.

COOK'S TIP
This makes a delicious and elegant starter for a dinner party. Alternatively, make cocktail-size pancakes and serve as part of a buffet supper.

INDEX

NOTES

NOTES

NOTES

NOTES

NOTES

NOTES

NOTES

NOTES